THE VICTORIANS AND SPORT

The Victorians and Sport

Mike Huggins

Hambledon and London

London and New York

Hambledon and London

102 Gloucester Avenue
London, NW1 8HX

175 Fifth Avenue
New York, NY 10010
USA

First Published 2004

ISBN 1 85285 415 4

Copyright © Mike Huggins 2004

A description of this book is available from the
British Library and from the Library of Congress.

Typeset by Carnegie Publishing, Lancaster
and printed in Great Britain by Cambridge University Press.

Distributed in the United States and Canada
exclusively by Palgrave Macmillan,
a division of St Martin's Press.

Contents

Illustrations

Preface

What did the Victorians mean by 'sport'? In 1837 the word was still closely identified with field sports, especially hunting, fowling and fishing. Of the many hundred book titles including 'sport' published from then until 1901 most used 'sport' adjectivally to suggest game hunting, as, for example, in *Powder, Spur and Spear: A Sporting Medley* (1889). Often coupled with nouns like 'adventures' (usually abroad), 'sketches', 'reminiscences', 'stories', 'rambles', 'world', 'scenes' and 'notes', such use suggests that imperial Victorian hunters found a ready market for their real or exaggerated exploits. Books on sporting 'guns', 'firearms', and 'rifles' signified an interest in the technology of killing. A vicarious sense of place was conveyed when 'sporting' was coupled with 'resorts', 'tour' (in the Highlands, India or elsewhere), 'trip' or 'guide'. Other writers produced books on 'sporting characters' or the 'sporting calendar'.

During the Victorian age, however, another use of the term emerged. The earlier 'manly games' and 'healthful recreations' gave way to 'sport', now associated with 'athleticism' or 'athletic sports'. Even in 1852 George Sala was praising 'athletic sports' as ones which 'send our lads (from Eton to charity schools) forth to do yeoman's service all over the globe'.[1] This more modern sense of a game or competitive activity involving physical exertion, usually outdoors and often played with other young men, is the main focus here. The *Oxford English Dictionary* first cited this secondary meaning in 1863. By the 1890s it had become generally used.

Sport involved many Victorians, and is therefore worth studying for that reason alone. Indeed, modern competitive sports may well be their most long-lasting legacy. The British pioneered many of the sports which later spread round the world. Sport was one of the most significant European cultural practices of the late nineteenth century, and the study of Victorian sports has much to teach us. The leading social historian Harold Perkin once famously pointed out,

> The history of societies is reflected more vividly in the way they spend their leisure than in their politics or their work. Sport in particular is much more than a pastime or recreation. It is an integral part of a society's culture [and] gives a unique insight into the way a society changes and impacts on other societies.[2]

The Victorians and Sport explores the rise of Victorian sport and explains how, from the 1860s to the century's end, Britain experienced an almost revolutionary transformation in the scale and nature of its sporting culture. New sports such as association football, rugby, golf and tennis became widely popular, though different social groups approached their sports in very different ways. Sport caused divisions and conflicts concerned with amateurs and professionals, betting, alcohol and temperance, the sporting treatment of animals, Sunday play or women's participation. At the same time, sport could bind together members of the same social class, and be a major form of conspicuous consumption. Some sports became increasingly commercialised, and a sports industry emerged, fed by a rapidly expanding and vibrant sporting press. Sports stars such as the cricketer W. G. Grace or the jockey Fred Archer became world-famous. Soccer and rugby began to make their own unique contributions to the formation of local, regional and national loyalties and identities.

An overview such as this, which attempts to look at all levels of society, from the monarchy to the working classes, has clearly had to be selective. There was so much change over the Victorian period, and so many possible themes and sports that could be covered, that much has unavoidably been omitted, or been cursorily treated. Some sports, such as croquet or swimming, for example, play minor supportive roles. In terms of coverage, this book is primarily a study of mainland Britain, rather than the United Kingdom. Scotland and Wales have largely been treated as part of the overall British experience rather than as separate entities.

Sports history is now a popular element of sports studies, as well as a sub-division of broader social history. So *The Victorians and Sport* provides both a synthesis of existing work and an introduction to my own ideas on sport in Victorian society, in an accessible and readable form.

This book rests on what is now a very substantial base of excellent monographs and articles on Victorian sport, containing the fruits of insightful research conducted, analysed and published by other scholars, as well as my own researches and painstaking combing of Victorian primary sources.

Wherever possible I have tried to seek balance, with examples drawn from across the class structure and the period, from regions and locations throughout mainland Britain, from both men's and women's sporting life, and from a wide variety of Victorian forms of evidence, ranging from medical school prospectuses and sports club archives to films, 'penny dreadfuls' and census material. The chosen format has placed limits on references, so my indebtedness to friends, colleagues and other writers and scholars can only be inadequately expressed, but I would like to thank specifically Professor John Mackenzie and Dr Martin Johnes for their helpful comments on chapter drafts. Whilst I have tried to make myself familiar with what they have written, and tried to set sport firmly within a wider framework of Victorian cultural attitudes, I have attempted to open up the history of sport to a wider readership by eschewing explicit reference in the text to theory and other researchers, and using everyday language wherever possible.[3] To those who feel I have still failed, those who would have liked more explicit academic rigour, and those who are disappointed not to see their names in print I must of course apologise. I can only say I thoroughly enjoyed writing this book.

1

The Rise of Sport

A British sporting culture already existed before Queen Victoria ascended the throne. Spectators, sports professionals, gambling and charges for grandstands or other viewing facilities were all present in the late eighteenth century in sports as diverse as cricket, horse racing, pedestrianism (foot racing), prize-fighting and wrestling. Despite such commercial development, much village and small town leisure was integrated in a small-scale, communal way of life. Formal sporting activity was infrequent. Recreations were often ritualised and bound by custom, and sports were governed by rules, albeit generally local ones. Sporting periodicals such as *Bell's Life in London* came into existence as the volume of both activity and expenditure in organised sport expanded between the 1790s and 1850.[1]

Even so, sport was not central to early Victorian life. It operated more on the margins, being irregular but not rare. Some sports involved challenges, and would happen over the year, with individuals and clubs competing on a number of occasions. Major events occurred only occasionally in individual towns, being looked forward to for months before. Some, like race meetings, were commercial in approach. Others were holiday events, linked to religious, seasonal and regional calendars, held at a time of an annual weekday fair or wake. Far more people watched than actually competed, and crowds were usually from all classes. Vigorous young men were the primary sports competitors, spearheading sporting participation. They had time and energy and usually occupied positions without responsibility.

The processes of evangelicalism, urbanisation, industrial capitalism and rapid technological change meant that sports in the 1830s and 1840s underwent a period of change, although the extent of that change is debatable, and on balance their impact was more positive than negative. More supposedly rational recreations were increasingly approved of.

In Scotland, golf faced problems, with the nadir point in the 1830s. Alongside conservative alarm at criminal activity, working- and lower-middle-class Chartism and other political activism, there was opposition to working-class activities seen as sinful, or where large, potentially unruly crowds assembled. Cruel sports and working-class betting, whether on racing, steeple-chasing, pugilism or pedestrianism, were obvious targets. In racing, attempts to fix results or welsh on bets received much publicity. Some of the titled had always done so. But their increased realisation that other classes were also exploiting such opportunities was not well received. Around this time working-class sports were poorly covered in the national press. In 1838 the London *Times* had articles, as distinct from results, on only nine sports. By 1847 this had dropped to seven sports, although these still included racing (and betting at Tattersall's Rooms), hunting and cricket. Awareness of the need to provide more positive, uplifting activities for the poor led to some provision of more 'rational' recreations.

Attacks by reformers on sports such as cockfighting or bull-baiting were relatively effective. Popular sports and betting proved far more resilient.[2] Annual local football matches, often staged on Shrove Tuesday, as at Ashdowne, were sometimes curtailed, but others, such as that at Alnwick, simply moved away from town centres. They employed a wide variety of local rules. Some allowed a great deal of handling, others put an emphasis on kicking. The occasional inter-village matches, still being played in the 1840s and 1850s around Sheffield and elsewhere, were an important precursor of modern soccer. The modern football codes, which diffused downwards from the public schools, were able to expand partly because of this pre-existing cultural base.[3]

Sporting continuities were also facilitated by further commercialisation of those sports, like racing, already partly commercialised. Commercial gardens and enclosed public house fields allowed the charging of admission for sports such as pedestrian races, cricket matches and pigeon shooting. Between 1800 and 1850 many sports saw growth. There was an increase in leisure opportunities for many people, especially for the wealthier. Amounts subscribed in towns for events such as racing, rowing or wrestling rose. So, probably, did crowd size, though before turnstiles crowd size is difficult to estimate. By the 1840s

Bell's Life was quoting over forty events each year with attendance figures explicitly above a thousand, many in the tens of thousands, with racing, steeplechasing, and pugilism attracting the highest figures, followed by pedestrianism, cricket and wrestling. Most descriptions were vague, but had 'big', 'large', 'crowded', 'numerous', 'biggest ever', 'immense', 'huge', 'many', 'a goodly muster' or similar terms, implying substantial crowds.

Early industrialisation had a limited impact in many towns. It was a protracted and diverse process. It was regionally confined. Some upper-class support for town sports previously supported as part of an obligation to provide local patronage was beginning to be withdrawn. The wealthy were spending more time in London, and abandoning their provincial houses. The changing circumstances of the 1832 Reform Act meant voters in towns sometimes rejected the candidate representing an local landed interest. There was more dishonesty in the running of sports. But upper-class cash was usually replaced by that of other patrons such as innkeepers, tradesmen or local businessmen, often more interested in speculation than local status and glory. Working-class sports often based on cash challenges, with the winner taking the money staked, still flourished in the 1840s and 1850s. These put the competitor in control, organising his own challenges and choosing his own opponents. Prize-fighting temporarily gained new vitality. While maintaining its focus on more gentlemanly sports, in the 1840s *Bell's Life* increased its coverage of working-class sports including pedestrian races, sculling, knur and spell, wrestling, quoiting, potshare bowling, rabbit and hare coursing, and shooting at pigeons and sparrows.

Sport was extensively watched and played by the mid nineteenth century as part of a vigorous popular culture.[4] It could be portrayed as a powerful distraction to Chartism and other working-class political disaffection. When a thousand people of 'all ranks' attended a pugilistic exhibition, for example, it was contrasted with 'the recent unhappy display of "physical force" Chartists at Bethnal Green', and forced upon the reporter

> the conviction that if the innocent and manly sports of the humbler classes were encouraged instead of being everywhere suppressed and hunted down by the tyrannical prejudices of puritans, we should see and hear much less

of those fanatical outbreaks we have of late had so much reason to deplore and which fills the country with well-founded alarm.[5]

Blood sports like bull-baiting, badger-baiting and cock-fighting, which had always been well-organised but occasional events, were the main public targets of such 'puritans'. Such sports were in clear decline. Bull-running at Stamford finally ended in 1840 after several years of pressure from the military, magistrates, the RSPCA and respectable reformers. That year *Bell's Life* only reported up to five cocking mains a week, mostly in Lancashire, the Sheffield region, and parts of the midlands. A further law against cock-fighting was passed in 1849, though it continued in attenuated and clandestine form for much of the century.[6] This was partly because it was by no means merely a working-class activity. Like dog-fighting, it had the attractions of betting, excitement and illegality. In 1866 writers bemoaned that 'cruel sports are still engaged in, not only by the lower orders, but by those whose position in society and education ought to make them blush at seeking their pleasure in such brutal, disgusting and degraded pursuits'.[7] A cock-fighting meet at Aintree in April 1875 attracted many supposedly occupying high positions. In Cumbria and elsewhere it continued throughout the century, usually on farms and in rural villages.[8] Policing was ineffective against activities supported within the local community, whether cock-fighting or cash betting.

Even in the period from 1840 to 1860 there were slow but significant changes in sporting patterns. Sport was already of increasing interest to sections of the middle classes by the 1850s. Horse racing attracted middle-class 'sporting men'. So did angling, cricket, hunting, coursing, yachting, rowing and shooting. By the 1850s there were more sports clubs, often but not always socially impervious. Cricket club playing membership could be cross-class, including both the gentry and professionals, although most clubs were predominantly middle class, and there were already some working-class sides. Most cricket teams still only played a few games a season, and, as Richard Daft, the cricketer, wrote, 'the match was the topic of conversation months before the event took place'.[9] There were more events than there had been previously. They were held more frequently. Crowd numbers at leading events increased. Cricket professional sides began touring the country. Sports became more competitive, rather than just being means of displaying

Lord's Cricket Ground, 1837.
One of the very earliest matches between the North and the South.

skill or strength. Wholehearted enjoyment was becoming subservient to winning.

Betting was increasingly popular amongst young and unmarried working-class males by the 1840s. They followed horse racing, adopted the technical slang of the boxing ring by reading the sporting press, boasted of their bets, wore suits of the latest sporting cut, tried to associate with and treat minor local sporting celebrities, occasionally attended Monday events at the enclosed suburban running grounds to watch events such as pedestrianism, cycling races, wrestling and boxing, and organised their own more informal races and fights.

From the 1860s to the century's end there occurred what can be described as a great sports boom or even a sporting revolution.[10] Its historical significance cannot be over-estimated. Britain experienced a notable transformation in the scale and nature of its sporting culture which helped make it the 'birthplace of modern sport'.[11] The middle classes, who were the main motive force, significantly increased their participation, in part due to public school example. The magazine *Land and Water* pointed out sport's increasing popularity there, suggesting some teachers feared 'the unaccountable furore of athletics which transforms the most promising pupil into an ardent votary of the cricket field, river and gymnasium, and renders him insensible to the charms of the classics'. It noted too the increased press coverage, and that 'since the volunteer movement, not only have the old forms of athletic sport been practised with redoubled energy, but new forms have been introduced and a spirit of system and organisation has been infused into athletics generally'. In total an 'athletic fever' had been created.[12] Amongst middle-class adults new sports such as mountaineering proliferated. Association football, rugby, tennis and golf were all key leisure innovations. *The Times* featured nineteen different sports in 1874, and twenty-seven by 1901, and included far more articles on individual sports. Numbers of sporting clubs, governing bodies and other institutions grew rapidly. Older sports had had local and regional variants. Now, in all sports, new rules were increasingly recorded, standardised and regularly modified to suit players' and spectators' needs. By 1901 the new sports had become institutionalised, codified and international in scope. The number of participants grew. This went together with increased commercial investment in sport, from stadiums to equipment.

In its top reaches, sport was already often highly professionalised, but the late nineteenth century saw the emergence of professionalism in newer sports such as rugby, soccer or cycling.

Yet notions of a revolution can be overdrawn. Many traditional working-class sports continued. In north-east England, for example, some sports, such as quoiting or potshare bowling, expanded over the second half of the century. Moves towards codification, commercialisation and institutionalisation varied from sport to sport. There were also substantial continuities from the earlier period and some older sports were sufficiently adaptable to fit the requirements of a new age. Localised versions of football survived across Britain, usually as annual events, changing and adapting to change. At Dorking in Surrey, for example, its traditional annual football match was still being played in the public streets in 1888.[13]

It is also important to remember that both sporting participation and spectating were still minority interests even at the end of the period. At soccer's nineteenth-century peak in the Stirling area only one in four males aged between fifteen and twenty-nine belonged to a club, while cricket, cycling, and rugby had far fewer adherents. But large numbers of the male employed population increasingly enjoyed sport, although the involvement of women and unskilled males was limited in its extent. Sport came to mean excitement, social prestige and modernity.

These changes can be briefly illustrated by data on the complex patterns of sporting participation and on crowd numbers. In most elite sports participatory growth was relatively slow. There were only about 800 active hare coursers in 1842; less than 1500 by 1901. There were 135 packs of foxhounds in England and Wales in 1850; nearly 180 at the end of the century. There were 1213 racehorses on the flat in 1837, and 3506 in 1897, when there were about 1300 active owners. There were about twenty yacht clubs in 1840 and around 116 by 1895. The number of cricket clubs increased substantially over Victoria's reign, but membership of the more elite county cricket clubs grew only slowly until the late 1880s. Surrey Cricket Club still only had 230 members in 1885 but had 4000 by 1899.

A more substantial growth in participation came in the new sports of the second half of the nineteenth century, although the trajectory of growth varied. Golf, for example, only really took off from the later

1880s. In 1850 there were only seventeen golf clubs and societies in the United Kingdom, but in 1898 there were 1460 clubs, with slightly over half of them in England. The Cyclists Touring Club was founded in 1878 with 142 members, but had 60,000 in 1899. There were less than fifty soccer clubs nationally in the 1860s, but Sheffield alone had 880 soccer clubs in 1899. The Rugby Football Union had twenty-one members in 1871. It had over 430 in the early 1890s, and many more clubs were unaffiliated. The Northern Union, with its more professional rugby game, had twenty-two clubs on its formation in 1895–96 but over a hundred by 1899. Women's active involvement in sport was growing, although for most still largely confined to schools and universities, and it was the better off who carried it into adulthood. Golf and tennis clubs attracted women in some numbers.

We lack systematic data on spectator numbers. They were probably at their highest in comparison to the local population in the first half of Victoria's reign, when large crowds seem to have been common at what were often rare events. Annual race meetings attracted very large crowds, especially to Epsom and Doncaster. Even for the small Blackburn Steeplechase held in April 1840 the attendance was 'immense, the numbers having been computed at upwards of 20,000'.[14] Major rowing events, where spectatorship was free, also attracted large crowds, often claimed as between 50,000 and 100,000. Although divisions of time and income within families usually ensured that only men could afford to attend gate-money events, the unenclosed sports grounds, where entrance was free, still attracted families. Women would watch the rare sculling races on the Tyne or Thames, and crowds at race meetings were always a mixture of men, women and children. At Aintree, 'hundreds' of little boys lay down on the grass and put their heads between the legs of the crowd to see the race.[15]

The British population increased rapidly between 1841 and 1901. Even if the level of involvement stayed the same, crowd numbers should have risen. The actual proportion of occasional spectators in the national population may well not have increased substantially over the period. Certainly large crowds attended what were perceived as 'national' events. In 1871 the Eton v. Harrow cricket match attracted 20,000 select spectators on the first and 18,000 on the second day. There were about 2000 spectators at the first English FA Cup final in 1872 when

DONCASTER RACES.

THE MANSION HOUSE, DONCASTER.

LIGHTS AND SHADOWS OF THE LEGER DAY.

Among the truest of all aphorisms is that which declares "there is a tide in the affairs of men." According to historians, the popular flood sets from east to west—at all events, that is the way the stream of gentility flows in the great metropolis. Occasionally, of course, there are exceptions to the general rule, as to all others—the latest variation it is our purpose to treat of in these presents. During the current week the north has been the fashionable point of the compass. The Court is away in bonny Scotland, exchanging the regal for the rural purple—"pomp and circumstance" for health and heather—the imperious ermine for the dun deer's spoil. But all this is to be a sealed book to the million; it is the Queen's pleasure that none intrude on the privacy of her Highland home; and shall not that wish be our law? Turn we then to another northern tryst, where the public was welcome in the exact ratio of its extent. Our scene is Doncaster Races—a rare rendezvous, such as erst it was in the time of the autocrats, the Fitzwilliams, the Harewoods, and similar worthies. The meeting of 1844 was the most brilliant within moderate memory. The recent fomentation of the turf has left it more bright and sparkling than ever: things had come to the worst and they have mended.

On Monday last the Great Northern Meeting commenced, and ended yesterday. Our affair, however, is with its principal feature, the renowned Leger, and, consequently, the time of action is limited to one day. That was Tuesday—which somewhat heavily, with clouds, brought on the fortunes and misfortunes of full many that in anxiety witnessed its dawn. By a very early hour the human tide had begun to flow, and long before noon it was high water—hot water in the rooms. There all who could were betting—these to make their book, those "to mend it, or be rid oa's," (which means "going for the gloves"). All sorts of casualties had been

busy with the field, so that, at the last hour, out of 109 entries, only the poor units remained—and nine were declared to start. First of these was the Curé, a goodly steed, though small (and having an ungainly right font withal), backed at even to win, and next him Foigh-a-Ballagh, the champion of Ireland, alone, just before the race, at 3 to 1. Others also had friends at miscellaneous estimates, as will also here be seen. Precisely at three of the afternoon clock the coursers began to appear—among the first being the pair aforesaid—"Foigh" looking as like a clipper as anything lately exhibited in horse-flesh. Thus, the cynosure of all account, the "nine" paraded before the stand, and eventually passed at for the great essay in the following order:—Foigh-a-Ballagh, first by a length; The Curé, The Princess, Lightning, Red Deer, the Amulet colt, Bay Momus, Little Hampton, and Godfrey. The usual functionary started them, the matter being too uncomplicated to call for the aid of my Lord Bentinck. Godfrey made what they called the running, which was a bad substitute for an exercise gallop: in fact, the speed all through was, as Jim Robinson called it, "paltry." Of course, the lot came together to the straight ground. There Foigh-a-Ballagh was in front, with the Curé on his quarters outside, and the brace began to do their endeavour in earnest. Both were flagged—the latter deserving all he got, for he bolted half-a-dozen lengths from home, and finished a cur as well as a loser. The Princess was a good third. Her gallant owner called for an investigation of the winner's mouth in the morning. Won't there be wigs upon the green if requests like these are to become common? There is a story of a Parisian and a Gascon who were playing a game of piquet, together when the Frenchman exclaimed, "Halloa, monsieur! you're cheating!" "Very likely," replied the provincial, with a horrible face, "very probable; but, observe, *I don't like to be told so.*" Unless we are wrong, here and there men will be found who won't relish an imputation

DONCASTER RACES.—THE ST. LEGER.

Doncaster Races. The St Leger, 1844.
Huge crowds of men, women and children thronged such early events.

fifteen clubs entered, but 69,000 in 1900 and 110,000 in 1901. Crowds at Scottish cup finals averaged nearly 8000 in the 1870s, and over 17,500 in the 1890s. The 1899 Northern Union rugby challenge cup attracted 15,763, the 1901 equivalent 29,563.

Crowd numbers at other than national events did not rise as rapidly. Indeed, where sports grounds became enclosed and people had to pay for their pleasure, the numbers of spectators initially went down, not up. Horse racing crowds dropped in the later 1870s once admission to the course itself was no longer free. Other sports with strong betting connections also drew smaller crowds.[16] Crowds for pedestrian events were often estimated as in the thousands in the 1840s when access to moor or road was open. Thereafter, as they increasingly took place in enclosures, crowds were usually lower and rose only slowly, fluctuating with the local economy and local interest. At Aston Cross in 1862, that 'some 300 persons, chiefly from the Black Country, paid admission' was seen as 'proof of the interest attached to this match', and that it was 'seldom that speculation has reached such a point'.[17] Many reports for the rest of the century did not give figures, but, of the minority which did, the vast majority of pedestrian crowds were between three hundred and a thousand. Only a very tiny minority were over three thousand except at holiday times. Predominantly male crowds at wrestling matches, rabbit-coursing and dog-racing 'gate money' events were nearly always below a thousand over the same period. Cycle racing was one of the few events regularly to attract crowds of well over a thousand from the 1870s, mainly in the Birmingham and Wolverhampton areas.

Since sporting events were held far more regularly in the 1880s and 1890s, those who could afford to watch sport went more often simply because there was more sport to watch. Teams played more often. Sunderland FC, for example, played only six matches in the 1880/1 season, but fifty-five matches in 1889/90, regularly attracting large paying crowds.

On any one Saturday afternoon in 1900 far more sport would have been watched, by far more people, than in 1837. The average number watching Blackburn Rovers matches was 5505 in 1888/9 and 6725 in 1899/1900. Average attendances at Football League First Division matches were approximately 4600 and 9500 for the equivalent seasons.

Even a small club like Northwich averaged crowds of 1325 during 1893/4.[18] In county cricket, in 1899 Worcester averaged 3525 spectators a match, Leicester 4436, Derbyshire 4569 and Yorkshire 16,617, although since matches lasted three days this was far less than soccer per day.

For much of the Victorian period the leading British sport was racing. It attracted the largest crowds and largest financial investment, and underpinned a massive betting industry. It was still an age of horse ownership, and racing provided a particular and characteristic source of pleasure. Frith's satirical panorama painting of *Derby Day*, exhibited at the Royal Academy in 1858, was so popular that railings had to be set up to keep back the crowds. Cricket began to assume its place as the universal English summer game from the late 1870s. By 1882 C. W. Alcock believed that thousands recognised in cricket 'the national game', not least because all classes played and watched.[19]

Rugby and soccer competed for the position of leading winter ball sport through the 1870s and early 1880s, when in many places, including West Yorkshire and the West Country, there were more rugby games. By 1882, however, there were claims that soccer was 'our National Winter Game' and was 'becoming more popular each year'.[20] Even so, Frederick Gale, in *Modern English Sports: Their Use and Abuse* (1885) still included a chapter on 'Football and Lacrosse', while the Badminton Library of Sports and Pastimes series published a book on *Athletics and Football* in 1887, both of which suggest that football's leading place was not yet assured amongst the more literate sporting public. Most still saw it as less popular than cricket. Soccer became the leading winter spectator sport in the 1890s, due to the competitive excitements of the FA Cup and Football League, though in 1896 the journalist A. E. T. Watson still believed 'that football has the steady vitality of cricket may well be doubted, and it certainly has not the well-nigh universal popularity of the latter game'.[21] Even in Scotland, where football spectators as a proportion of the total population were about double those in England, less than 14 per cent of the male population of localities attended in the 1890s, and bad weather was always a deterrent when a majority of stands were open.[22]

Sports provided a seasonal pattern to the year. In the first half of Victoria's reign sports using the winter months were fairly few – fox hunting, hare coursing, and the relatively new sport of steeplechasing were the most commonly reported, with their beginnings in September/October and endings around March. These were more for the wealthy, who could afford warmer dress and changes of clothes, although the steeplechases, being annual events, attracted all classes. Curling was popular in Scotland. Steeplechasing peaked in March, and early April saw the close of the winter sports season. Summer-orientated sports such as rowing largely but not exclusively used the months from March to October or November. In late March and April yacht squadrons began sailing again and the Boat Race was contested. Cricket, tennis, archery and flat racing all began in April or early May. But some sports such as pedestrianism, popular in London and the north, as was pigeon shooting, were carried on throughout the year. There were very occasional pugilistic or rowing contests even in December, January and February. Sports like bowling, quoiting, handball, dog-racing and golf, although much more common in the summer, could be year-round sports.

Sport also gave a pattern to the week. Hunting and coursing took place on any weekday, although Monday and Friday were slightly more popular. So did regattas, trotting, horse-racing and pigeon-racing. Pedestrian races could be found on any weekday in 1840 but the enclosed events of the 1850s and 1860s more commonly used Mondays with some Saturdays, reversing the priority thereafter. Enclosed sports grounds favoured the same two days for a whole variety of activities, including knur and spell, cycling, dog racing and rabbit coursing, through the century. By the 1880s most more amateur sports, including yachting, cricket and amateur athletics, used Saturdays for over half of all events. The next most popular day was Monday. But even in early August 1882 twenty-five out of sixty-two cricket club matches reported in *Bell's Life* were on the other four weekdays.

In 1837 racecourses, cockpits or bowling greens were exceptions to the general rule that most sports did not have to have specialised, full-time, regular locations. Events were held on moors, commons, beaches, wagonways or specified roads, all places open to public view. Most ubiquitous of all was land beside the public house, a chief sporting locus, providing news, entertainment and social and cultural life. Landlords were the first leisure entrepreneurs. Most pedestrian matches took place on roads, where reasonably accurate measurement was available between milestones, and *Bell's Life* would give references such as 'the Black Bank mile'. They also occurred, less often, on racing or cricket grounds.

The increased growth of towns meant existing places of play were taken over as property became privatised or more exclusively used for botanical gardens, museums or promenades for the rich. Commons were enclosed, patches of open ground were infilled, and streets became congested. In Sheffield, in 1843, a cutler commented on 'the want of places for healthful recreation', claiming that 'scarcely a foot of these common wastes remains for the enjoyment of the industrial classes ... we have a noble cricket field, but entrance to this must be purchased'.[23] A Hampstead letter bemoaned that land where 'our boys have played cricket and football' had been sold for building.[24] Such pressure on space, for residential, commercial and industrial use, forced the development of enclosed sporting grounds.

For the later team sports, access to fields in crowded urban areas was vital to their viability. While clubs scrambled for available grounds, rapid rent increases were common. By 1900 even poor Manchester fields awaiting building could cost £5 for a season's rent, expensive for working-class teams.[25] Drainage could be a problem too. Most landowners were indifferent to the demands by clubs for space. Clubs could easily find themselves without grounds. Yet the pace and effects of building development varied significantly and can be exaggerated. Lincoln's commons, for example, were maintained throughout the nineteenth century, and were often used for organised sport. Cricket was being played on the South Common from an early date; by 1895 Lincoln Golf Club was playing on the West Common. Equally, rural enclosure did not necessarily mean the loss of sport. The racecourse at Richmond in Yorkshire was specifically excluded from the local Enclosure Act. Nevertheless, densely urban, increasingly heavily-policed areas placed far more limits on formerly popular mass sports like the various varieties of football. Conflict over the right use of space often ended in their repression, although impromptu children's street versions of sports continued in streets despite police attempts to curb them.

The expense of private fields meant Victorian parks were often used for sports. Victoria Park in Whitechapel had facilities for cricket from 1846. Professional clubs, including Tottenham, Clapton, Millwall and West Ham, were initially established on or close to public football pitches. Sheer weight of use often forced local authority restrictions. Many shut on Saturdays in the winter at 4.45 p.m. or even earlier, and Manchester's parks were very little used for winter games.

Growth in sport's popularity, prevalence and importance reflected changes in Victorian society. Sporting involvement increased thanks to a variety of interlocking factors. The two key ones were money and time. The productivity gains of the industrial revolution created an economic surplus which first and most directly benefited the middle and upper classes, and allowed more money and time for sporting activities. The period of unprecedented economic wellbeing between about 1850 and 1873 spread prosperity across all forms of economic activity, from foreign trade to farming. Its benefits were diffused throughout the British population. A general improvement in living standards took place. From the mid 1830s to the 1870s prices were relatively flat, although with cyclical swings, which explains some of the difficulties entrepreneurs initially faced in expanding the working-class audience for sport.

Demand expanded fastest in favourable periods of the trade cycle, such as the early 1870s. At these times more people were drawn into sporting habits that continued, although at a lower level, during the subsequent trough. Real wages rose fairly steadily over the Victorian period at a long-term trend of about 1.2 per cent per annum. Although the wide spectrum of wages amongst the employed had implications for access to sport, per capita wages were about 50 per cent higher in 1901 than in 1851. So it is unsurprising that for those with spare disposable income their consumption of sporting leisure increased, part of the wider rise of a consumer society.[26] By the 1880s a better-off working-class audience aided the emergence of mass national spectator sport, even though this had its roots in the 1850s and 1860s. The increased penetration of market forces into sport led to its increased commercialisation. The last two decades of Victoria's reign saw a distinctive and modern leisure landscape. It was a period of further sporting change, with sport occupying much more of some people's emotional thought, effort and time than previously.

Having more time was also important to sport's expansion. Middle-class salaried professionals had always enjoyed a flexible working week and some holiday time. By the later nineteenth century entrepreneurs had junior staff or managers to cover absence. Some firms allowed weekday early closure or time off to male staff for appropriate sporting recreation. But for most people at the beginning of the Victorian period, a working week of six full days, with long hours, often meant little time free for sport, except perhaps on Sundays, which was often literally a day of rest. In many trades six day weeks of sixty hours or more continued to be common. The common practice amongst occupational groups on piece rates of Monday absence from work made it a very common day for sporting activity up to and often well beyond the 1850s. Increasingly through the period, however, larger numbers of the employed population enjoyed approved leisure time. Some of this was due to active attempts by workers to reduce working hours, or favourable periods in the economic cycle when workers took extra free time. Some was due to the responsive activities of the state and of employers.

In the early years of Victoria's reign working days lasted until around six o'clock. Work hours in a range of major trades, including building and engineering, were dropping in many of Britain's largest towns from the 1860s, and the 1867 Factory and Workshops Act extended the sixty hour week beyond the textile industries of Yorkshire and Lancashire. The boom economic conditions of the early 1870s allowed many unionised workers to achieve a nine hour day through the exercise of industrial muscle. By the 1880s the British working classes had more leisure time than anywhere else in Europe, and there were moves in some industries towards an eight hour working day. By 1900 the working week had reached a mean of 52.3 hours for the building, engineering, footwear, furniture and printing trades in Britain's major cities.[27]

There was a slow repatterning and reconfiguring of sporting time towards Saturday afternoons. Many offices and commercial premises began closing at noon on Saturday from the 1840s, and it was the middle classes who first had sufficient time to develop the new weekend sporting innovations such as soccer, which needed regular scheduling. The 1850 Factory Act allowed textile workers a Saturday half holiday starting at 2 p.m., which had an impact on the emergence of works cricket teams in Lancashire, and for the next decades both Mondays and Saturdays were popular, especially summer, leisure days. Opportunity for sport varied with occupation, although piecework with its incentives for higher productivity meant some workers chose shorter working hours to gain leisure time. Skilled workers in the manufacturing trades were the first to receive a Saturday half holiday, and those towns dominated by single manufacturing industries were the first able to make use of Saturday afternoon. Some firms were closing at 1.00 p.m. as early as the 1850s in London and Birmingham. By the 1860s skilled and lower middle-class workers in the railways had followed suit. The Factory Act of 1878 gave all factory workers the same right. Unskilled workers and shopkeepers and their assistants, by contrast, were more likely to have to work through. Local variations meant different trajectories of sporting opportunity, and for most of the working class outings to watch or participate in sport were still constrained by income even as free time increased. In Birmingham the 1 p.m. finish was general by the late 1870s, reaching 12 noon in 1890. The effect on Saturday soccer was major. The area only had twenty district soccer teams mentioned in the press in 1876 but 155 in 1880. In areas like Liverpool, with its low proportion of skilled workers, or the north east with its heavy industry, Saturday half-days were uncommon until the mid 1880s. Here soccer took off more slowly. Even so, the shorter working week and the Saturday half-day, along with an annual holiday were unique in nineteenth-century Europe, and helped Britain become a dominant influence on global sport.

By the later nineteenth century the democratisation of leisure was well underway. Sports activities were increasingly capitalised. They were better marketed through the press. They were held more regularly, and much more commercial in their approach. The rise of these commercialised sports forms was hugely aided by an increasingly concentrated urban market, aided to a large and growing extent by the formation of an essentially working-class culture, tough, resilient and adaptive with a collective self-consciousness, well able to appropriate some sports into their own cultural life.[28] The population of England and Wales rose from about fourteen million in 1937 to almost twenty-nine million by 1901. Britain was still a rural society in 1837, but by 1901 an urban revolution had occurred, with huge industrial towns intruding into the rural agricultural landscape. Sporting activities were fostered by new class subcultures, while, first in London then elsewhere, the suburbs developed their own sporting life. British cities provided space, capital, paying spectators and participants for sport, while, as in the USA, sports grounds provided a context for recreation, an image, an identity and a haven which allowed urban residents to escape the strains and stresses of urban living.[29]

Other factors influencing sport are returned to later, and are only touched on here. The expansion of the middle classes, with their generally positive attitudes to sport, was clearly important. The Victorians re-emphasised the spirit of competition and the need for a commercial approach to profit, and applied such notions to their sports. Local authorities provided facilities such as parks, baths and recreational grounds as part of a wider civic project, and as another way of asserting their own status compared to other towns. It is also often forgotten that Victorian society was a young society. In 1851 half the population was under twenty, and only 25 per cent over forty-five years old. This too aided the potential demand for sport. The slow spread of literacy also enlarged the audience for sporting texts. New printing and telegraph services aided its spread, as did new techniques of advertising.

Other new technologies had more limited effect. The railways helped top professionals travel further, but usually simply replaced earlier forms of transport for spectators. The railways' impact on away games in soccer largely came only in the 1890s. But sports organisations were aware of the importance of railway transport, and the new 'first-class' cricket counties of the 1890s all had county grounds near a mainline terminus or on a trunk rail route. Within cities trams and omnibus services made sport more viable.

These changes in Victorian society and sport are now well understood, but they raise further questions. What did sport actually mean to the Victorians? What part did it play in the lives of the various social groups of the period? What did the pursuit of sport as spectator or participant reveal about their cultural values? Why did it cause such debate? Why did they enjoy it? How commercial was it? What role did the media play in its expansion? How important were stars like W. G. Grace or Fred Archer? In what ways did sport contribute to the formation of local, regional and national identities? How did British sport become a major element of British cultural imperialism, as British sports were exported globally? The following chapters try to provide some answers.

2

Class and Sport

Victorian sporting experience was largely a product and a reflection of social class. Factors such as the nature of the job, the size and location of the home, the amount of free time and people's leisure interests denoted their class, created divisions of power and inequality and dictated leisure activities. Class, like gender, respectability or the division between the urban and the rural, was a major fault line in sporting culture.[1] In yachting or polo participation was only open to the wealthy *par excellence*. In 1899 golf cost about ten shillings a week to play, plus club membership fees. Artisans, if admitted at all, often only played during special hours reserved for them.[2] Clubs like the Newbiggin Working Men's Golf Club (1884) were rare. Amateur rowing required day-time leisure to practice, so was more common amongst university or medical students and professional men. Choice of sport thus helped define status. In cross-class sports like cricket, *Bell's Life* reports carefully clarified this by the 1840s. County and MCC players were variously titled, of military rank, either 'Esquire' or 'Mr' if amateur, or given their surname if professional. Public school or ex-public school sides like Old Carthusians were all 'Esquires'. In military sides ranks from 'General' down to 'Private' were scrupulously noted.

Few if any sports were confined to a single class. Sporting participation and watching intersected with class in complex ways. Cricket, riding to hounds, hare coursing and race meetings drew on middle- as well as upper-class financial support. The middle and upper classes dominated racehorse ownership and peopled the grandstands, yet the working classes saw local meetings as an annual carnival and attended in large numbers.[3] The football codes attracted mainly middle-class members to the grandstands but working-class supporters to the terraces. County cricket attracted the leisured spectator, but the Saturday Yorkshire and Lancashire leagues of the 1890s were far more cross-class.

Fishing was supposedly 'a sport that in one form or another, comes within the means of all', but game fishing, with a short stretch of river costing £1 a day to fish, was priced out of reach of the lower middle and working classes, even more so after the introduction of excise licences in 1879. Workers mainly went coarse fishing.[4] Geography made a difference too. Rugby union was largely a middle-class game in England and lowland Scotland, but was a mass sport in Wales, and to an extent in the Scottish borders. While most sports were administered by the upper or middle classes, governing bodies varied considerably in flexibility.

Few sports were purely amateur, purely middle class or purely working class in active membership. In professional football and in cricket, for example, there were both middle- and working-class players and spectators, even if the working-class professional was treated differently in each. To play three-day county cricket regularly as an amateur, or to watch a whole game, required a great deal of free time, and few could afford this. The proportion of Britons actually participating in sport was quite low, largely confined to the male upper, middle and skilled working classes for much of the period, while younger males provided the perennial spearhead of change. Few women took an active role.

Wealth, income, work and free time all influenced but did not necessarily determine sporting participation or spectatorship. There were also complex, fluid and socially constructed vertical divisions of 'respectability' and 'disreputability' or 'reformist' and 'conservative', although these could be differently defined in different leisure contexts.[5] A good illustration was provided in 1860, by which time pugilists faced real difficulties in setting up a fight without warrants being issued by reforming magistrates for their arrest for a breach of the peace, and bad publicity over fixed matches and seedy pugilistic maneuverings had supposedly made the public distrustful. Yet the *Illustrated Times* echoed most contemporary sources in arguing that the fight between the British champion Tom Sayers and the American contender John Heenan had 'been the subject of conversation in every circle of society for a month past', and that the people were 'all in favour of the fight coming off', as was 'well known to everybody who has gone through London with his eyes open'. The complicit 4 a.m. South-Eastern Railway train 'carried ... the upper classes to the fight' and had 'numbers of both Houses in plenty. Authors, poets, painters, soldiers and even clergymen were present'.[6]

Lord Palmerston attended. *The Times* published a stirring account. Two years later, when Mace and King contended for the championship of England, 'distinguished noblemen and gentlemen who have done the state some service' were again supposedly on the train to the match.[7] But bare-knuckle pugilism was increasingly described as debased and brutalising, and further action quickly had 'a decided and crushing' effect.[8]

Despite such complexities, Victorian sporting culture provided a crucial way in which class was articulated in the nineteenth century. To construct a picture of the different ways in which sport was approached, the rest of this chapter attempts to draw out six overlapping sporting cultures characteristic of the period.[9]

By far the most powerful, wealthy and high status group in Victorian society was what was sometimes termed 'Society' itself, a self-confident 'leisure class' whose power was largely based on pedigree, state service and land ownership, and which comprised less than one in two thousand of all British families. It comprised the aristocracy, gentry and squirearchy, together with some members of a newly-rich industrial, professional and mercantile plutocracy.[10] In Britain's relatively stable and cohesive society sport helped foster upper-class identity and unity. In 1847 their yachting, shooting, hunting, coursing and racing interests dominated *The Times* sporting columns, together with cricket and rowing, including the Henley and Thames Regattas. Their political, social and economic dominance gave them powerful prestige. The image of the Victorian gentleman, with his concern for sportsmanship, fair play, fellowship and discipline, became an archetype. Anthony Trollope, in *British Sports and Pastimes* (1868), praised them as the 'largest and wealthiest leisure class' of any country.[11] From the 1860s onwards their power slowly diminished due to the growth of towns, political reforms and increased taxation. Despite their less powerful role in forming leisure tastes they were still admired and envied for their conspicuous consumption of sport. Even in 1901 they continued to play a major sporting role, although press coverage of their activities had declined. Elite sports (like polo at Hurlingham or Ranelagh) were still mentioned, but it was newer, more 'modern' sports that now predominated, and many, such as football and rugby, had middle- and working-class followings.

The leisure class was numerically relatively small. In 1880 there were just over 1100 peers and baronet families each owning at least ten thousand acres, while *Burke's Landed Gentry* (1883) listed a further 4500 families.[12] Some were very wealthy. The Duke of Buccleuch had Scottish land worth £217,163 per annum in 1883.[13] The Duke of Westminster, with much London property, had an annual income of perhaps £290,000.[14] Others were far poorer. In broader cultural terms they had sufficient common interest to be recognisable as a powerful element within British society, despite their varied interests.[15] Country squires and the titled both stressed the differences between themselves and the new industrial and commercial rich, yet they themselves had conflicting and contradictory attitudes, being variously involved in making or spending money, interested or uninterested in estate productivity, public-spirited or not, liking 'town' or 'country' pursuits. Some, like the seventh Duke of Devonshire, a devout low churchman, had little interest in sport. Others were more frivolous, arrogant and self-indulgent, dissolute gamblers and 'rakes' doing their bit for the decline of the industrial spirit. The sixth Duke of Newcastle went bankrupt in 1870 with debts of about £200,000 from his racehorse ownership and betting activities. Lord Glasgow spent nearly £90,000 on racing over forty years without ever winning a big race. The Prince of Wales, without a clear constitutional role, spent much of his sporting leisure hunting with the more exclusive hunts, enjoying shooting parties at Eastwell, Sandringham or Lord Londonderry's Wynyard Park, attending race parties at Goodwood, Newmarket and elsewhere, and occasionally fishing, although he also became a patron of the Rugby Union in 1887.

Such men, with no need to work and ample private means, could enjoy conspicuous, self-indulgent leisure. They were looked up to as 'true sportsmen', with 'less vice', who could run horses, play games honestly and bet for fun.[16] This was a naïve view. The early expansion of cricket, racing and pugilism was largely because the rich were already prepared to support bowlers, jockeys, racehorse trainers or boxers to indulge their sporting pleasures and win their bets. Cricket and racing continued to enjoy their broad support. But their main sporting interests derived from land ownership. In 1882 some 4217 landowners owned 54 per cent of the land of England and Wales, and 66 per cent of all the British Isles was held in estates of a thousand or more acres.

Newly wealthy or newly ennobled business men also invested in land, increasingly, as fashion dictated, purchasing sporting estates to aid their entry into society's higher levels.[17] Land provided income from rents and the exploitation of mineral rights, visible evidence of status, and shooting and hunting. Good sport was a chief benefit and reward of ownership. Shooting rights could be exploited commercially, especially during years of agricultural depression.

Sporting involvement was usually first learnt at home or at public school. The three to five months of the London 'Season' was punctuated by trips to attractions such as the race-meetings at Epsom, Goodwood and Ascot. In the 1840s and 1850s the MCC, under the patronage of Prince Albert, brought their season to a conclusion at the beginning of August, ready for grouse shooting which began on the twelfth. The annual Eton versus Harrow cricket match at Lords was a leading social fixture by the 1880s, a glittering occasion where wealthy families could watch and, equally importantly, be watched. Although the titled pro-portion of MCC membership was by then dropping, it was still about 15 per cent. It had the Prince of Wales as its patron, and, although overall it was more upper middle class in its composition, almost half its com-mittee was generally upper class.[18]

Further elite involvement was based around estates or holidays at resorts in Britain or abroad, where they could look down on *nouveaux riches* vulgarians and middle-class townsfolk. Country house parties came together for local race-meetings, for hunt balls, or for shooting, although tennis, archery and croquet provided social enjoyment for the youngsters. The sporting squire, a hunting, shooting and fishing coun-tryman, is an enduring image of the Victorian age. Riding was learnt in infancy, and the self-contained stable-block was often the most splendid of the estate buildings after the main house. A billiard room, smoking room and gun room were increasingly part of a masculine suite within country houses from the 1860s.[19] At the seaside, where only the very rich could afford expensive yachts and exclusive yacht club membership, Cowes week became increasingly popular socially.

Landlords preserved game for their own pleasure or as a source of pleasure for others. Occasional shoots were sometimes allowed to unqualified freeholders and farmers, and at least one Methodist tenant farmer in the 1870s was exasperated by his fellow farmers' obsession

"BEG PARDON, SIR! BUT IF YOU WAS TO AIM AT HIS LORDSHIP THE NEXT TIME, I THINK HE'D FEEL MORE COMFORBLER, SIR!"

The *nouveau riche* shooter in 1890. Such cartoons pointed up
the social incompetence of inexperienced young men.

with shooting and hunting with landlords.[20] Game might be distributed to tenants, estate workers and hospitals. The fabric of estate landscape was shaped by aristocratic sporting pursuits quite as much as aesthetic and economic interests and preferences, and they continued to exert traditional authority, and flaunt their wealth and status, through field sports. The social rituals of shooting house parties, with correct clothing, equipment and *après*-shoot activities, were well-established.

After the 'Glorious Twelfth', grouse could be shot on the wing on the moors of the northern uplands and the highland zone. Partridge and pheasant were shot in ploughed or grain-growing areas, especially Norfolk and Suffolk. Sandringham, bought by the Prince of Wales in 1863, became one of Britain's finest shoots, with enormous 'bags'. On one day the Prince alone killed 229 head of game, including 175 pheasants, a somewhat excessive demonstration of his 'masculine' prowess. The stress on game preservation, the controlled rearing of birds, the creation of coverts, the regular shooting parties, were all typical Victorian developments, although at the expense of making poaching an endemic feature. Shooting also relied on the availability of cheap local labour – beaters, gamekeepers, and other staff, and led to the destruction of birds of prey.

The large numbers of brace shot by these upper-class, competitive, obsessively record-seeking 'big shots', sometimes in grand *battues* where birds were driven in large numbers over the guns instead of away from them as in rough shooting, were carefully noted in game books. The game room, with its stuffed game and fish, became an architectural feature. Pigeon shooting was widely popular up to the mid nineteenth century and even in the 1860s there were House of Commons teams. Seven titled rifle-shooters and three MPs contended for the 'Great Aristocratic Handicap' at the Welsh Harp Grounds near Hendon in 1866, although Hendon soon had a Tradesmen's Club. An Aristocratic Pigeon-Shooting Club was formed in 1868 at Fulham's Hurlingham estate, purchased for £20,000, and attracted 123 entries at £5 entry fee each in 1869 for its main competition. The Prince of Wales was a keen member, stimulating the republican Charles Bradlaugh in 1872 sarcastically to describe the Prince's greatest attainment as the shooting of tame pigeons. From 1874 the Hurlingham Club also organised polo, and its Polo Committee became the ruling body of the game. The Hurlingham (and Harrington Park) grounds remained socially exclusive venues for watching enthusiastic titled and military pigeon shooters up to the 1880s, regularly reported by *The Times*.[21] By then Hurlingham Club had 1500 members, but only 200 were shooting members.

Most exclusive of all was deerstalking, a strenuous 'millionaire's sport', mainly pursued in Scotland and costing nearly £100 a day. Landlords cleared crofters to replace them with grouse and deer, and stag heads were soon mounted in all the best country houses.[22] Others went overseas to enjoy 'noble' hunting. The seventh Earl of Aylesford, 'Sporting Joe', enjoyed tiger shooting. Hugh, the fifth Earl of Lonsdale, 'The Sporting Earl (also 'The Yellow Earl', after his racing colours), dissipated a huge fortune, a then annual income of over £80,000, on personal extravagances, foreign hunting and British sporting interests that ranged widely from racing and shooting through to boxing, to which he donated the famous Lonsdale belts.[23]

Hunting, for foxes or (far less frequently) stags, otters and hares, was another major obsession, especially in the midland counties of Northampton, Leicester and Nottingham, where foxes were numerous and where better drainage and hedged fields enhanced riding. The more exclusive, fashionable and elite hunts could be found there. Their hierarchical ordering, their invented traditions, uniforms and expensive hunting boxes all stressed breeding, bloodline and inheritance, as did many of their well-bred horses and hounds. Masters of Foxhounds were often aristocrats and gentry, more rarely purse-proud *parvenus*, not least since it cost an estimated £1800 to maintain a pack in 1858 and in 1899 one Master quoted £2300 each season.[24] Many upper-class families were hereditary hunters. The winter hunt balls were glittering annual social occasions for the county set, with numerous house parties attracting distinguished visitors and well-known hunting people from other hunts. There were usually large fields on the day following. The 1899 East Cheshire post-hunt ball meet at Willesden Hall saw a marquis, an earl, three barons and nine titled women as well as many members of the squirearchy.[25] Hunting supposedly knitted rural society together and reinforced county leadership, although not all farmers welcomed the hunt riding across their fields, damaging crops, walls and fences. It became ever more necessary to treat farmers gently and attentively, paying compensation for trespass and damage, and for using posts and rails instead of barbed wire. In Ireland, where tensions were at their greatest, the violence, disruption and sabotage of hunts, especially at the height of the Land War during 1881–82, made hunting so precarious that many gave up.

For some gentlemen shooting or hunting could become almost obsessive hobbies. The typical week of the country squire Colonel Davies Evans, for example, usually included at least three days shooting and one riding. During the hunt season he hunted up to four days a week with various packs, and he had friends visiting to shoot on his estate on a regular basis.[26] Others took to shooting as they grew too heavy to hunt. But increasing costs took their toll by the late nineteenth century. The Duke of Rutland was forced first to ask for subscriptions and then to cut his hunting back from five to four days a week in 1891, before he retired as Master of the Belvoir in 1896. The squire Henry Chaplin, who combined a political life with much horseracing and hunting from the early 1860s onwards, and still rode when over eighteen stone, was forced to sell his hounds in 1883 and his estate soon after.[27]

The huge financial costs of active sporting involvement at this level increased through the patronage of the sports that the leaders of society supported. Patronage helped to consolidate their social position in much the same way as their contributions to public utilities or education, but 'liberal' or 'zealous' support was expected by a wider public. Wealth and influence matched community conventions and traditions, but was confined to the regions of their estates, where they provided subscriptions to sporting events from horseracing to local sports. Some members of the elite, perhaps exercising social controls, appeared supportive of traditional values, although towards the end of the century financial pressures forced some retrenchment in sports from wrestling to racing.[28] They acted as stewards at horse races, coursing meetings or even athletic meetings, especially those of high status or held in rural surroundings where they could rely on a more deferential reception. Field sports, patronage and official positions as stewards provided regular occasions for shared enjoyment with tenants, helping to create a rural community, although at times fox hunting, and especially the increased unwillingness of some tenants to allow the hunt passage over their lands, created tensions.

Country house cricket was getting under way by the later 1840s, with teams of travelling fully-amateur 'gentlemen' clubs with fancy names such as I Zingari – the Gypsies (founded 1845), who owned no ground, but played at any country house where they were offered suitable hospitality and entertainment. Enthusiastic owners sometimes enlarged their houses to accommodate them. The 'cricketing wing' added to Ballywater Park in Ulster in the 1890s appropriately had twenty-two bedrooms.[29]

Some sports also allowed the elite to indulge their passion for pleasure and pageantry alongside high spending. Horseracing had its origins in aristocratic sport, and allowed the cream of aristocratic society to display itself at Ascot, Doncaster, Epsom and Newmarket. Queen Victoria took part in the royal procession at Ascot until Albert's death in 1861. The Prince of Wales became a member of the Jockey Club in 1864 and by 1890 was attending twenty-eight meetings a year, encouraging a wider sense of royal populism. More generally the leisured classes played a major role in breeding and racing throughout the period, and were particularly successful in the high-status classic races. They were central to racing's organisation, bought shares in grandstand companies, subscribed towards prize money, had private stands at meetings, owned a majority of top horses, and many bet heavily. Some were intent on making their racing pay, but many went racing for reasons of status and sociability, as members of racing clubs or as part of the racing house party.[30]

The widespread persistence of a belief in hierarchy, and lingering deference, ensured that the claims of birth, rank and privilege enabled the upper classes to be prominent on many ruling bodies in sport, even if their actual power was often less than it appeared. Lists of the landed dominated the Jockey Club, the MCC and the more select yacht clubs. Membership of Brooks, the Reform Club, the Turf Club and other important centres of betting in Victorian west and central London was also dominated by the landed and very wealthy. The clubs were also home to a large number of bachelors, who spent their idle hours there.

It was the expanding urban middle classes, especially those in the handsome houses, villas and other private residences of the growing urban suburbs, such as Birmingham's Edgbaston, Glasgow's West End and Nottingham's Park Estate, who were the main beneficiaries of the sports facilities and the new, modern sports of the second half of Victoria's

THE DERBY DAY, 1868.

Getting to the Derby, 1868.

reign. Glasgow's fashionable West End, for example, had curling and skating ponds, cricket and rugby grounds, bowling greens and tennis courts.[31] Their high income and discretionary free time allowed the middle classes wide choice in how they played or watched sport. They could afford entrance to commercial sports and were more likely to live near the suburban parks, golf courses, tennis courts or sports grounds, or own houses with tennis or croquet facilities.

They were a powerful cultural force, a highly significant and rapidly growing group in numbers and wealth. In the early Victorian period between a tenth and a fifth of the population of most large towns were already middle class.[32] By 1867, when some 90,000 solid middle-class families enjoyed incomes of £300 a year or more, and found working hours shortening, they were well placed to enjoy sporting leisure, although under 2 per cent of the families in England and Wales. Many of the far larger percentage of the lower middle classes (around 24 per cent), had incomes of less than £100 a year. But by 1904 some 3,750,000 people were living in the 'comfort' of over £160 annually.[33] More importantly, their social position and influence were extremely high in proportion to their numbers.

The Victorian middle classes were property-owning, engaged in occupations usually connected with manufacturing, trade and the professions, abstaining from manual wage labour. Classic studies have argued that they were marked by a powerful sense of class cohesion, a powerful work ethic and strong emphasis on respectability. Yet they were also marked by profound divisions.[34] From the 1840s and 1850s there were distinctions of wealth, religious identity and political rivalry, soon followed by a further separation between a landed, commercial and financial elite of imperially orientated 'gentleman capitalists' based on London and an industrial manufacturing interest with its strength in the north.[35] The rise of the professional group was a key feature of the later period. There was specially rapid growth in England and Wales, with 647,075 in 1881 and 926,132 in 1891, though this included army and navy officers.[36] This too was already, however, as the 1881 census remarked, 'a most heterogeneous class', something that became increasingly marked, although with a widening inequality gap between them and the working classes from the early 1880s.[37] Thus in sporting terms there were social pressures contributing to conformity but also divergent tendencies.

The middle classes took up sports and games with enthusiasm from the late 1860s onwards. In so doing, they made a unique contribution to national and world sport as a political, cultural and social entity and, more broadly, to British, imperial and global culture.[38] Their enthusiasm and energy for sport impacted on recreational culture, career access and the formation of class cultures and relationships. Their own sports had to be justified, and to have a sense of purpose, so supporting ideologies were created, even if sometimes characterised by hypocrisy, compromise and extension.

Pressures for conformity came from a number of directions. Most of all perhaps, it came from the public schools, where the cult of athleticism was the most telling of all influences.[39] The older public schools took increasing numbers of the upper middle classes, and they were followed by many of the newer public schools, a mixture of old and newly-endowed grammar schools, joint-stock proprietary and denominational schools. Together they diffused gentlemanly and public service ideals and new forms of games. Eton was playing cricket against both Westminster and Harrow by 1805, and by the 1840s competitive cricket was widespread. More systematically organised games out of school hours were encouraged by mid-Victorian masters like Charles Vaughan of Harrow, G. E. F. Cotton of Marlborough and Edward Thring of Uppingham. Pressure of numbers, disciplinary problems and educational idealism all played a part. Athleticism became a civilising offensive, aiding Christianity and education in the character-conditioning and health of sometimes badly-behaved, brutal or brutalised pupils, and promoting school identity.[40] It legitimised controlled confrontation in sports and games, thus aiding order and discipline, encouraging unselfishness, loyalty and team spirit, fostering leadership qualities, and grooming pupils for future working life. It also supposedly took adolescent minds off sex. The school house system, playing fields and team game competitions, cups and colours gave a major boost to the systematisation, reorganisation and regulation of modern sports, as former public school boys carried their sports into the wider world. From the mid nineteenth century public schools began to transform the nature and purpose of sport. Complex concepts such as those of 'manliness' or 'athleticism' were developed to aid the process, with notions of 'fair play' added later, and linked to imperialism and militarism. The games ethic became dominant across the public school system only by the 1880s, when school advertisements began featuring their facilities for cricket and outdoor sports ahead of their academic strengths. By the end of the century the more athletic school houses stressed virile toughness, sometimes coupled with flogging and sadism. Games were compulsory. The sporting elite of 'hearties' and 'bloods' was favoured and looked up to. The academic or aesthete was neglected or even reviled.

By the 1880s athleticism was penetrating the training colleges and grammar schools.[41] In the universities field sports retained a following amongst upper-class undergraduates, but a degree of devotion to healthy exercise, especially in its cricket and rowing manifestations, was encouraged, sustained in and then diffused from larger colleges like Trinity and Jesus at Cambridge, where many dons were supportive.[42] Between 1855 and 1900 about 80 per cent of Oxbridge students were former public schoolboys and it was here that the various local 'football' forms were slowly amalgamated in order to allow them to play together. Harrow's 'kicking' game and the Rugby 'handling' game proved the most significant. Colleges took their sports seriously, and intervarsity matches extended their range. Students may have been amateur, but the best took training seriously. By the later nineteenth century, the number of cricket coaches employed at Cambridge was approaching twenty. 'Blues' for cricket, rowing, and other athletic sports became a mark of amateur sporting status. Athletically inclined graduates in turn became sought after by the expanding public school system. Medical students were also in the forefront of sporting activity. By 1900 medical school prospectuses regularly made reference to their various athletic, cricket, football and tennis sports clubs as an added attraction of study.

City businessmen and plutocrats increasingly modelled their lifestyle on that of the leisure class. By 1862 the Royal Thames Yacht Club had a membership owning 240 yachts, but only a minority owned land. The vice-commodore was the shipowner Richard Green.[43] Many wealthy middle-class Londoners enjoyed the bucolic pleasures of hunting in the shires, an exodus growing with railway expansion and subscription packs. Political aspirants and social climbers enjoyed mixing with the county set, and numbers of packs increased. The famous Quorn Hunt was saved by a millionaire shipbroker in the 1870s. Provincial cities followed suit. By the 1890s 'hundreds of Birmingham magnates and

MENTOR AND TELEMACHUS.

Unsuccessful Oar. " I SAY, MUSCLES, HOW DO YOU ACCOUNT FOR MY BREAKING DOWN ?"

Trainer (reproachfully). " O, WERY EASILY, SIR. YER *WOULD* READ WHILE YER WOS IN COURSE O' TRAININ', AND I ALWAYS TOLD YER THAT BOOKS AND LITERATOOR AND THEM THINGS SPILED THE 'ANDS, AND WOS DEATH TO A GOOD EDUCATION."

Unsuccessful rower and his trainer, 1872. Coaches for rowing, cricket and athletics were to be found at some Oxbridge colleges to raise the standards of 'gentlemen amateurs'.

businessmen' devoted a large part of their leisure to the Warwickshire, Staffordshire and Worcestershire Hunts.[44]

Voluntary societies were a feature of Victorian Britain and sport was no exception, with, for example, racing, archery, coursing, yachting and cricket clubs even in the early Victorian period. Members were usually elected and predominantly upper and middle class. Meetings were infrequent, but club houses were already being set up. The Royal Yacht Squadron, for example, met monthly at its club house in Cockspur Street.[45] Tattersall's, at Hyde Park Corner, was the leading subscription betting club, with a membership around two hundred in the late 1830s. Elite sports clubs were largely run by the middle classes, exercising their educational and organisational skills. The middle-class Weatherby family provided a highly lucrative system of advice and support to the Jockey Club throughout the century, preserving the illusion of upper-class power while enjoying its fruits.[46] Sports clubs grew in number from the beginning of the period. In the Stirling area, for example, there were twenty-five clubs in the 1830s but already fifty-one in the 1840s.[47] By the 1870s and 1880s growing middle-class wealth, and increasing suburban spread in larger towns, combined to create enormous numbers of sports clubs in these areas catering for a wide range of amateur sports. In Stirling, even where club membership was more diverse, public service and professional men dominated the ranks of club officials and function attenders.

The pattern of middle-class involvement in sport was highly complex. Middle-class sport could be socially exclusive. Anxiety over the extent to which the growing democratisation of leisure obscured traditional class markers was revealed in the way some clubs and sports made great efforts to restrict contact with those they regarded as their social inferiors: through rules, prohibitively high entry, annual subscription or other costs, through blackballing systems of secret ballot election to membership or by only competing against social equals. It could also be done by high entrance fees. The first Wimbledon Tennis Championship, in 1876, cost a guinea to take part in. Up to the 1870s cricket was a relatively exclusive summer urban sport. New sports with no aristocratic roots emerged, like golf, tennis, amateur athletics, amateur rowing and cycling, and such clubs proliferated later in the century. Their membership was often relatively exclusive in class terms.

Where such clubs were set up in middle-class suburbs, well away from working-class areas, this was inevitable. Improvements in rail transport soon saw an expansion both of the middle-class seaside holiday and of commuter resorts. Both created a demand for golf links courses and tennis courts, recreating suburban leisure life at the seaside.[48] The numbers of more exclusive clubs, however, were far exceeded by those with a more cross-class membership. Success rarely went hand in hand with exclusivity. Golf clubs, tennis clubs or harriers clubs which did not compete with other clubs, but only amongst themselves, could afford to be exclusive. In sports like football or cricket, cross-class membership, especially when seeking the best players of whatever class, was far more common.

By the 1860s the middle classes had adjusted to leisure, however conceptualised. Some saw it as an extension of work, others as an antithesis to work, or something quite different. Many saw their sports as 'improving' of body, health and character, a form of 'rational recreation'. Physical fitness was seen as an antidote to sedentary middle-class urban life. Sport helped to teach morality, build character and promote the social order. Vigorous activity helped to prove the manliness of the growing numbers of office workers of all kinds. This increased sporting enthusiasm was thus partly in pursuit of physical, social and moral health. Competitive sporting struggle within agreed parameters, with sufficient hazard to promote manliness, became a positive force in society. Amateur sport became a medium of personal, communal and national virtue. At the same time it was sociable, entertaining, uplifting and complemented work and labour.

Not all the middle classes wanted to distance themselves from the working classes. The sporting paternalism and 'welfare capitalism' of the upper middle classes sometimes involved organising sports clubs for the workers, and the workplace played an important role in encouraging working-class participation. Sometimes this was because owners or managers themselves had a strong interest in the sport. The Coleman mustard family were keen cricketers at Norwich in the 1840s; the Pilkington glass family enjoyed rugby in the 1880s. In other cases initiatives often came from workers, with the industrialists providing grounds, and sometimes subsidising equipment on the 'muscular Christian' basis that a healthier workforce with higher morale and sporting identity would be more productive and efficient, and counteract the temptations of drink, gambling and violence. Sir Titus Salt (1803–1876), the Bradford industrialist, founded the cricket club, and later boating and bowls clubs, at his Saltaire model village. At Bourneville the Cadbury brothers played cricket with their men in the 1860s. They provided football and cricket facilities in 1879, opened a recreation ground in 1896 for the Bourneville Athletic Club, and built open-air baths with covered dressing rooms in 1898. Cadbury's women workers were required to learn to swim for cleanliness, but the company provided sports facilities 'to develop manual dexterity and visual awareness which are the commercial object'.[49] Arsenal, West Ham and Newton Heath (Manchester United) all originated as works sides. Breweries also sometimes organised sports clubs for their employees. Railway companies, and railway towns like Crewe, often encouraged involvement in sport amongst their workers. The London and North-Western Railway provided a cycle and running track, football pitch, tennis and bowls courts for Wolverton Railway Carriage employees in 1885. Directors and employers saw playing and watching sport as a source of social control and stability, keeping workers from drinking and betting, and encouraging a sporting sense of 'fair play'.

While actually competing against the lower orders could be awkward, respectable capitalists were leading investors in more commercialised sports, pursuing profit as well as pleasure. Businessmen, politicians and publicans all saw opportunities for profit, prestige and political opportunity in sport. Publicans, with brewers, were a particularly formidable vested interest, organising sporting activity from early in the period, but increasingly almost all the major sports involving professionals, especially those popular with working-class spectators, were organised, run and financed largely by the middle classes.[50] Without their financial 'sporting investment' in football, cricket, rugby and other clubs, these would certainly never have got off the ground.[51] Wanting to compete, and be successful, against the best was important to such men, and here there was far less support for amateurism.

Ice-rinks, racecourses, professional football clubs and general recreational companies wanted all classes involved to maximise profit. Equally some middle-class groups very much enjoyed watching these more commercial sports. Such spectator participation could act as a safety-valve from their more respectable, decorous public roles. The

increased emphasis on spectacle was part of a heightened urban awareness of the ways in which social roles could be differently assumed,
played out and performed in different contexts. Sport provided an outlet for profuse emotions and created an enjoyable fantasy world. The
middle classes could be found in the grandstand at racing, professional
football or pedestrian events in significant numbers. At larger First
Division grounds there were more than 3000 grandstand seats by the
mid 1890s. At northern events, hooting and booing seemed in some
grounds 'to be even more plentiful on the grandstand than the plebeian
field', although actual stand disturbances were unusual.[52] At Derby, for
example, there was reportedly regular abuse of visiting soccer teams
from the 'toffs', those 'well-dressed cads and Johnnies that bellow
from the pavilion steps ... who from appearances should be models of
propriety'.[53]

Middle-class respectability was never particularly strong, even
amongst the middle classes. The clear pressures for convergence, coming often from social contexts such as the domestic arena, were often
balanced by divergent tendencies, pulling middle-class sportsmen in
different directions. Some initially select clubs like London Athletic
Club moved toward more mixed membership to increase membership
or success. Many middle-class men, including sporting journalists,
clergymen, teachers and other professionals, were keen to spread sport
amongst urban workers and play alongside them too. Middle-class
complaints, appeals against results and highly competitive approaches
all indicated that winning could be as important as sport for its own
sake or 'playing the game'. There was also a very significant middle-class
group which enjoyed less respectable sporting activities such as betting
or pugilism, and in a number of sporting leisure contexts less
respectable middle-class behaviour was quite common.[54] What consti-
tuted the rational and respectable was not always agreed upon, and the
united social front based on contained sociability, amateur values and
expanded sporting repertoires was more apparent than real.

The later Victorian middle classes became even more protean and
amorphous with the expansion from the 1870s of what was beginning to
be called 'the lower middle classes' of small entrepreneurs, wholesalers,
tradesmen, shopkeepers and clerks, as well as industrial, commercial
and poorer professional families.[55] This was a far larger group, with

many members earning less than £100 a year, trying to maintain middle-class standards on inadequate income. Some desperately clung to status, to membership of separate middle-class clubs; others exploited the expanding opportunities to enjoy more bohemian and less conformist pleasures.[56] The growing numbers of clerks faced particular problems. Clerking was an unheroic and non-manual occupation, like that of the male shopworker, and one sometimes presented as implying diminished masculinity.[57] The new organised games of the 1880s saved the manly reputation of many such men, preventing such 'counter skippers' from being unsexed.[58] Whilst the costs of purchasing the paraphernalia of sporting gentility were too high for many, this group played soccer or rugby, rowed or cycled in significant numbers. With 300 cycling clubs in London alone in the 1890s, most members were lower middle class.[59] Lower middle-class elementary teachers, the products of the various training colleges, were, with older pupils, often key figures in the soccer sides of the early 1880s.

While sensitive to their respectability, some had less to lose by acts of nonconformity. Bachelor clerks, single shop assistants and unmarried commercial travellers were often caricatured as a restless, disruptive and socially threatening group found in music halls, pubs and urban streets, but they also played hard in sporting terms, and were to the fore in the social activities of sporting clubs.

The religious and secular branches of the cross-class reformist group were the most 'respectable' in Victorian society, exercising vociferous pressure from both above and below against much sporting activity. Victorian sports were shaped within the constraints and pressures which such reformers generated, even though by 1851 church attendance was already falling. They helped to impose standards and expectations on many sports, and had some positive impact on sporting honesty while setting sports within firm limits of time. Their supporters amongst the middle classes sought a paternalistic and well-intentioned disciplining and civilising of public space, time and popular sporting culture, attacking hedonism and excess. A radical and politically-conscious wing of the working classes, including some Chartists and Owenite Socialists, tried to live out a genuine, all-embracing alternative culture, emphasising seriousness, sobriety and self-improvement.

The reformers shared a core of beliefs even if there were differences in their access to power and cultural capital. Working-class improvers were often suspicious of the motives of apparently liberal reformist philanthropists. Their active numbers were relatively small, and reformist culture was plagued by discontinuities, divisions and rivalries, but they were potentially powerful, claiming the support of a supposedly silent majority, and making sport a matter for serious critical debate. They tried to construct a more respectable, 'rational' approach to all forms of recreation, one more in tune with the economic and social order now emerging.

Reformists adopted a strongly self-improving approach to sport. Some middle-class reformers were driven, by fear of the working classes and concerns about popular radicalism or Chartism, to avoid or to oppose those sports and games perceived as unnecessarily cruel, brutal and uncivilised, potentially boisterous, disorderly or violent, or fermenting unlawful assembly, potential riot and property damage. Such sports were popular amongst the young, and fear of the dangerous potentiality of such activities made opposition the more vigorous, particularly during the politically unstable 1830s.

Religious belief was an important axis of respectability, strongest in its assurance amongst Methodist chapel-goers of whatever class, with the Church of England occupying a middle position. Churches embodied spiritual authority, and virtuous reformists were driven by evangelical Christian belief, zeal and concern for personal salvation to attack manifestations of worldly pleasure-seeking conviviality and brutality, a form of moral imperialism whose manifestations in press, pulpit and public administration were often evident if their actual impact was perhaps less clear. They were hostile to gambling, the drinking of alcohol and a morally degrading sporting life. To the most puritan, all sport was improper use of God-given time. As the incumbent of St George's in Leicester told his captive congregation, at a special religious football service in 1892, 'exercise thyself rather unto godliness, for bodily exercise profiteth little'.[60]

Fervent reformists avoided the playing of sports, emphasised a domestic sociability which circumscribed the extent to which women could leave the home, and actively opposed sports involving animal cruelty. The *Liverpool Mercury* was not alone in castigating not only

steeplechasing but 'cockfighting, bull-baiting or any other popular pastime which is attended by the infliction of wanton torture', and the
latter sports were stopped or the subject of strong enough disapproval
to lose much of their popularity.[61] Bull-baiting in the Midlands ceased
in the later 1830s and early 1840s. Mass football at Derby became seen as
'rude and brutal barbarism' and was suppressed.[62] At Stamford, the bull-
running, a long-customary part of the recreational calendar, formerly
supported by local MPs and members of all classes and defended on the
grounds of parish-based rights of custom, labour, practice and place,
was eventually stopped in the 1840s, largely through external reformist
pressure. In the village of Tysoe some thought that 'Methodism had
killed the [old] sports because the best sportsmen had been converted'.[63]

By the mid-Victorian period this seriousness of purpose, emphasis on
domestic leisure and suspicion of pleasure had already begun to slacken.
Muscular Christian principles began to allow limited respectable sporting involvement, although the more earnest still played sports, if at all,
for spiritual and mental recreation. Some, driven by enlightened social
reform, implied that sporting recreations could and should be brisk and
purposeful; but, even so, the more reformist, high-minded prim moral-
ists still wanted all sports to meet Evangelical and dutiful purposes.
Urban streets such of those of Merthyr were cleared of informal foot-
races or prizefights to curb such 'brutal practices' of their persistent
popularity.[64]

More rational recreations were a way of remaking and improving
working-class activities, behaviours and values. Educational activities
provided associations for reformist sympathisers. Key leaders of church
social clubs or mechanics institutes were often reformers who saw some
sports as a 'rational' alternative, a missionary endeavour drawing the
young away from temptation and vice by offering self-improving physical, healthy and wholesome outlets for their misdirected energies. At
Blackley, for example, the Mechanics Institute called on the 'respectable
inhabitants' to restrain drunkenness, gambling, quarrelling and fighting,
to encourage exhibitions of running, leaping and climbing, and to
organise sports and games.[65] The Bristol YMCA had a cricket team in
1862, a gymnasium in 1879, and by the 1880s it offered swimming, cricket,
soccer, hockey, harriers and cycling. Sports became viewed as ways of
stressing the middle-class values of hard work, cooperation, courage and

honesty. Respectability had an impact on the commercialisation of sporting leisure too, placing pressure on organisers of sports grounds to conform, and to display notices about the banning of betting or swearing in order to avoid public condemnation. But such moves had limited success. The middle classes were not fully committed in support, while working-class resistance was more powerful than expected.

Elevating 'rational recreation' often meant a denigration of the sheer enjoyment of some activities associated with sport. The rowdy and unrestrained behaviour of crowds at sporting events, and their association with alcohol, was a challenge to Christian moral precepts and principles, and a focus for the Temperance movement. So many teams played on public house pitches or changed at public houses that in Sheffield local Sunday schools soon formed their own association. Opposition to betting united both religious and secular strands, but preaching, petitions, press articles, anti-racing demonstrations, counter-attractions and educational trips all had only very limited success.

Reformist attitudes to sports themselves became more positive from the 1860s. Sport slowly became an important focus of recreational activity for young churchgoers of whatever class. Sunday schools for the young were seen as nurseries to extend adult church attendance. Religious clubs and associations increasingly offered sport, especially football and cricket, as a key attraction, a rational sectarian recreation to help evangelise the poor, although even in the 1890s the Methodists were much less likely to do so than other nonconformists, and the Anglicans led the way. Wakefield Trinity, for example, as the name suggests, was originally a church rugby club. Rented 'mission houses', with professional lay missionaries, were established in the slums. In Scotland Queens Park (1867) grew out of the YMCA, Hibernians (1875) out of the Catholic Young Men's Society. In the 1880s and 1890s the YMCA, the Church Army, the Boys' Brigade and Church Lads' Brigade all used sport for such purposes. Boxing, under the Queensberry Rules, appealed as character building for such youths. Playing team games encouraged co-operation and discipline. Indeed, the first north-east soccer club to reach an FA quarter final (in 1885/6) was Redcar and Coatham YMCA.[66] Perhaps as a response to the growing use of Sundays for sports such as rowing, croquet, tennis and golf, Anglican and nonconformist churches in large urban areas increasingly encouraged the involvement of working lads in Saturday team sports. Sport's temperate attractions became part of such practical Christianity, providing medicinal obligatory attendance at a Bible-class, with cricket and football to take the taste away. Even so, soccer and other games were still being denounced by some as a thoroughly demoralising influence, a 'madness', at the century's end.[67] The regularly repeated, unbending nonconformist equation of worldly leisure and pleasure with sin, and a belief in total abstinence, meant its members found it difficult to accommodate sport's role in popular culture within their world view. It contributed to their marginalisation.

In mid Victorian England and Wales about 14 per cent of families were those of skilled artisans, a group that had a strong sense of pride in its craft culture, and was more able to defend customary practices. Artisans did not thoughtlessly take on 'respectable' middle-class values and aspirations. They accepted middle-class money and sponsorship but not its ideology. They invested their own meanings into sport. Their 'respectability' was concerned more with status and self-respect within their own group. They saw themselves as self-confident and able to make their own choices as to how they lived, which limited the effect of pressures from above or reformists' schemes of more 'rational' recreations.[68] Even in the 1840s artisans, especially in the handicraft trades in towns like London, Sheffield, Nottingham and Birmingham (where small workshops still dominated), were still able to regulate their own hours. At Windsor, in 1840, it was those 'sons of Vulcan', the local blacksmiths, whom *Bell's Life* classically described as able to get up friendly cricket matches.[69]

In such areas, along with the Potteries mines and brickfields, and the South Wales ironworks, an almost institutionalised 'St Monday' absenteeism was used for much of the century to enjoy a variety of more informal sporting leisure, sometimes at the expense of working in the evening or at night after.[70] Skilled workers had the time, money, work security and control over work conditions to play and watch sport, although not every week and not always on Mondays, though miners in Warwickshire, who were paid fortnightly, might take the following Monday off. But around mid-century matters of 'universal' sporting interest like a prize fight might only be five or six such occasions all summer. Artisans helped provide the large and regular paying clientele which provided a critical mass for those commercial sports which were best able to integrate and accommodate the features of earlier traditional forms. Along with the wealthier they attended the early enclosed running tracks in the 1840s and early 1850s, such as the Hyde Park Grounds in Sheffield, Belle Vue at Manchester, or the Copenhagen House, Red House and Royal Oak grounds in London. An 1870 visitor to the Hyde Park Grounds saw it as filled with 'groups of sturdy artizans, all resolutely breasting the hill and paying their money', while all top pedestrians had 'maisters', who backed their men'.[71] On London's Isle of Dogs during the summer skilled artisan workers in the ironworks, shipbuilding and marine engineering works spent much of their leisure time in practising, supporting or promoting boat-racing, footracing and other athletic sports, and following pugilism.[72] In Stirling, in the early 1880s craftsmen, tradesmen and skilled workers provided a majority of participants in football, quoiting, athletics, and cricket, and a significant minority of those identified as anglers and curlers. Football crowds nationally by the 1890s seem to have been disproportionately made up by artisans, coming together in a boisterous mass to enjoy the game. Skilled workers were often the first semi-professional players of soccer and rugby.

The best off were well capable of appearing respectable, hard-working labour aristocrats, serious members of reputable bowls or cricket clubs. But they could also play hard, enjoy less respectable recreations, be indifferent to their 'betters', and show an active refusal of upper- and middle-class patronage. Some were attracted to heavy-drinking sports. Even in the 1860s some of the best paid were claimed to be 'notorious for their addiction to drunkenness and to brutal and brutalizing sports'.[73] They did not turn to the temperance movement in great numbers. Betting, most especially on the horses, attracted many.

If such men joined the Volunteer forces, it was often for the non-military activities such as sport they provided.[74] Where they joined middle-class clubs, they adopted an instrumental attitude to respectability and amateurism. They enjoyed sporting success in part for the self-esteem and higher community standing it brought. They were the vanguard of working-class inclusion in sport, working their way onto middle-class clubs and teams because of their earning power, providing the bulk of spectators at commercialised sports, and aiding the development of professionalism. In Scotland, the North and Midlands between 20 and 40 per cent of shareholders in the 1890s soccer clubs were skilled working men. In the north east, for example, they made up 22 per cent of Sunderland Albion's shareholders. At Middlesbrough Ironopolis the figure was 45 per cent. Glasgow Rangers in 1899 had over 30 per cent.

In the early part of the century England was still a rural nation, but by 1901 only about a fifth of the population lived in the countryside. We know less of the sporting world there than we should, since rural popular culture from the early nineteenth century was often only recorded in the accounts of the unsympathetic, as it came under threat from enclosure, and the increased disapproval of gentry and farmer patrons. Rural culture and traditions such as the foot-races, sack-races, women's smock races, climbing the greasy pole, or chasing a soap-tailed pig often found at local races and sports slowly disappeared, although this varied from region to region. Many recreational sporting traditions, especially the more cruel animal sports, and turbulent customary rough sports like wrestling and backsword, were undermined by moral reformers.[75] Later writers spoke of them nostalgically. In the Thames valley the old sports and festivals 'used to brighten up the year for farm people, and if they were rude and simple, noisy and boisterous, they served their purpose very well, and were always hailed with unfeigned joy and delight'.[76] Sports like cockfighting disappeared underground, sustained by families who had often been involved in the sport for generations.

Almost certainly, opportunities for sport in the countryside varied as greatly as rural settlement. In the Lake Counties and the upland northern Pennines, many villages sustained traditional athletic sports and games, including wrestling, usually organised by local committees, with local landowners subscribing prize money. The strongest shepherds, quarrymen or masons could supplement income by competition in a number of such events annually.[77] Further south there were agricultural areas of mixed farming, wood pasture and open pasture. There were 'closed' villages dominated by single landowners.[78] There were also 'open' villages, where the landlords and clergy were unable to exercise firm control.[79] Then, too, there were industrial villages, with much in common with urban popular culture, though in rural settings. In the mining villages of south Northumberland the increased free time of the mid-Victorian period allowed miners to compete with other miners in a wide range of sports: potshare bowling, dog racing, foot races, pigeon flying and quoits. Traditional sports survived too. In the 1890s, most Durham coursing clubs still bore the names of collieries. The north-eastern mining villages began competing in football cups in the 1880s, when their cricket teams began playing teams from outside the mining communities. The Nottingham framework knitters, working in their village homes at hours of their choice, were able to organise work to enjoy cricket practice. Bill Underwood, the proprietor of Ruddington's cricket ground in 1881, was a framework knitter, and Ruddington was famous for the number of its men who became professional cricketers during the summer.[80]

In most villages, farm workers had six-day weeks and poor pay. Recognised holidays were rare, perhaps only Christmas and Good Friday. There were very few recreational sporting opportunities, beyond occasional angling or hunting small animals for food. Quoits might be played on summer evenings. In Norfolk, many public houses had a quoit bed, and one public house used to play against another.

Annual celebrations often offered sporting opportunities. In 1871 Francis Kilvert, the Radnorshire curate, observed that after the parish harvest festival dinner, 'all the men played or rather kicked football at each other ... till it grew dark, when the game ended in a general royal scuffle'.[81] In the south many open villages had a Sunday cricket team, providing there was common land available or a field could be found. In the early summer, before the harvest began, with the longer summer evenings, it was not unusual to see a number of the younger men at play at cricket in the meadow with the more active of the farmers.[82] Cricket sides could accommodate the deferential relationships and social variety of rural society relatively easily. John Reid's 1878 bucolic painting, *A Country Cricket Match*, shows a Sussex scene with local gentry and shepherds sitting around a table and milkmaids grouped nearby. The cricket field soon ranked with the alehouse as the symbolic centre of rural life. Even the 'quarry roughs' of Headington had a 'rough sort of cricket – not much style ... plenty of barrels of beer'.[83] In larger villages, with a cricket club and ground, it was richer farmers and skilled men who were most likely to play. By the turn of the century there were more permanent village cricket fields, replacing occasional use of the local landlord's.[84] During the winter informal football, using a pig's bladder, was sometimes found. In areas with a nearby race meeting or steeple-chase, contemporary pictures, newspaper descriptions and even novels indicate that local farm labourers often took, or were given, time off to attend. Sports days were occasional events in some villages. In some areas they survived, or were repatronised and reorganised by middle class committees. The Methodists often provided sport as a secular satis-faction to parallel the spiritual pleasures of preaching and worship. In some rural areas, membership of the Volunteers provided access to sporting participation.

Country folk were better able to read sporting press reports, often in their local inns, by the later nineteenth century, when the culture of the countryside became more affected by urban sporting patterns. Improved communications and better transport of railways and cycles meant rural recreational culture was becoming less distinct.

Some hunting fiction suggested that fox-hunting involved local vil-lagers, straddled class lines and brought the classes together. But the hunting village blacksmith or carrier must have been a rarity, and other village workers, let alone farm workers, were hardly in the hunt.[85] They may have enjoyed its spectacle, but it was they who felt the constraints of the game laws, leading to a wider sense of social injustice and a con-tempt for the law.

Up to 1901 sport was largely an urban phenomenon, and still often more middle class or relatively exclusive. Although a majority of workers lived in towns, urban popular sporting culture was regularly enjoyed only by a small minority of workers. It was often localised, isolated, conserva-tive and fragmented, oriented more towards pleasure than politics, and often portrayed (by the middle classes) as distinguished by physicality, sensual excess and threatening behaviour. While the urban working class had internal divisions, and could be seen as fragmented, not least through regional and ethnic differences, pressure from above drew the working classes together.[86] During the nineteenth century urban popu-lations expanded enormously, both as a consequence of an influx from the countryside and through natural growth, yet the typical worker was more likely to be a domestic servant or craftsman than a textile worker.

Most of the unskilled were time-poor and cash-poor, though the last quarter of the century saw an increase in real money wages thanks largely to reductions in the price and taxation of foodstuffs. This rising plane of prosperity for those in regular employment meant, according to Charles Booth's 1892 survey, that over half of London's population were both working class and comfortably off, living in more 'respectable' housing, and with additional opportunities for leisure and sporting recreations.

In towns, most workers watched rather than participated in sport. Lack of space, the cost of equipment and reformist opposition all limited opportunities for participation, except for the outstandingly athletic in a job such as professional waterman. Angling was perhaps the most common working-class participatory sport, most especially in London. Around Stirling, from 1880–83, the semi- and unskilled only participated significantly in athletics, quoiting and football, and made a very modest contribution to angling, cricket, and curling.[87] Club membership was relatively rare. In the early Victorian period spectator sports such as race meetings, traditional football or wrestling championships were rare, usually annual urban events, often on unenclosed common ground, looked forward to and discussed for months beforehand. Most local men and women, boys and girls might attend. Rational recreations had little appeal to them. Later, urban popular culture was increasingly composed of enclosed, gate money spectator sports. Working-class spectatorship, like participation, became largely male, a economic activity requiring the purchase of services. Publicans organised a variety of more regularly held events, pigeon shooting, pedestrianism or even rabbit coursing, charging admission and selling alcohol. In professional rowing, where there were many free vantage points, crowds were still large in the early 1880s before declining, as successful association and rugby football sides began to attract larger skilled working-class male followings and charge admission.

The culture of athleticism and club development had some limited impact, but many working-class participant sports were self-initiated. Workers created their own sporting culture with support and organisation rooted in the local community or neighbourhood, and were relatively resistant to pressure from above.[88] They entered sporting urban space in larger numbers by the 1880s, working upon it, imitating, rejecting or subverting it for their own ends. Their sports were often highly competitive, pursuing status and prizes, and the bowling, whippet racing, pigeon racing or handball in the mining communities of Northumberland or Derbyshire provided examples. Crown-green bowling, quoiting and professional pedestrianism often had gambling connections. Betting continued to be a key part of working-class sport, and women as well as men could be found in urban areas playing a role in the making and taking of bets. Even angling, probably the most widespread working-class participant sport, with its many urban angling clubs, had much competition and betting associated with it.

The semi-skilled and unskilled urban working classes, living in the slums, with no surplus income or discretionary time, and with most public recreational areas some distance away in the suburbs, found fewest opportunities for participation and spectatorship. Larger towns with a predominantly working-class population, such as Jarrow or Wallsend, had very few sporting successes. Even late in the century major enquiries suggested that not all had shared the economic prosperity of the age. The surveys of Charles Booth suggested that 8 per cent of Londoners were living in primary poverty between 1886 and 1892.[89] B. S. Rowntree proposed a figure of 10 per cent for York in 1901.[90] A figure close to a further 20 per cent seems to have been living at a level of secondary poverty, where extravagance or ignorance meant wages were spent unwisely. Involvement must also have been affected by the trade cycle, and unemployment increased in the 1880s. For many workers, tiredness, lack of money and time meant little opportunity for playing or watching, and cultural barriers locked working-class women out almost entirely. The substantial group of domestic servants, whether male or female, equally had little time for sport. Their employers sometimes believed that their employees did not need or desire exercise. This did not necessarily mean a lack of interest in sports. Even the unemployed might still show an interest in betting on racing results. In the larger towns, slum communities like Whitechapel provided a shelter for more traditional sports such as pugilism, dog fights, rat-killing, or even cock-fighting and badger-baiting in 'sporting' pubs, regularly reported on by mid-Victorian observers investigating 'low life'.[91] Working-class urban children played football through winter and summer in streets and yards, making goals from lamp posts and coats, and using 'tanner pills' or tightly rolled paper balls, though reformist pressures ensured that the street became increasingly policed. When eleven 'juniors' were prosecuted in Dowlais in 1890 the magistrate expressed the hope that they 'would all turn out good footballers' but fined them and told them to 'practice elsewhere'.[92] In Manchester, lads were forming their own teams from the ages of ten to twelve by the early twentieth century. They showed far less interest in playing cricket, a game not taught in their schools. Even so, according to one lads' club secretary they nearly all took a great interest in county cricket press reports, and 'scores of boys' could 'dispute, with no little knowledge, the chances of the various counties'.[93]

In the new leisure world of later Victorian Britain, working-class sports tended to emphasise aggression and playing to win. Animality, excess and boisterousness, fierce parochialism and indifference to amateurism continued to be features of popular sport, now seeing increased numbers of working-class professionals and the hero-worship of top sportsmen.[94] Later chapters will explore in more detail working-class involvement in sport, including the nature and scale of sporting urban commercialism, the place of betting on sport, the large crowds, the emergence of stars and professionals, and the role of the sporting press in fostering such interest.

3

Amateurs and Professionals

Sir Arthur Conan Doyle, himself a keen cricketer, argued that the main reason for playing cricket and other sports was that it kept men 'fit for the serious duties of life'.[1] Sir Henry Newbolt, the famous poet of late Victorian sporting imperialism, went further, arguing that even how the 'game' was played was important for social and moral salvation, and that playing should not be for actual or symbolic reward.

Only a minority espoused such sporting values, although their greater access to power and dominance aided the diffusion of their views. Sport was a primary fault line in Victorian society, creating and reflecting cultural and ideological tensions, divisions and conflicts amongst players, spectators and wider society, and raising problems of class, status and authority. Ownership of particular sports, their core values and the place of competition and winning were all debated. Despite the growing competitiveness of sport at the higher levels, the idea of serious competition was denied by some sports club members. Such men claimed extrinsic rewards were unimportant, boasting 'we are not overwhelmed with mortification when we lose, or puffed up with pride when we win. We play for play's sake far more than for victory'.[2] But for others, in sport as in industry, winning and success increasingly mattered, and became matters of status and potential gain. Money, in a commercial age, caused major strife. By the 1870s it was accepted that 'at important meetings and in all important races the prizes must be of substantial value'.[3] Equally, when the middle classes played they often played violently, in ways many had learnt at public schools. And winning was important. In their football games of the 1870s, before the introduction of neutral referees, teams argued amongst themselves, and games were often marred by gamesmanship to help them win.

Sport reflected Victorian social divisions. Social reformers and powerful groups within the expanding upper-middle classes wanted to impose their sporting meanings and fight off perceived threats. Sport articulated, debated and developed ideas about behaviour and social norms. Class, gender and region all affected the cultural dilemmas, ideological conflicts or the perceived meanings of and extent of commitment to terms like 'amateur', 'sportsmanship' and even 'manliness'. Some wanted the pace of change to quicken, others opposed any change.

The 'amateur question', and attitudes to working-class players and spectators, emerged at different times in different sports, it was a middle-class way of marking social difference, confirming class boundaries, controlling property, organisations and membership and asserting power. In 1800 the terms 'professional' or 'professor' had been indicators of a high level of expertise, and could apply to any class. By the 1830s 'professional' referred to individuals of lower social status earning money from sport. 'Amateur' in 1800 was a synonym for an upper-class patron or sporting enthusiast (whether or not earning money from sport). Later the term was sometimes expanded as 'gentleman-amateur'. But after mid century 'amateurs' were participants in sports the middle classes were appropriating. 'For practical purposes', claimed an 1889 editorial, amateurs 'may be said to have been invented at the time of the athletic revival, rather more than a quarter of a century ago.' They had 'gradually grown in numbers, and have come prominently into notice', and their status and activities had 'been a good deal discussed'.[4] Amateurism was of less interest inside working-class culture, failing to surface, for example, in music-hall songs about sport.

Even in the equipoise of the mid-Victorian period a more class-based society saw some middle-class members beginning to define themselves as different in terms of their values and attitudes, partly because of threatened inroads from the working classes. Inclusion and exclusion became major concerns. Some sports, previously more popular, such as rowing or athletics, became increasing appropriated, organised and controlled by the middle classes, even if their rhetoric still claimed that sport promoted patriotism, and helped bring 'peer' and 'peasant' together in class conciliation. Growing middle-class unease about wider social unrest, the impact of the cotton depression of the 1860s and the later Great Depression, and the growth of new unionism, reached a

OUR ANNUAL HOLIDAY.

Mr. Punch. "AH, DEAR BOYS! THIS IS BETTER FUN, THAN ABUSING ONE ANOTHER AT WESTMINSTER."

Politicians at Epsom, 1868. Prime Ministers, leading politicians
and Mr Punch all enjoyed a day at the races.

further peak in the 1890s. In the context of anguished conflicts over how sport should be approached, the status of 'amateur' and 'professional' sportsmen was increasingly important.

Amateurism, accompanied by snobbishness, hypocrisy and double standards, became emblematic of class.[5] In swimming the National Swimming Society (formed in 1837) included professional swimmers, but, later in the century, London records of the Metropolitan Swimming Association and the Swimming Association of Great Britain both contain much matter relating to discussions of amateur status and the need to ban professionals. This forced teachers of swimming and swimming entertainers to form a Professional Swimming Association in 1881. In a more fluid society, as traditional markers of social division eroded, a central concern to many social aspirants was to establish clear lines of status hierarchy in the new sports. It led in rowing and athletics to rival competing bodies, and in rugby to mutually exclusive codes.

Yet making money from sport was not new. In Georgian England gentlemen cricketers often hired professionals. Racehorse owners employed lightweight professional jockeys, and prize fighters and pedestrians helped employers win bets. Spectators and betters cared little about their status, so long as their man won. In the 1840s and 1850s the term 'amateur' was occasionally applied to enthusiasts who played simply for love of the game, regardless of standard or class. In rowing, for example, the Northern Rowing Club on the Tyne had both amateur and 'professional' members, and many elsewhere viewed this in a broad and tolerant manner.[6] But, even at this time, it was always important to clarify players' social standing. In cricket gentlemen amateurs and working-class professionals did not mix socially. Professionals ate their own food with the spectators. Amateurs ate with the committee and members in the pavilion dining area.

The key distinction was between 'gentlemen' and the rest, limiting and stabilising the democratic thrust of Victorian society. In racing, for example, some races were restricted to 'gentlemen riders', to avoid competition with the lower orders. In the 1860s such riders included those 'persons generally received into Society as Gentlemen', those belonging to a select list of London clubs, officers on full pay, magistrates, peers, or those bearing a courtesy title, or simply those balloted in by the National Hunt Committee. The aristocracy were as anxious as the bourgeoisie to

distance themselves from inferiors. Being paid was not the major crite-
rion, even if gentlemen supposedly did not take money for riding or
travelling expenses. Indeed it was well known that some happily took
money for riding. 'Gentlemanly' status was based on title, education and
land. Money gained by trade had lower status. This was the traditional
snobbery of those who already possessed such attributes. *The Times*, for
example, initially castigated steeplechasing as 'set up by publicans and
horse-dealers to pillage the unwary and enrich themselves'.[7]

Predominantly middle-class sporting clubs emerged in greater numbers in the 1840s, creating opportunities for public status display. These
clubs sought further exclusivity, keeping people out, not letting people
in, on the model of Jockey Club or MCC membership or entry into the
royal enclosure at Ascot. In rowing, for example, entry to the Henley
Regatta, established in 1839, with winning a matter of honour not
reward, was confined to 'any crew composed of members of a College
of either of the Universities of Oxford, Cambridge, or London, the
schools of Eton or Westminster, the officers of the two brigades of
Household Troops or of members of a club established at least one year
previous'. The more provincial and thus slightly less elite organisers of
Lancaster's 1846 regatta might perhaps allow a crew of 'master tradesmen' to compete, thought *Bell's Life*, but certainly not journeymen or
working mechanics.[8] There was to be no entry of the lower classes into
these symbolic centres of bourgeois leisure.

From the 1850s the aspirant middle classes entered urban sports, especially in London, in larger numbers. Increased access to public school
and university provided an introduction to the rhetoric of leadership,
respectability, character, moral fibre, sportsmanship and fair play, coupled with belief in the gentleman amateur. Their socially powerful clubs
extended 'gentleman' to include, for example, the Civil Service. Some
clubs with impeccable credentials, such as the Alpine Club, still kept out
those in trade in 1901. The term 'gentleman' slowly dropped out of use,
partly perhaps because self-ascription was rendering the term less mean-
ingful. It was increasingly replaced by 'amateur', already being used to
distinguish those who competed in sports also enjoyed by the lower
orders.

There were still clubs such as Blackheath Harriers (founded 1868) that
stipulated that their membership was for 'gentlemen only'. Even in the

1870s the elite London Rowing Club distinguished between 'gentlemen amateurs' and 'tradesmen' amateurs, and was keen that 'the barriers between them were not broken down'.[9] The word 'select' as in Hove's Select Lawn Tennis Club (founded 1881), fulfilled the same function.

In cricket the 'players', and especially professional touring sides like the All-England XI, remained a major attraction in the 1850s and 1860s. Amateur writers, for whom cricket was a game not a business, felt that they had become 'unserviceable servants', 'spoiled by success and flattery', 'petted and cherished' by many clubs. They might be individually respectable and civil, but were assertive about what they would or would not do. Required 'order and discipline' were maintained only at Lords.[10] Amateur-governed counties reasserted their control over professionals from the later 1860s. Some, like Lancashire or Surrey, were really leading club sides who employed professionals only for their county games. Some, less first-class, were fully 'gentlemen' amateur sides such as the Yorkshire Gentlemen or Carmarthenshire, who did not even accept 'tradesmen' members. Yet others like Nottinghamshire and Yorkshire, had the best sides possible, retaining amateur captains, and had paid officials, committees and subscription lists. Professionals knew their place, although in cricket mythology amateurs were supposed to bat, professionals to bowl. This was only partially true. By 1896 there were forty-three professionals in the first-class bowling averages and only twenty-one amateurs. But eighty-eight professionals figured in the batting averages and only seventy-five amateurs.[11]

As workers gained increased income and time from the 1870s, the mixing of classes caused increased concern. The several different forms of amateurism which emerged were attempts to stop middle-class sports being contaminated. Amateurism became a question of power, of ensuring middle-class control, a way of keeping working-class players in their place or keeping them out.[12] Working-class players threatened middle-class playing pre-eminence. Professionals, or those working in mines, factories or other relevant physical jobs, had better strength and skills and outclassed those working in sedentary ways during the week. Golf's Open Championship, for example, founded in 1861, was dominated by Scottish professionals, so that an English Amateur Championship had to be founded at Hoylake in 1884/5. In racing, according to the Earl of Suffolk, the leading 'gentlemen riders' could become at best 'very fair fourth-class jockeys over long distances'.[13] By 1895, when Aston Villa reserves played Cambridge University at soccer, they simply toyed with their opponents, with enough 'comic business' and physical 'gag' to show how far removed their play was from the amateur.[14] Successful amateurs increasingly used their free time and money to train as hard as professionals. In 1895 the 'gentleman rider' Captain Lee-Barber was 'rowing every day, and walking and running round the Park, doing fifteen to twenty miles every day, and sparring for half an hour three times a week'.[15]

As the sports boom accelerated middle-class members, playing 'for sport alone', experienced rowdy and partisan crowds, prepared to pay to watch and fanatical in their support, exhibiting very different working-class norms. Working-class players supposedly had no respectable reputation to lose, so their arrival was viewed with concern. Cash prizes for challenges were a standard expectation in working-class communities, and money in working-class hands was threateningly disruptive, a potential source of moral corruption. Professionals had to satisfy spectators, employers or patrons by winning, so the result was more important than aesthetic pleasure or entertainment. Amateurs pointed to professionals' win-at-all-costs mentality, their more aggressive and violent approach and their sharp practice, deceit and cheating.

Professionals were supposedly prepared to collaborate with book-makers to fix results or swindle the public. In athletics, for example, 'to see the betting which goes on, and to see the terms the competitors are on with the betting contingent, is quite enough to satisfy anyone that a victory means something more than mere honour and glory, and not to the winner alone, but often to the loser as well'.[16] A *Yorkshire Post* letter in 1886 suggested the professional in football 'would encourage idleness and would engender betting, while men would naturally sell their services to the highest bidder'.[17] Professionalism became increasingly maligned. The headmaster of Harrow, for example, claimed that 'against professionals as men I do not sat a word, but professionalism is the bane of athletic games'.[18]

To some extent, such attitudes simply reflected class prejudices, a failure to see the extent to which some in the middle and upper classes exhibited similar practices where betting was concerned. This was most obvious in racing, where middle-class practice was far from pristine.

Likewise, poaching of players, gamesmanship strategies, a strong emphasis on winning and constant disputes were a constant feature of the amateur soccer and rugby games of the 1870s and 1880s, as changes of rule to combat this revealed.

Amateur concerns also reflected class attitudes to work. Many of the middle class believed in the duality of work and recreation. Sport was supposed to be played for enjoyment and not for money. 'If', as one rugby administrator remarked, '[a man] cannot afford the leisure to play the game he must do without it.'[19] Leisure should be earned by working hard in the factories through the week. The *Sporting Chronicle* believed that 'the right to play is the reward of work' and that 'the man who works during the week and plays football on the Saturday is always the fitter and better conducted man' than 'the idler and loafer'.[20] Professionalism in football was associated with competition and cup matches, which were 'a great injury to the game and give greater encouragement to the professional element and betting'.[21] 'Pot-hunting' for cups meant that 'the glory of the pastime and the exercise it provides are smothered by a morbid unhealthy desire to win'.[22] Professionalism weakened work discipline, since professionals would give up their full-time work and fail to develop useful work habits and skills. Professionals were claimed to be unwilling to take risks, lacking amateur spontaneity.

Such problems could be avoided by choosing opponents carefully. In 1880, for example, the establishment of a national Amateur Athletic Association (AAA) brought together leading clubs and organisations to encourage friendly competition against other purely amateur clubs, although it soon dropped the exclusion clause against working-class amateurs. Invitation events likewise allowed amateurs to compete only against their equals. Or there could be separate amateur and professional competitions and championships, as introduced in speed skating from 1881. From the 1870s even rural sports sometimes had different events for 'amateurs', 'tradesmen' and 'professionals'. Cartoons in *Punch* and other magazines increasingly pointed up the incompetence and social gaffes of the unknowing.[23]

But the best way of keeping out workers was by controlling club membership. Many socially aspirant middle-class sports clubs became increasingly exclusive. In the 1860s and 1870s select rowing and cricket clubs were joined by large numbers of amateur athletics, swimming, rugby, soccer and harrier clubs. Membership forms often asked for bank and occupation. Members were usually elected, with blackballing a further safeguard. Moseley United Quoit and Bowling Club in 1867 was one of many who stipulated 'one black ball to exclude'. Elite yachting clubs used a confidential system of references. High membership fees helped too. Lancaster's cricket and boat clubs both charged a guinea in 1870.[24] In larger associations, workers could be banned from affiliated clubs and events. Class legislation could be overt and savage. In the 1860s 'tradesmen, labourers, artisans and working mechanics' were banned from rowing clubs, partly to keep out professional scullers, even if they were 'landsmen' not watermen. The Amateur Athletics Club (AAC) kept out all those who had participated or assisted in the pursuit of athletic exercises as a means of livelihood. In 1867 it temporarily introduced further clauses explicitly debarring 'mechanics, artisans and labourers' from membership. This was counter-productive. Their exclusion simply made some even more determined to supplement their earnings with payment for sport, further threatening the amateur ethic.

Alongside such formal exclusion, there was an increased middle-class stress on the unacceptability of competing for money. Victory should be its own reward. Concerns about the taking of money and prizes asserted themselves more prominently from the 1860s. The AAC defined 'amateur' to exclude any person who had competed in any open competition, or for public money, or for admission money, or with professionals for a prize. In rowing, the Henley Rules of 1879 excluded from its competitions anyone 'who had ever competed in an open competition for a stake, money or entrance fee', or 'competed with or against a professional for any prize', or 'ever taught, pursued or assisted in the practice of athletic exercises of any kind as a means of gaining a livelihood', or 'employed in or about boats for money or wages'.[25] Some rules banned any contact with professionals, and made the punishment of professionalism a life-long ban. Amateur organisations increasingly restricted their prizes, with honorary prizes being the most pure. In athletics, for example, the AAA discouraged 'pot-hunting' by forbidding prizes worth more than £10.

This, of course, applied only to the working classes. The wealthy still considered that 'the bare fact of contending for a prize ... either wholly or in part money' was not enough to deprive a gentleman 'of his right to be considered an amateur'.[26] It was the amount that mattered. So 'gentlemen' could still win substantial sums in sports such as horse racing or yachting where the working classes did not compete. Many of the less rich 'amateurs' also found ways of benefiting financially. Checking and enforcement of rules was not always stringent. In 'open' swimming competitions prizes, not cash, were offered, but winners could nominate someone else to purchase them and the supposed 'purchase' was never checked.[27] Symbolic prizes such as an ornamental clock could be sold, and it was significant that 'amateur' athletics publicity always specified their value. Expenses could be inflated and exploited too. Ex public school rugby sides demanded lavish expenses to play in the north. In professional athletics and cycling, amateurs sometimes competed under assumed names. In 1894 the Scottish Amateur Athletics Association was forced to have an Athletic Abuses Commission, so wide were practices of betting and race fixing in the sport.

Cricket had many such 'shamateurs', the term itself dating from 1896. By the 1880s amateur county players allegedly received much more in expenses than professionals received in wages and expenses. Although it was 'simply absurd', suggested the *Cricketers' Companion*, if 'a gentleman playing for his county is to be at liberty to drink Chateau Yquem with his dinner, and to smoke shilling cigars at the expense of the Club', some clearly did.[28] The 'amateur' W. W. Read played for Surrey for twenty-five years. He was appointed Assistant Secretary, and received first £120 and then £150 annually, plus a railway season ticket, while playing full-time. He toured Australia in 1882–83, and received £250 as a token of his play on his return, far more than the professionals received. He was given regular £100 bonuses, and a gift of £250 and a piece of plate as a wedding present. His 1887/8 Australian tour netted £1137 in expenses. A testimonial match was arranged for him in 1894 which raised over £800, including a Surrey contribution of £200.[29] In soccer, N. L. Jackson established the Corinthian Football Club in 1882 to assemble middle-class amateurs to play regular 'friendly' games against professional sides. It had a membership restricted to fifty, no subscription fees and no ground, but since they demanded (and received) 75 per cent of gross receipts for 'expenses', by 1889 they were a professional side in all but name.

Amateurism was never all-pervasive. Some members of organisations were almost fanatical in their keenness to keep their sport pure: others quietly took money. The *Athletic News* claimed in 1879 that the 'dodges, shifts and evasions, the down-right lies and unequivocal frauds that are perpetuated under the cover of the term "amateur athletic" are a crying disgrace'.[30] Indeed, in May 1881 it dropped its subtitle, 'a weekly journal of amateur sports'. Likewise, amateur clubs were prepared to exploit professionals, paying them to attend and provide exhibitions to raise money to maintain club facilities, attract interest or boost membership. The Amateur Athletic Club was founded in 1866 specifically to avoid 'gentlemen amateurs' having to mix with professional runners. Yet, while its Lillie Bridge ground staged the inter-varsity match and the national amateur championships, it also staged professional meetings and charged gate money, becoming the acknowledged centre of working-class pedestrianism, with crowds of over 20,000 in the 1880s. Amateur approaches were inconsistent. Some sports allowed movement between amateur and professional status, others not. And amateurs wanted to win, proving their superior status by defeating their social inferiors or demonstrating club pride by defeating other clubs. The annual Eton versus Harrow cricket match at Lords, or the inter-varsity matches, whether cricket, rowing or athletics, were all characterised by a highly professional approach and a clear desire for excellence. Professionals were condemned for training, yet before the Boat Race Oxbridge's 'amateur' rowers were in strict training for months and employed professional trainers. The Cambridge University Athletics Club employed Jack White, the former pedestrian 'Gateshead Clipper', in the early 1890s as a club servant to coach them. Leading public schools all employed coaches too. Crowds at the Eton versus Harrow cricket match exhibited as much partisanship as the players, quite comparable to working-class games. In 1873 the MCC called for old boys to ensure matches were more orderly, and in 1874 warned against 'undue exhibitions of party feeling'.[31]

The middle classes were fragmented. Some were elitist, others increasingly emphasised class collaboration and social links. The former valued rank and nobility or wealth and position. The more liberal valued skills and achievement of whatever class, or were influenced by muscular Christianity. From the 1880s onward efforts to keep amateur sport respectable redoubled, but there was also more concern about the public image of gentlemanly exclusivity. Distancing from snobbish excesses became more common. When England's amateur soccer captain failed 'to recognise his men on a long railway journey [nor]speak to them in any way', while travelling 'in a separated compartment' and behaving 'as if he was a superior sort of being', en route to a match, he was reminded by the *Athletic News* that 'sport levels all classes'.[32] Some clubs began to widen their membership, following the example of the London Athletic Club, which admitted 'tradesmen' in 1872, initially losing sixty members. It had nine hundred members by 1874. The National Amateur Rowing Association in 1890 was anti-professional and strongly amateur but accepted clubs whose members included respectable manual workers. In the north and midlands many clubs became much less socially exclusive as sport widened its appeal. In some places there were simply too few middle-class members to be found, or they would only play at home. High status and wealthy Huddersfield Cricket Club found success elusive, complaining that 'the principal difficulty is getting players to travel'.[33] Athletic and cycling clubs with a more working-class 'amateur' membership sometimes allowed individuals to shift back and forth according to circumstance, and held both amateur and professional races at the same event, although sometimes at the expense of national organisational membership.

By contrast, as middle-class fears of socialism, industrial conflict and the growing power of unions began to surface in the 1880s, there was increased class hostility and more opposition to egalitarianism. Clubs re-emphasised precepts of gentlemanly sporting conduct, ethical notions of fair play, courtesy, courage, self-control and playing the game. In this climate the idea of 'professional' created more not less antagonism. Further amateur bodies sprang up like the Amateur Boxing Association, the Amateur Swimming Association or the Lawn Tennis Association, all banning any monetary recompense, and trying to cleanse sports of elements considered impure, immoral or dangerous.

The two football codes provided a useful case study. Here middle-class administrators, concerned with survival in a changing environment, made differing responses and followed contrasting approaches once they saw their ideals apparently betrayed.

Up to 1881 most leading soccer clubs came from the south. Players were largely former pupils of famous public schools or private schools in the London area. Many were former or current university students. They were 'establishment' figures from elite, wealthy backgrounds, largely with 'amateur' ideals. Of the 158 southern players involved in the early Football Association Cup Finals (to 1881) thirty-nine were involved with the law. Thirty-eight were army officers. There were sixteen clergymen, fourteen schoolmasters (including some of the clergymen), eleven in banking and finance, eight brewery directors, managers or wine merchants, six civil servants, two doctors and two professors. Many others were directors of companies or described as 'gentlemen'.[34] Most relied on the close dribbling learnt at school. Felix Barry, a Clapham Rovers cup winner in 1879–80, was described as a boy who 'dribbles excellently' but sometimes 'goes over a great deal of unnecessary ground by dribbling from side to side'.[35]

In the late 1870s, however, some northern clubs such as Darwen, Blackburn Rovers and Blackburn Olympic were taking a different, more serious approach. Cup matches attracted crowds, but to achieve success good players were necessary and, especially in Lancashire, they were increasingly semi-professional, enticed (often from Scotland) by offers of better-paid jobs and pay for time off work from middle-class committee members. Gentlemen and office workers were free on Saturdays, but working-class players, regularly sacrificing pay of 5s. or 6s. a day to train or travel to away games, expected compensation from 'gate money'. By early 1879 the Old Harrovians were already demanding that only 'amateurs as defined by rules to be drawn up by the committee' should compete in the FA Cup.[36] Working-class players also trained more seriously to raise fitness standards, and Scots had learned to use space more effectively, spreading play across the field in a more fluid and coordinated team game. In 1882/3, for the first time, London and southern entries for the FA Cup were outnumbered by those from Lancashire, Cheshire, Yorkshire and the Midlands.

As the Lancastrian 'professional' teams succeeded, traditionalists, north and south, portrayed their tactics as unfair, ungentlemanly, tricky and deceitful. Professionals supposedly claimed fouls or feigned injury and 'the glory of the pastime and the exercise it provides are smothered by a morbid unhealthy desire to win'.[37] Professional sides were disparaged. When the Old Etonians defeated Blackburn Rovers in the March

1882 final of the FA Cup, *Bell's Life* was delighted, claiming their victory was 'a popular one', 'not only well received in the south, but ... in every part of the kingdom ... the causes of this satisfaction are not difficult to seek. It was practically a contest between an eleven of amateurs, in the strictest sense of the word, and a team mostly composed of professionals, some of them, according to the ordinary acceptation, of the most pronounced type'. The 'by no means pleasing odour of betting which pervaded part of their associations' was stressed. So was the 'excessive zeal' of their supporters, which contrasted with the self-restraint and masking of enthusiasm in victory expected of the public school athlete.[38]

The same paper also complained that 'many northern association clubs go in for imported talent', hoping that a special commission of the FA would ask them to leave.[39] There was some hypocrisy in this. The London amateur club the Wanderers, Cup winners five times in the 1870s, had always imported players from other clubs, and in their first Cup Final fielded 'A. H[arrow]. Chequer' from the Chequers club. But more amateur sides' complaints initially lacked evidence. When Accrington was expelled from the Association in 1883 and Preston was excluded from the FA Cup for professionalism in January 1884 it brought matters to a head. Preston's manager admitted professionalism, claiming that the practice was regionally common. The same year, Hearts became the first Scottish club punished for professionalism. Some more liberal FA administrators, including southern luminaries like Lord Kinnaird and Charles Alcock, were coming round to the view that professionalism was inevitable but should be controlled. Rules were somewhat modified in June 1884, allowing clubs to pay a day's lost wages. Veiled professionalism was hard to prove, and Alcock felt that while 'the distinction between amateur and professional players should be clearly marked ... professional football will have to be admitted sooner or later, and the sooner it is recognised and legalised under proper conditions, the better it will be for the game'.[40] *Sporting Life* argued that 'the recognition of professionalism is a certainty'.[41]

This alarmed amateurism's supporters. In October the FA Council demanded that members should provide full details of all imported players, including wages. In response some seventeen Lancashire clubs threatened to form a separate association. Aston Villa and Sunderland representatives attended their discussions. A rival British National

Football Association (BNFA) was formed at Blackburn, informing the FA that it would only dissolve if professionalism was introduced.

It was clear that the game could split. On 19 January 1885 Alcock proposed that professionalism should be legislated for under stringent conditions, but this did not get the two-thirds majority, although 113 were for and only 108 against it. At a second meeting in March the motion was lost again. But in a less well attended meeting, on 20 July 1885, with many amateur delegates away, 70 per cent of delegates accepted professionalism, but under tight regulations. The BNFA, which had grown to some seventy members, faded away. Professionals were allowed to compete in cups provided they were qualified by birth or had lived for two years within six miles of their club, and had been registered. They could only play for one club in any one season. This was similar to cricket regulation. During these debates strong support for professionalism came from most Lancashire clubs, but also from some delegates in London and elsewhere. While London delegates were generally opposed, there was also opposition from regional FA bodies outside London. The Sheffield Association wanted to insist on payment only of 'legitimate' expenses, and was prepared to carry on without Lancashire clubs. The Birmingham Association was opposed, even though the practice was prevalent there. So initially were the Welsh and Scottish FAs. They felt that it led to a drain of players from smaller town and rural clubs to larger urban clubs. Scottish opposition initially meant that more talented Scots were paid illegally in Scotland or went south to earn money, but such poaching forced professional recognition there in 1893. The amateur/professional debate was largely a conflict within the middle classes about how to deal with the incursions of the working classes into middle-class soccer. An FA elite supported professionalism to retain their power and influence, although at the expense of ensuring most amateur sides were no longer able to compete.[42]

The FA elite did not last long. Poor southern club attendance at its 1886 annual general meeting allowed pro-professional representatives, who attended in force, to depose the existing predominantly amateur-inclined committee. It was subsequently replaced by a more representative council composed of officers like Alcock and divisional representatives elected by the clubs, a group some bemoaned as composed of 'a class of men who followed football as a business quite as much as professional footballers'.[43] In 1889 the formation of the Football League showed that league organisations, with their more commercial considerations, could provide a strong impetus to further professionalism. In the north east, a Sunderland general committee including two clergymen and two local preachers 'renovated' their team with Scottish professionals in 1887, and the last remaining powerful regional amateur side, Middlesbrough, was forced to turn professional in 1890 following its failure to compete with professional sides in the Northern League.

The opposition to professionalism retarded the southern game, but by 1901 even London had professional sides, and top soccer was part of a wider entertainment industry. Professionalism in football reached London in 1891 when Woolwich Arsenal began to pay its players. Millwall and Southampton followed soon afterwards. Ostracised by the London Football Association, Arsenal instead played professional sides in the north and midlands and joined the Football League in 1893. Seven other southern professional clubs formed the Southern League in 1894. The FA's Amateur Cup, introduced in 1893/4, was supposed to offer more opportunity for teams like old Carthusians or the Royal Artillery, but it was soon dominated by northern, ostensibly amateur clubs like Bishop Auckland. Occasional amateur critiques of the professional game continued through the 1890s, in the columns of the *Badminton Magazine*, *Contemporary Review* or *Gentleman's Magazine*.

The debate raged with equal intensity in rugby over the 1880s, when it was still the dominant English football game, but with very different results. Soccer's leading administrators had been sufficiently conscious of their social position that they were able, in a period of relatively stable industrial and political relations, to make concessions.[44] By contrast, class conflict and division first fragmented then fractured rugby in the 1890s, during a period of 'new unionism' and militancy.[45]

Clubs like Richmond or Blackheath preferring a handling game had separated from the Football Association in the 1860s, and the London-based Rugby Football Union (RFU) was founded in 1871. It was initially unconcerned about professionalism. Nearly all players were middle class, the sport being spread through schools and universities, and there was no gate money. Early northern clubs were similar to southern ones. Liverpool and Manchester had rugby sides in the 1850s, composed of ex-public schoolboys, university graduates and some ex-grammar school boys. In the 1860s Bradford (1863), Leeds (1864) and Huddersfield (1869) emerged. Greater press coverage and publicity began to attract working-class attention, especially in West Yorkshire, but also in Lancashire, Cheshire, Cumberland and South Wales.

Although the RFU committee was opposed to cup and league competitions, it was forced to allow various county committees flexibility. The successful introduction of the Yorkshire Challenge Cup (1877–78) by the Yorkshire County Football Club (YCFC), attracted large numbers of spectators paying at the gate. The South Wales Cup started the same year. Northumberland and Durham followed suit in 1880, when Yorkshire's top ties sometimes attracted over 14,000, about triple those in London. The YCFC adopted the MCC rules on amateurism, allowing 'gentlemen' to claim legitimate expenses. Its leading committee members shared the instincts of their southern colleagues, and were opposed to payments of any sort to working-class players, although happy to pay the expenses of visiting amateur southern sides. But further down, at club level, the cup's gates provided funds for compensating players or attracting new ones, and veiled professionalism soon appeared. In some clubs secret monetary payments to working-class players became increasingly common, as did inducements to sign, and players demanded payment for taking time off work to train or travel to away games. Crowds with very different life-styles, value systems and expectations began to watch. Playing standards in the Yorkshire Rugby Union soon improved. Cash payments to good players increased. The YCFC committee still banned professionalism, limiting competition to amateurs as defined by the MCC, and wanted to preserve their game's gentlemanly status, but by 1884 pressure from some committee members allowed 'actual expenses' to be 'defrayed', a phrase which allowed flexible interpretation.

The battle for rugby began to focus on differing attitudes towards working-class players. In those areas where rugby had a mass working-class base, from South Wales and the south west to the Scottish borders, there were increasing violations of the amateur ethos. This alarmed the national committee, which was still strongly resistant to such moves. In the south there was little interest in cup competitions amongst clubs, and the game's followers were more middle-class. A sub-committee drafted more explicit rules against professionalism for the

October 1886 AGM, in order to 'meet the evils existing in Yorkshire'. This banned:

> any player who shall receive ... any money consideration whatever, actual or prospective, for services rendered to the club of which he is a member ... including any money consideration paid or given to any member, whether as secretary, treasure or other officer of the club, or for work ... of any sort with the club's affairs ... any player who receives any compensation for loss of time ... any player trained at the club's expense ... any player who transfers his services from one club to another ... on the promise to find him employment.[46]

Despite resistance from clubs such as Dewsbury or Newport, these moves were given overt support by leading club administrators, the national committee and the sporting press, even that in Yorkshire. The stern, self-important Reverend Frank Marshall, head of Almondsbury Grammar School, referee, treasurer (from 1888) and then president of the YCFC (from 1890), convened regular investigations of alleged breaches in kangaroo court style. Covertly clubs ignored them, and the debate increasingly focused on how middle-class control of the game was to be retained. Some club committees found their success attracted huge crowds, to whom winning was everything. Crowds resulted in higher expenditure on enclosed grounds, and clubs were happy to purchase further success. Some committee members made personal profit from the sport. Club numbers increased, and by 1890 there were 150 clubs in Yorkshire affiliated to the national body. Rugby, not soccer, was the 'people's game' in Yorkshire, and professional soccer made only a belated entry into the West Riding textile region.[47]

Rugby's middle-class leaders felt their control was being lost with the sheer influx of working-class players. Some felt professionalism would increase club costs and reduce club profits; others were opposed to professionalism on principle. Some were ex-public school men unsympathetic to industry and its workers, others were self-made industrialists. Others were prepared to compromise to control professionalism, and were sufficiently confident and self-sufficient to push a view that driving able working-class players out would lose clubs enthusiastic working-class support, damage civic pride and wreck rugby. In September 1893, by which time the RFU membership had risen to 431, a Yorkshire motion proposed payment for *bona fide* broken time. It was defeated by more than two to one, as contrary to the interests and spirit of the game. Increasingly attitudes hardened. In Yorkshire, Huddersfield, Leeds and others were suspended in 1894. In Lancashire, led by a similarly virulent opposition, Leigh, Salford and Wigan were suspended. In London, in September 1895, when 67 per cent voted for refusal yet again, more draconian anti-professionalism rules were drawn up. There was an intransigent witch hunt to seek out any financial payments, including the awarding or receiving of medals without RFU approval. Any club even accused of professionalism was suspended.

This final straw forced over twenty senior northern clubs to form the breakaway Northern Rugby Football Union (NU). By 1896 it had fifty-nine members. Its leading decision-makers, like their opponents, came largely from business (many owned their own businesses), the professions or trade, with textile manufacturers, for example, found on both sides. The NU leadership shared a background and outlook with some commitment to amateurism, still trying to avoid full professionalism and exercise control, but with more acceptance of the free market. They were more likely to be political Liberals. Unlike the original leadership of Yorkshire and Lancashire rugby, which was firmly based on the public school and often Oxbridge educated, none had been to public schools.[48] They were under strong local community pressure to produce successful sides. They saw working-class participation as profitable, but wanted to retain a measure of amateurism while reinbursing those players on a day wage for 'broken time' of not more than six shillings a day. In 1898 a working clause stipulated that players should have a respectable full-time job outside rugby, not involved with club jobs, billiard markers, betting or the selling of alcohol. In that sense the NU shared some of the RFU's values and were trying to prevent full-time professionalism.

The RFU responded even more firmly, making all members of these clubs professionals, and even making professionals of those 'refusing to give evidence ... when requested by this Union ... signing any form of the Northern Union ... advocating or taking steps to promote Northern Union or other professional football'.[49] By 1898 unrestricted professionalism soon followed in the NU, as imported players demanded more in a competitive bargaining situation, although the full-time employment clause was retained. This added to the clubs' financial problems, as crowds fell due to a combination of a depressed local economy and negative play by weaker professional sides, while the game became increasingly played and watched by the working classes.

The high-minded RFU initially had little difficulty keeping its weakened base in line after the northerners left. Some clubs were exclusively middle class: fear, and anxiety to show their amateur credentials, retained others. To purge further impurity, there were fines for code breaches, while affiliated clubs could be banned from competing with non-affiliated ones. Even so, by 1899 the *Sporting Chronicle* suggested that there was 'no doubt that professionalism in a veiled form exists amongst English amateur clubs'.[50] Perhaps such remaining threats made the public schools wish to reassert their ownership of the game. It was in 1900 that, in a fine piece of what may well have been invented tradition, Rugby School publicised the story of William Webb Ellis, who supposedly caught and ran with the ball in 1823, and set a commemorative plaque in its Headmaster's Wall. By 1902 the RFU had only 244 members. Wales, where rugby's symbolic unifying role led to a more socially inclusive approach, showed overt concern for amateurism, while covertly legitimising informal payments, in order to stay within the British system and international rugby. It increasingly became a strong rugby nation, with its top sides, many strongly working class, equal to leading English clubs. Ireland, too, despite limited numbers of clubs, and a strongly amateur base, managed to capture the triple crown in 1894 and 1899.

If professionalism was the major area of sporting debate, views on betting, drinking, cruelty and violence were not far behind. One attraction of sport was the opportunities it presented for betting. In 1837 betting was already common amongst 'sporting men' of whatever class, with clubs like Tattersall's facilitating credit betting on horseracing. The Jockey Club took betting for granted but had rules to minimise cheating. From the 1840s working-class cash betting became increasingly common, mainly but not solely amongst skilled workmen, with a more rapid expansion from the 1870s, which made it a dominant leisure feature of working-class urban life. Betting could now even help the popularity of a sport. As the *Swimming, Rowing and Athletic Record* noted, 'an infusion of the betting element contributes to a very great degree in improving a sport's status'.[51]

Reformers took a different view. Horse racing attracted strong opposition from those variously concerned about betting, the language and behaviour of race crowds, absenteeism, or the traveling criminals who followed the races. The 1853 Betting House Act was an attempt to stop people placing cash bets in offices and pubs. It was not seen as applying to enclosed courses, although the Jockey Club was unsuccessfully prosecuted in 1874 for allowing betting at Newmarket. Prosecutions were rare, and fines low, although large numbers of 'betting pubs' existed. Local authority by-laws attempted to stop street bookmakers. Preaching, petitions, anti-race demonstrations, counter-attractions and trips all tried to meet the challenge of racing and betting. A National Anti-Gambling League was founded in 1890 backed by groups including the Protestant churches, the more respectable middle classes and some employers, together with progressive social reformers. Some papers, such as the *Northern Echo* or the *Manchester Guardian*, were reluctant to carry betting information. None achieved much success. This was a minority movement, although a few racecourses were shut down. Betting's hold on society was strong. In the 1860s sporting papers were already claiming that 'the police would be far better employed in seeking out real criminals' and that most bookmakers were 'most respectable members of society'.[52] Later organisations such as the Sporting League, first set up by the *Sportsman* in 1897, lobbied parliamentarians hard to support racing.

Bookmakers could also be found at pedestrian, horse and dog racing, coursing, pigeon shooting and other events. As betting became more popular in society as a whole, it became increasingly disapproved of by respectable sports administrators. It was perceived as problematic, and potentially criminal, although bookmakers, or ground lessees, were rarely prosecuted by the police unless pressure was brought to bear, and reformers had relatively few successes. The problem was that, where working-class sportsmen were involved in sports with an associated betting market, betting commerce led to corruption, and to ways of earning money through the fixing of results. In pugilism, like pedestrianism, there were regular allegations of match fixing. In 1862, for example, spectators were 'dubious as to the probability of battles being finished fairly', and boxers' only creed was supposedly 'to go for the money (by fair means or foul)'.[53] In racing, the Jockey Club banned jockeys from betting, although this was widely disregarded.

In Cumberland and Westmoreland wrestling, despite the efforts of its various local wrestling organisations to control the sport, there were regular allegations of 'barneying', the fixing, buying and selling of matches, throughout the period. Rules had little effect. The 1859 Carlisle and Cumberland Wrestling Association rules stated that any wrestler 'attempting sham wrestling, personation, buying or selling a fall, getting into any weight to which he is not entitled or otherwise misconducting himself or in any way attempting a barney ... shall be at once expelled ... and debarred from again contending in the Carlisle ring'. Despite constant complaints, and increased regulatory stringency, losing a fall was unproblematic when friends could back the winner, and the winner might share the prize money. Reformers viewed this as fraudulent practice showing a lack of moral fibre, but had had little sense of the wage uncertainty which made such practices common. In pedestrianism, non-trying so as to deceive the handicapper, and so increase the chances in a later race, was very prevalent, while in exhibition matches fixing the result made for better entertainment. Non-trying was even more common for horseracing handicaps, and often encouraged by upper- and middle-class betting owners.

Although bookmakers were used by the upper classes for their own credit betting, betting disappeared publicly from the higher status amateur events. Up to the 1860s the press sometimes reported the odds at cricket matches but then stopped.[54] But even at 'amateur' university matches, admitted *Cricket*, 'when local patriotism is interested ... a few sovereigns change hands'.[55] In commercial contexts, almost all enclosed grounds satisfied the law by exhibiting notices that betting was not allowed, despite its prevalence. And in the north east, by 1887, it was being reported that 'betting done on the important matches in the Cleveland district, is gaining ground rapidly ... as strong in football as it is [in] amateur athletics'.[56]

The public house and alcohol played a key role in sport. Yet early Victorian temperance supporters were active in opposition to both. The pub's supposed drunkenness and vice, like the prostitution and drinking associated with the tents and booths of race meetings, provided particular targets. The 1853 Betting Houses Act in part was passed because betting facilities in pubs attracted the working classes.

Refreshment tents at race meetings or athletic sports encouraged drunks to roll round the public streets afterwards, a practice to be roundly condemned. The temperance movement had little success in stopping such drinking. As the 'rational recreations' of cricket, football and rugby began to develop, especially in their earlier more 'respectable' regulated forms, they attracted temperance support as alternatives to the lure of liquor. Playing was healthier, while spectating, as evidence from some chief constables seemed to confirm, kept men out of the pub. Some players believed that athletics and strong drink did not agree, and it was very noticeable that some of those who led the expansion of professional soccer in the midlands and north came from a Methodist temperance background. The Church of England and nonconformists increasingly became involved in encouraging the formation of sides. Soccer bonded religious allegiance. By 1900 church and Sunday school leagues had been founded in large numbers.

By this time the churches faced another problem, that of Sunday sport.[57] Sport increasingly contributed to the secularisation of the Sabbath. In the early Victorian period, long working weeks had forced working men to use Sundays for informal sporting recreation. Sunday activity was limited by law, with the Sabbatarian movement, particularly strong in the 1850s, exerting pressures at local, regional and national level against most popular leisure forms. Legislation had banned entertainment venues from charging on Sundays since 1780. Both the Temperance movement (founded 1829) and the Lord's Day Observance Society (1831) were very active in opposing Sunday sport. Although substantial numbers of manual workers did not attend church, attempts by the Leicester Secular Society to stage Sunday cricket in 1885 failed when a thousand turned out to obstruct their play.[58] Traditional sports, such as racing or field sports like hunting, never used Sundays. Later, newer national organisations such as the AAA or the National Cycling Union also took care not to allow Sunday events at their affiliated clubs. Derby Rowing Club even expelled a member in 1883 for rowing recreationally on a Sunday.

But by late century Sunday play was infiltrating the new suburban sports such as golf, croquet or lawn tennis, which could be played on private club premises, or in the gardens of the wealthy, despite church pressures for self-regulation. Other sporting Sabbath-breaking was recreational but only too visible: small-scale yachting and coastal cruising on the seas, rowing on the rivers, and cyclists on the roads, although some, like Blaydon Amateur Cycling Club, had an annual church parade to satisfy consciences. Sport variously brought out caddies, caterers and spectators, while some working-class angling clubs made Sunday their main day. A few clubs changed their rules. Wimbledon All-England Lawn Tennis Club allowed Sunday tennis from 1888, but with no ball boys. Alarmed evangelical churchmen preached about moral degeneracy and corruption of the young, seeing sport as both cause and consequence of secularism and increasing middle-class apostasy.

Another major area of Victorian debate was about the nature of manliness, appropriate manly behaviour and the acceptable levels of sporting violence. Sport was instrumental in shaping a middle-class male world view. Most sports were, in a much used term, 'manly' activities, even in the early nineteenth century. In the 1870s and 1880s football was 'this manly sport', while cricket was 'the best and most manly of our outdoor sports'. Tennis, which could be played by ladies as well, was thus an 'effeminate amusement'.[59] Manliness was initially manifested in seriousness and self-denial, but by the later nineteenth century shared beliefs about robust masculine strength, skill, steady perseverance and stoic acceptance of the result were becoming central.

For some fans their athletic vision of manliness incorporated adulation of necessary roughness, hard physicality or even violence. Being able to give out and receive pain unflinchingly developed courage and character. Violent sports had particular appeal, especially for men, in part satisfying the need for curiosity, thrill seeking and excitement, allowing an element of cathartic relief, helping to assert masculinity, yet allowing the spectator himself to be safe, with strong elements of ritual and local identity in its encouragement. There was probably also, to some, a sadomasochistic appeal. Pre-Victorian football was rough and often violent, as was pugilism. Not all, however, shared such views. A 'civilising process' in terms of manners and customs, as more constrictive codes of behaviour and etiquette percolated through society, can be discerned through the century.[60] Such restraints were resisted by certain minority groups. The question became what level of socially sanctioned savagery was acceptable.

Reformers fought hard to modify and regulate belligerence, violence and cruelty, and sanitise, civilise or eradicate the more vulgar, disorderly elements. As we have seen, violence by humans against animals became a major concern. Cockfighting, bull-baiting and similar activities, which had preserved some local popular support, were attacked by more respectable locals, joined by reformers from outside the local community, in the late Georgian and early Victorian period. Initially the RSPCA, founded in 1824, avoided a direct attack on field sports, not least because some of its own members supported them.[61] They showed more interest, and had more success, in attacking the cruel sports of the poor, though there was some opposition to steeplechasing, seen by the *Liverpool Mercury* as the 'infliction of wanton torture' on participating horses at Aintree in 1839.[62] From the 1860s there was some limited moral and political opposition to aspects of hunting, shooting and coursing.[63] In 1871, for example, the RSPCA prosecuted Lord Middleton's huntsman and others in the East Riding for causing the deaths of two horses through harsh and careless treatment. Local magistrates dismissed the case, while this attempt on 'the finest of English manly and womanly sports' was described as 'hypocrisy and mock philanthropy' and 'morose cant' by its defenders.[64]

In June 1884 landowners founded the National Sports Defence Association to get the public to resist aggressive measures against countryside sports. Such aggressive measures were typified by the more radical Humanitarian League, founded in 1891, which became especially active against blood sports.

The regulation of human violence also began to generate more interest. Prize fighting provided an example. Despite its dishonesty and corruption, pugilism maintained its popularity among sporting men and some sections of the general public in the first decades of Victoria's reign. Lord Palmerston, for example, was a staunch supporter. But reforming magistrates increasingly used the rural police to aid the prosecution of pugilists for disturbing the peace. Publicly-held fights were defined as riotous assemblies. By the 1850s boxers were also occasionally being prosecuted under assault laws because of the potential for serious injury. If the location could be discovered, magistrates could call police by telegraph. In the late 1860s the Home Office determinedly began granting countrywide warrants against fights, while the Regulation of

Railways Act of 1868 banned the provision of fight excursion trains. Pugilism's supporters responded by reforms which gave it the appearance of a safer sport, re-emphasising its skill and 'art', encouraging indoor sparring, with time-limited, gloved and regulated fights by both amateurs and professionals over the next decades. Boxing even began to be taken up in the public schools.

Pugilism contrasted with the very different sport of football. In the case of pugilism police and magistrates intervened. This was rare indeed in soccer and rugby. Even in football's early stages, middle-class masculinity was the dominant ethos. By the late nineteenth century the ritualised violence of the public school games field was tolerated and sanctioned, part of an increasingly militaristic, athletic and muscular ideal, while in the wider world the level of violent play amongst 'fair-playing' amateur football sides suggested that sporting violence had become legitimated, endorsed as manly virility. It was a safeguard against effeminacy, an outlet for excess energy, and a way of promoting muscularity and character.

Wider public attention focused on the extent to which hacking of shins by opponents should be allowed, and how far sports injuries were tolerable. Even in the 1860s, Blackheath and other supporters of rugby rules still wanted to retain hacking. This helped split the newly-formed Football Association, taking it in the direction of the kicking game. The question for administrators was about how to retain football's masculine ethos in a suitably restrained form. By 1867 some influential rugby-playing clubs were rejecting hacking. Older players could not afford the possible social and financial consequences of injury. Leading articles in the press, following an injury in a Rugby School house match in the 1869–70 season, led to demands for rules to limit rugby injuries. When the Rugby Football Union was formed, in January 1871, it promptly banned both hacking and tripping, though Rugby School itself retained hacking. Codification here eliminated one aspect of violence, though still institutionalising other aspects of manliness and morality.[65]

The death of a Stockport player in 1876 created further panic about rugby's 'brutality' in the daily papers.[66] Some felt violent play was brutalising, demoralising and dangerous. Even without hacking, rough play and injury probably continued to be common in the 1880s and early 1890s, especially given the increased stress on winning and the use of unfair and intimidatory tactics. The sources, nature and variability of the statistics make it virtually impossible to be certain, but there were a number of articles in the *Lancet* and *British Medical Journal* about the physical damage done by rough play in both soccer and rugby. *The Times* regularly reported such accidents and correspondents' comments in the early 1880s, and there were flurries of letters in local papers about over-aggressive play. Fractured collar ones, dislocated shoulders, broken ankles and legs, ruptures of livers or intestines, concussion, neck and spinal injuries, heart attacks and occasional fatalities were seized on. In fact, however, most severe injuries occurred amongst younger and less skilled players, or amongst older men who took limited exercise, and there were more serious accidents in riding, cricket and cycling than football in the early 1890s.[67] Violent players were occasionally banned. In 1886, for example, the Birmingham and District Football Association expelled one player and suspended two others for excessive roughness. Violence shown by working-class players was much more problematical, especially that levelled against middle-class teams, when it could be redefined as unfair, intimidatory and thoroughly demoralising. Amateurs argued that crowds at 'gate money matches' incited more wild play and pitch fights, as did gambling and the desire to win at all costs by setting out to injure good opposing players. When a largely Maori 'Natives' rugby squad, wearing their all-black strip and performing their *haka*, toured Britain in 1888, generating large crowds, they suffered a series of injuries, prompting the following verses in the *Northern Review*

> Fifteen Maoris, at Burton-on-the-Trent
> Three very soon to the right-about are sent.
>
> And then twelve Maoris, trying to hold their own;
> Six break an arm or two, or else a collar bone.
>
> Half-a-dozen Maoris, of all save pluck bereft,
> Fight one more battle, and then none are left.
>
> Four and twenty Maoris, damaged beyond measure;
> All swear there's nothing like a football trip for pleasure.[68]

Supporters dismissed objections. C. S. Coleman, writing in the 1896 *Badminton Magazine*, claimed that 'nonsense' was talked about roughness, and insisted that 'without a certain amount of danger or pain no

sport can pretend to rank'.[69] Others saw it as fostering moral and physical development, and accepted a certain amount of risk as inseparable
from contact sports. It made men manly. Injuries were marks of the
craft, to be accepted with fortitude, teaching lessons of courage and
character where sport was played and watched with good temper.

But the 'games cult' version of manliness was only partly successful
amongst working-class crowds. Male working-class cultural life was
traditionally centred round pride, male aggression, chauvinism, loyalty,
solidarity and local community. Rough and ready violence was part of
being able to look after yourself, and working-class communities
generated and sustained this in a world of subordinate power relationships. Generally violent behaviour appears to have been rare, and
most crowds behaved with decency and physical (but not verbal)
restraint.[70] Certainly 'disgusting', 'filthy' language, 'shouting', 'rowdy-
ism' and barracking was relatively common, but disorder in football
grounds and race meetings only rarely included violent, anti-social
attacks on officials or opposition fans. There were occasional examples
of political grievances becoming associated with sport, such as the
riots at Lancaster races in 1840, which were both a resistance to the
police's attempts to stop gambling and an attack on the Liberal policies
of the council. Frustration when spectators' expectations were
thwarted, and emotional arousal accompanying unexpected victory or
defeat, were the two most common triggers of disturbance. When the
market town of Yarm's soccer team, was heavily defeated by a local
mining team the crowd blamed the referee, whose later report described
how:

> the Yarm people were dancing madly around crying for the 'bleed' of unfor-
> tunate me ... the position was very touchy. After blowing the whistle I
> walked smartly away from the crowd ... For a minute all was quiet, then hor-
> rible yells rent the air ... at a good pace came streaming like Red Indians at
> the charge a couple of hundred reckless hobble-de-hoys and half-drunken
> men. Quickly throwing my overcoat into the face of the first assailant as a
> feint, the next moment I most courageously took the open country at top
> speed ... I soon lost the foe, and gained the shelter of a kind and friendly
> house.[71]

Resentment between local, religious or ethnic rivals also led to con-
frontations in sporting contexts. In 1868, for example, drunken

Welshmen and Irishmen in a refreshment booth at Stockton races fought for some time before being brought under control.

Almost always, middle-class reporters blamed such disturbances on the unrestrained intensity of feeling shown by the working-class mob, variously described as 'noisy, brawling fellows', a 'crowd of roughs', the 'turbulent section', 'unruly hobbledehoys', 'excited mob' or the 'football mobocracy'.[72] In the late 1890s, many famous Welsh rugby clubs, including Aberavon, Cardiff and Llanelli, were suspended for having rioting spectators. Middle-class groups were unable to establish their own code of manliness amongst working-class crowds whose way of life was based on a competing definition.

Victorian sport was predominantly a male phenomenon. Women of all classes had always been amongst the crowds at the rarer events of the eighteenth century. This certainly continued through the nine-teenth century at unenclosed and rarely held events such as regattas or horse races, as a wide range of evidence including letters and diaries, pictures and photographs and music hall songs confirms. Attendance was largely a function of cheapness. Once payment for entry was expected, far fewer women attended, although where, as at Sandown Park racecourse from 1875, male members got free grandstand tickets for women, their attendance rose. Many of the top semi-professional soccer clubs of the 1880s still allowed the wives, girlfriends or female relatives of members free entrance to their grandstands, so match reports made regular reference to the 'fair sex'. There were 2000 women at one 1885 Preston North End match. When clubs began to charge, this tailed off.

Women's actual involvement as sporting participants was modest and restricted, although growing.[73] Working-class women had little time for leisure. For those who worked there was little opportunity and less money for play. In a small working-class rented home, housework and family care was exceedingly time-consuming. It was only upper- and middle-class women who had the time and opportunity for sport.

Despite the increased emphasis on health and athleticism, and demand for more freedom, women's participation aroused male anxi-ety, fear and hostility. Sport was considered a *masculine* activity, through which a man developed skills of stamina, perseverance, team spirit and

competitiveness which could be used at work. Sport would unsex
women, rendering men effeminate. A whole series of powerful cultural
forces collided over the whole question of women's participation in
sport, with late century debates and arguments from doctors, physical
educators and others in the press. Male stereotypes about women
stressed their supposed medical vulnerability, emotional nature and
physical limits, arguing that women required only delicate exercise and
that robust fitness was vulgar. On the other hand, some women could
argue that 'nerves' or 'headache and vapours' could be corrected by
education and physical exercise. Initially males suggested that female
interest in sport was counter-productive and would ruin their repro-
ductive capacity, but by the end of the century women's physical fitness
was being linked to national efficiency and female fertility. By this time
demands from women to extend their political, educational and professional aspirations, and the right to use their bodies as they and not men
wished, were being linked to sport. There was strong male resistance
from some, but other men began to take a much more favourable attitude to women's involvement as spectators, players and patrons, and
made efforts to get them more involved.

In the 1860s participation in the hunt, archery, croquet and yachting were all relatively popular among upper-class or upper middle-class
adult women, secure in their femininity and high status. Increased numbers had been appearing in the fashionable hunts from the 1840s,
assisted by a secure pommel for riding side-saddle, non-slip girths,
safety stirrups and appropriate clothing. All such participation, while
problematic, was accepted largely because these activities were predominantly social and recreational. Women were only playing at
playing games, constrained by costume and custom. Such activity
had limited competitiveness, and allowed both men and women to
play and watch together, although women still had to 'play like
gentlemen and behave like ladies'. They had to play separately from
men, and be kept invisible in protected areas where male roughs could
not interfere. There were a few ladies' golf clubs, such as St Andrews
(1867), Westward Ho! and North Devon (1868). By the early 1890s
perhaps two thousand women were playing golf in Britain, most at
men's clubs, where they were confined to a subordinate role. Even so,
this intrusion, into what was seen as male space, caused concern about

the extent to which codes of social etiquette would be modified and morals affected.

Male ridicule was often clear in press comments about 'new women' and 'disreputable' sporting female behaviour. The sporting press generally reinforced traditional gender ideas and maintained prevailing ideologies. Sporting women were consistently denigrated. Cartoons reinforced male superiority by showing women playing a more passive role as spectators, looking admiringly at male athletes, or playing more gentle, 'respectable', 'ladylike' games such as croquet. They were drawn largely with the male gaze in mind. Their pictured clothing, the decorative and flamboyant wasp-waisted dresses, long and heavy trailing skirts, numerous petticoats, high heels and tight corsetry, were calculated to confirm their restriction and their conformity to the constraints of femininity and fashion. Dress reform was always part of the feminist agenda.

Sometimes cartoons suggested that most women were dizzy creatures with little interest in sport. Hunting, for example, was supposedly in pursuit of a prospective partner, not the fox. Women's interest was more in appearance, flirting and sociability, participating in a subordinate, restrained, maidenly and genteel way. In many of the cartoons and critical comments sexual attraction makes the disguised running, with flattery and flirtation from the men and banter and badinage from the women. For *Punch*'s 'Hurlingham Girl', for example:

> It is enough for her if, in place of historical dates, she knows the fashionable fixtures, while Sandown and Kempton, Ascot and Goodwood, Hurlingham and the Ranelagh, supply her with a variety of knowledge ... The interest she takes or pretends to take in racing is something astounding. For in truth she knows nothing about horses ... yet she chatters about them and their races and their races and jockeys, their owners, the weight they carry, their tempers, and the state of the betting market, with a glib assurance ... On the following day she will visit Hurlingham in order to be looked at as a spectator at a polo match, in which she has no interest whatsoever.[74]

Efforts by women to participate made better though still limited progress in educational contexts. Therapeutic gymnastics were introduced by the London School Board in 1885 and its training colleges had trained seven hundred teachers in this by 1887. Liverpool introduced gymnastics at the end of the century. The major changes took place in private schools such as Roedean, Wycombe Abbey and Cheltenham

Ladies' College, where athleticism's influence could be seen in the way hockey or lacrosse were used to build character, and outdoor exercises and games were daily events, although teachers often tried to restrict direct physical contact. Such schools often took teachers from the Dartford College of Physical Education organised by Madame Bergman-Osterberg. She combined a belief in team sports with the practice of Swedish gymnastics. Her pupils' influence spread to middle-class schools at Anstey, Bedford and Dunfermline. At Bedford High School in 1887 Margaret Stansfield had a shed for a gym and a small playground for games. After she got a field in 1900 pupils could play cricket, tennis, hockey and lacrosse.

Even in the 1870s, at Girton College, Cambridge, there was free time for 'recreation' each afternoon, although there was never the emphasis on athleticism of the men's colleges. Students soon played raquets, fives, croquet, badminton, gymnastics and tennis. It had a gymnasium from 1877, and a tennis club from 1878. Newnham College, the next women's college, was soon playing intercollegiate matches. At Oxford, tennis, croquet and badminton were played at the new colleges of Somerville and Lady Margaret Hall after 1870. Students at the later St Hugh's and St Hilda's were also expected by their principals to spend afternoon time outdoors. From 1883 there were private inter-university competitions. In the Scottish universities from 1892, when women first entered, hockey was the main game, followed by tennis and golf. In London, which opened up all its degrees to women from 1878, but had a mainly non-residential student body, women shared some facilities with men, and rowed competitively, although there was an emphasis on physical training through gymnastics.

By the 1890s middle-class women were playing the individual suburban sports of tennis and golf. These offered opportunities for flirtation as well as fun. Some were enjoying cycling and even climbing in Britain and the Alps as well as taking part in hunting and other field sports. The number of adult women participating in sport had increased, their sports demanded more competitiveness and physical exertion, and there was a move towards clubs and national governing bodies, although in terms of membership numbers were a tiny proportion of the male equivalents. There were even abortive attempts at professional cricket with the Original English Lady Cricketers in 1892, and a professional

London-based female soccer side in the mid 1890s. 'Lady footballers' attracted a gate of £100 at Bury but were criticised as having 'an elementary knowledge' and providing 'a travesty' of the game of football.[75] Male cartoons responded with an increased stress on women who challenged male boundaries as masculine, and thus unfeminine, freakish, over-muscular and overactive in their relations with men. Women who enjoyed sport were portrayed as over-keen, pseudo-masculine 'hearties', with 'masculine' bodies.

The end of the century, with its increased emphasis on women's suffrage and emancipation, saw the emergence of the 'new woman', as a recognisable cultural type, recognisable through intellect, education and devotion to tobacco and sport. Men began to see that women's enthusiasm and active intensity might potentially equal their own. A dominant image of this period, applied to a range of sports, was represented by a *Punch* picture of 'Our Ladies' Hockey Club' which showed a lively set of female players with their sticks thrusting at the ball while a man, with his cap just falling off, unavailingly tries to avoid them. The ironic caption announced that 'one of the inferior sex who volunteered to umpire soon discovered his office was no sinecure'.[76] By contrast, working-class women lacked access to facilities and faced restrictive social pressures.

4

Sporting Pleasures

Although the Oxford versus Cambridge boat race generated little public interest at its commencement in 1829, by the mid-Victorian period it was a major metropolitan festival. Sport, both played and watched, provided recreational time free from work, and, except for those rare days when it had to start early in the morning because of tidal conditions, the Boat Race was a great cross-class day out, a rush to the river bank by a mighty crowd of holiday-bent Londoners. Its patterns of behaviour had become traditional. It was a social event with ritualised and theatrical aspects, a cultural and communal expression of pleasurable leisure.

Men, women and children of all classes put on their finest clothes for the occasion. University colours were sported by apprentices, costermongers and others with not the remotest connection with either elite university. Steamers were massed with humanity. Public houses were thronged, as were the lines of boats and barges moored along the Thames's edge, and the houses behind. A seething multitude lined the banks. Others, such as gypsies, let out chairs, told fortunes or ran gambling games. Urchins perched on lime trees. It was a festive occasion, a day of laughing, chaffing and flirtation. As the boats passed there would be 'frantic shouting, amid a snowstorm of pocket handkerchiefs, and delirious ravings of purple-faced betting men'. Men and women would dance, bawl or turn away in sheer excitement.[1]

Later the same day, rowers and spectators celebrated in the wealthier West End, where the Boat Race dinner took place. Boisterous behaviour was almost legitimised. In 1871, for example, at Evans's Song and Supper Rooms, all chairs and tables were removed for the night for safety. In the Haymarket, where crowds were shouting, hooting, breaking the windows of cabs and pelting the police with oranges, three students were arrested for disorderly conduct and for inciting the crowd to rescue a prisoner.[2]

The Boat Race represented one of the key *continuities* in Victorian sport: its importance as part of festivity, celebration and ritualistic display. Major sporting occasions were secular festivals, with a carnival atmosphere. They caused reformist concerns yet like many pleasure fairs were too powerful and locally important across classes to ban. Interest in the Epsom Derby, for example, dwarfed interest in the Boat Race. Judged by crowd size, media coverage and attention to the result it appears to have been the first 'national' sporting event. It was a time when, according to *Sporting Life*, 'all London, nay, all England, goes (more or less) racing mad – princes, peers, parsons, peelers and peasants ... to see the Derby run men pack up their bags and travel from the Continent, America, and the burning zones of India'.[3] It was a major holiday occasion, an event which suspended routine constraints. Like the Boat Race it was heavy with ritual and symbolism, yet was also carnivalistic, a time of excess and licensed transgression. The French visitor Hippolyte Taine was astonished to observe that 'gentlemen' had gone up to a carriage containing ladies and young girls and there 'against the wheel eased themselves'. He estimated the crowd as of 'perhaps two hundred thousand people', with

> gypsies everywhere, singers and dancers grotesquely got up as negroes; booths for shooting with bow and carbine, cheapjacks selling watch chains with a torrent of eloquence, games of skittles, and Aunt Sally, all kinds of musicians, and the most astonishing procession of cabs, coaches, droskis, four-in-hands, each with its baskets of pies and pastries, cold meats, melons, fruit and wine, especially champagne ... Twenty-four gentlemen triumphantly set up seventy-five bottles on their omnibus – they had drunk them all. Parties bombarded each other with chicken bones, lobster shells and divots of turf. Two parties of gentlemen had got down from their omnibus and were boxing, ten against ten; one had two teeth broken ... One of our own party who stayed till midnight saw certain enormities which I cannot write down here. On this occasion the beast is unleashed.[4]

The many other word-pictures of the Derby presented its sporting pleasures as an abundance, with amenities in the grand style, an occasion for the relaxing of inhibitions, for gambling, sexual licence, overindulgence in food and alcoholic drink, loud music, fighting and folly. It also had much in common with Saturnalia, a point Taine makes explicit. He found a friend's usual coachman who had been invited to

BLOSSOM AT THE BOAT-RACE.

Blossom at the Boat Race, 1872.
Many people went to great lengths to see the race.

lunch with 'a gentleman, two ladies and a child', and given 'a friendly invitation to a glass of port, sherry, stout or ale'. Taine comments, 'On this day we are all things to all men: but only for one day, as in the Saturnalia of old. Tomorrow, distinctions of rank will be as rigid as ever'. This was certainly true. There was a general acceptance of drunken behaviour and widespread betting, but there were still tacit rules about the extent to which social rules could be broken, and any relaxation of the social order was temporary. The police were still on hand in relatively large numbers, even if few arrests were made, and these were usually of pickpockets, sharpers and other petty thieves. Even though classes had opportunities of mixing this was often less so than it appeared, as there were separate enclosures and stands with restricted entry or charging different admission prices.

Right across Britain annual race-meetings were seen by locals as a carnival equivalent, the social and recreational zenith of the year, family occasions and a main annual holiday for workers, who did much overtime beforehand to save up, and an opportunity for social meeting for rural and urban hierarchies. At Leicester, for example, observers commented on race week as the 'yearly break in the monotony of daily life', the 'great annual holiday, and 'the great carnival of the year'.[5] At Doncaster, the *Doncaster Reporter*, no friend to racing, accepted St Leger week as 'the Carnival of the North'.[6]

Such sporting events were key annual holiday occasions, like the fairs, wakes or rushbearings which still formed part of the traditional cycle of customary leisure, looked forward to for months beforehand and, like Christmas, used as events to date from. Their social significance was made even more clear in the two other commonly used images of sporting journalists, one of which was the 'annual reunion', and the other the term 'pilgrimage', with its obvious religious connotations. Victorian industrialists had little choice but to shut down, or accept major levels of absenteeism. Miners left the pits. Farm workers took time off from work. Schools found their pupils absent. Sociability was a central part of the experience. Accounts make as much, or more, of the journey there and back by rail, by horse-drawn vehicle or on foot, the companionship of the day and the eating and drinking, as the sporting event itself. This applied also to northern supporters 'up for the Cup', or even to the highly select Henley Regatta, where photographs of the noted riverside hostelries *en route* from town were being 'helpfully printed' by 1900.[7]

At Epsom, for the Derby, clusters of those who could not go would watch the passing crowds, and pelt and be pelted with nutshells and worse. Charles Dickens provided an 1851 Epsom picture of 'barouches, phaetons, broughams, gigs, four-wheeled chaises, donkey-carts, covered vans made arborescent with green boughs and covered with no end of people, and a cask of beer – equestrians, pedestrians, horsedealers, gentlemen, notabilities and swindlers, by tens of thousands'.[8] Large town courses like Manchester's would have 'a complete canvas city of public houses' covering the grass, selling a range of 'alcoholic liquors' and food which in 1867 consisted largely of 'pork pies and exceedingly brown and puky-looking ham sandwiches, with no end of dabby mustard'.[9] At more select courses Fortnum's food hampers and champagne were to be seen in the carriages.

Up to the 1870s, with most courses still unenclosed, women in large numbers, and from all classes, were to be found in the grandstands and on the course, and the respectable and unrespectable mixed for the day. According to the *Day's Doings*, the publican's 'missis', the 'costermonger's girl', the 'grass widow', 'foreign girls' from Soho and the 'Hyde Park horsebreaker' all figured, while in the celebrations in London after the Derby there was also a 'leaven of what is carnivalesque in it, there is an extra fastness in the fun'. The music halls and other entertainments were crammed, while up in the balconies 'Lesbias, with beaming eyes, are looking down on the scene and enjoying it thoroughly, while at times they fill the brimming beakers and dally with their attendant swains'.[10]

The Derby and the Boat Race were metropolitan and relatively recently founded events, yet British sport had long been associated with many forms of traditional festival.[11] The holidays around Christmas, Easter and Whitsuntide, which all extended over several days, were highly tenacious times for sport. Traditional football had often been played at Christmas. As the holiday increased in popularity, commercial interests, including those of the food and drink trade, began to promote it further. Other vigorous activities, such as prize fights and pedestrian matches, were being staged on Boxing Day by the 1830s onwards, attracting large crowds. In 1875, for example, a 'monster attendance' of about 18,000 watched cycling stars compete at Wolver-hampton's Molineux Grounds.[12] In the later nineteenth century both rugby and soccer games were regularly played then or even, occasionally, on Christmas Day. New Year's Day was an occasion for public house sports. As these declined in number, tours, especially by Scottish football teams, became more common.

In north-east England, by the later 1880s, there was no football on Christmas Day but matches in large numbers in the week following. In 1887, for example, there were 'eager anxious throngs at the football matches which have been looked forward to with so much interest for some considerable time', with visits from the Sheffield clubs and Scottish teams which included Glasgow Rangers, Hibernians, Linthouse, Third Lanark, Albion Rovers and Dumbarton Athletic.[13] The supposedly amateur Corinthians soccer side enjoyed tours to the north the same year, and by 1895 their 'annual Christmas tour' had become a tradition. It included first-class expenses-paid matches with Leicester Fosse, Sheffield United, Sunderland, Nottingham Forest, and a number of Scottish clubs, including Queen's Park.[14]

The following year the Corinthians toured the west of England at Easter, a period for recreation as much as religiosity even at the start of the Victorian Age, and one which saw a great variety of popular sport. Good Friday was a common law holiday, but its religious significance became more stressed by the respectable in the last third of the century. There was strong press pressure to avoid it: 'Football matches on Good Friday ... offend the deepest feelings of hundreds and thousands of people, many of whom are among the chief supporters of the game'.[15] By the later 1880s Easter Saturday, Monday and Tuesday had become the regular carnival period, one which saw soccer and rugby 'holiday' matches, tours by soccer, rugby and cycling clubs, and steeplechasing and rowing events.

The traditional festival of Whitsuntide gained even more impetus by being made a Bank Holiday in 1871, becoming one of the more central and sometimes the main holiday period for sports days, race meetings, and other sorts of sport. In Cumbria, for example, public houses, temperance societies, Liberal and Conservative associations, cricket clubs, and bodies of every description organised sporting events at this time, with their numbers growing during the period.[16] Athletic sports became major Whitsuntide holiday commercial attractions, widely advertised, and drawing large crowds, and there were deliberate attempts to promote sports to bring outsiders into the towns. The August Bank Holiday, newly created by Lubbock's 1871 Act, soon became the equivalent sporting day of high summer, with large 'gates' at events.

Further down the social scale there was much evidence of sporting continuity as well as change. Sport formed a part of many parish rituals, traditions and festivals, and there was strong working-class defence of custom and practice. Many sports had communal rituals and customs, but their functions varied. Some reinforced social cohesion and local community values. Religious festivals often had secular aspects, including sport, associated with them. Early Victorian events such as Whitworth Rushbearing often had wrestling or running races, sometimes accompanied by dog-fighting, cock-fighting or bull-baiting. Even after such 'rough and rude' sports had largely died out, fairs and wakes usually still incorporated sports such as athletics or wrestling, as they did, for instance, at Egremont's Apple Fair in the late nineteenth century. Even when there were attacks on such sporting occasions from outside the community they could often be resisted. The annual bull-running in November through the streets of Stamford was frowned on by reformers, yet it continued up to the 1840s, supported by a majority of the town, including usually the corporation and local MP, with blocked streets and bonfires lit. It celebrated their town, their bravery and their customs, and only foundered after a long, externally-driven campaign. Long-standing unenclosed race meetings functioned as a customary event in themselves. They afforded customary rights of labour absenteeism, they were relatively cheap, making them affordable holidays, and they were tied to specific places.

Earlier symbols and rituals of sport also continued to be used. The medieval knightly challenge survived in the large numbers of challenges to be seen in *Bell's Life* in the 1840s, made by pedestrians, pugilists and rowers. Some wrestlers, rowers, pedestrians, pugilists and other professionals still used the *Sporting Chronicle*'s columns in 1900 to issue such challenges. Even the FA Cup was originally a challenge trophy, with the winner of the earlier rounds meeting the previous holder in the final, while cups were initially to hold the libations of the winning team or athlete. The notion of the medieval champion was extended further in

Victorian times to create British and even world champions and championships in a whole variety of sports. In soccer, a relative late-comer, there was a contest between West Bromwich Albion and the Scottish club Renton for the title 'Championship of the World' as early as 19 May 1888.

To such traditional survivals, the Victorians added new forms of annual sporting event. Most of these were for the social elite. Attend-ance at race meetings such as Goodwood or Ascot, or rowing events such as Henley, soon formed part of the annual calendar, an opportu-nity for reunions, to meet old friends and reminisce, or to socialise and network. Some tourist centres on the county cricket circuit became beneficiaries of summer cricket 'weeks' or, as at Scarborough, 'festivals'. At Canterbury (from 1842) cricket formed part of a wider round of 'county' pleasures. These could include theatres laying on special enter-tainment, bands playing on the cricket ground and elsewhere, and the illumination of sports grounds and parks. In August 1899

> the ground had a large collection of private tents, including those ever-useful marquees erected by the Canterbury and Conservative club, whilst I Zingari had their tent, with the ancient intimation on the old card that it was exclu-sively for the members of I Zingari. Lord Harris, of course, had his own private sanctum, and as has been his custom on the first day, he invited the Lancashire team to lunch ... there were quite a large number of aristocrats present. During the afternoon the band of the Prince of Wales's own 10th Royal Hussars discoursed sweet music.[17]

Sport was also an occasion of display, a display at several levels. Pro-fessional sportsmen such as pugilists had always displayed their bodies and skills in boxing booths at fairgrounds, in sporting public houses and in circuses. They now did so increasingly in the music halls too. Their success brought new opportunities. When it was announced that the pugilistic champion Tom Sayers was visiting Liverpool in May 1860, shortly after his last fight, he was met at Lime Street Station by an immense crowd, 'all eager to get a look at the man who had supplied the great subject of conversation in all circles for a week past'. His more ardent admirers took the horses of his carriage out of the traces and drew it to his hotel, where he had to show himself at the window to respond to the deafening cheers of the crowd. His appearance at the Liverpool Exchange later also drew a huge crowd, and the officers of two

navy ships invited him to come aboard, while the sailors manned the
rigging and greeted him with loud cheers.[18]

Popular festivals had always celebrated the community itself, displaying its ability to put on a good show. By the later nineteenth century
whole villages were sometimes on display, not only to each other, but to
people from rival villages, and even to visitors who were increasingly
important as the tourist industry expanded. In Westmorland the
Grasmere sports became a glittering social occasion attended by the
leading gentry, with a date chosen to maximise the attendance of visitors
to the Lake District. Events were chosen to further traditional Lakeland
sports and local culture and to display them to visitors. Modern football was codified by the public schools and diffused down to the working
classes, but even in the late nineteenth century other localised versions
of football, some allowing a great deal of handling by players, and others more akin to soccer, survived across Britain, usually as annual
events, changing and adapting to change. The Workington Easter mass
football match, for example, between 'uppeys' and 'downies', created an
spectacle during which 'all disagreements during the last year' could be
'put off into this night to settle', an outlet for aggression that could
attract five thousand spectators, many of them brought by special train,
by the 1870s.[19]

Most sports relied on public display to provide an urban spectacle.
Middle-class public appearance was strongly ritualised and formalised,
something carried on into many sports. Sports may have been played for
pleasure, but many were also a way of demonstrating middle-class
moral, social and cultural authority and wealth, in the same way as
concert nights or civic processions. Political position could also be reinforced, and both parliamentary Liberals and Conservatives were
attracted to support sport. Only the socialists denounced it to any extent.
Prior to the development of enclosed courses, local MPs, especially
Conservatives, regularly subscribed to race funds. Council investment in
racing at Doncaster, Chester, Lewes and elsewhere also reduced rates.
Most politicians ensured their names were on subscription lists for
sports which chimed with their political interests, although the amounts
were seldom high. Carlisle's annual wrestling competition of 1876
attracted four MP subscribers, but the amounts were all of two guineas
or less. Mayors, aldermen and councillors supporting local race meetings

ally Sloper's Half Holiday

BEING A SELECTION, SIDE-SPLITTING, SENTIMENTAL, AND SERIOUS, FOR THE BENEFIT OF OLD BOYS, YOUNG BOYS, ODD BOYS GENERALLY, AND EVEN GIRLS.

Vol. II.—No. 63.   SATURDAY, JULY 11, 1885.   [ONE PENNY.

ETON AND HARROW.
THE WEATHER-BEATEN FABRIC A BOY AGAIN.

" We were all there, of course, and perhaps I might have almost enjoyed myself if it hadn't been for Pa and Ma—Pa going on anyhow, telling everyone that he well remembered being at Eton as a boy, and Ma, with a huge packet of ham sandwiches and a bottle of Bass, which she would persist in handing round to the girls from the 'Friv.'"   [EXTRACT FROM MISS SLOPER'S CORRESPONDENCE.

The Eton versus Harrow match at Lords was a leading social fixture,
a glittering occasion where families would display their social status.

Rugby in the 1880s. The physical damage done by rough play and over-aggression, especially by working men or professionals, was a cause for comment.

could be found in grandstands from early in the period. As the franchise extended and sport grew in popularity in the later decades, many also became involved in attendance and ceremonial at other sports. Leading local cricket, rugby or soccer clubs, for example, almost always had a mixture of the landed gentry and those involved in local government amongst their vice-presidents, taking an interest in club welfare, opening grounds, presenting prizes, making speeches and providing subscriptions. In north-east England, supportive councillors could be found buying shares in the Stockton and Gosforth grandstand companies or the soccer companies of Newcastle's West End, Middlesbrough Ironopolis and Sunderland Albion. Politicians also got involved more broadly in sporting activities. The mayor of Southampton attended and - welcomed delegates to a meeting of the National Cyclists' Union there in 1899.[20] There were limits, however. Sporting achievements rarely occupied much place in council chamber speeches.

Increasingly, the architecture of cricket, rugby and soccer grounds assumed a more monumental character, an object of awe and a backdrop for the display of sporting skills laid on by their bourgeois promoters. Sporting arenas were used to display the power and the wealth of the town's leading figures. For directors, patrons and others, they became as much sites of consumption and display as were the department stores and distinct central urban shopping streets for middle-class women. Soccer grandstands became tacitly gendered, with women, who watched less often than men, becoming restricted to parts of grandstands specifically reserved for them. Race-meeting grandstands had always had substantial numbers of middle-class and upper-class women. At the new park courses, male membership often allowed two women. Cricket members' enclosures and pavilions may have attracted more women by the century's end. By 1900, for example, Worcestershire had 823 male and 283 female members. Even cycle races could be an event for the fashionable, with the 'feminine element' featuring largely as spectators at Wolverhampton by 1873.

Ritual reinforced social power. Authority was demonstrated by the formalised, often ceremonial appearances of the rich and powerful at sporting functions, displaying their wealth and authority to a wider audience. At Ascot the Royal Enclosure and the royal procession along the course symbolised authority and hierarchy, the aristocratic hereditary principle, tradition, ostentatious display of wealth, prestige and aristocratic sporting interests. Ascot's processional pageant, first instituted under William IV, was soon recognised as pleasing the public. Victoria continued the use of the procession to the Royal Stand, and the Royal Enclosure was first created in 1844. After Albert's death, and Victoria's withdrawal from public life, the Prince and Princess of Wales instituted a royal drive, initially in semi-state. By the 1870s it incorporated the Master of the Buckhounds, the Queen's huntsman and whips, grooms, outriders and postilions, all in archaic dress, and had become 'one of the institutions of Ascot'.[21] Escorted coach processions, involving a display of gentry and aristocracy power and wealth, were also seen at a variety of 'county' race meetings up to the 1850s, but became less frequent from the 1860s onwards, largely disappearing by the 1890s, when aristocratic visitors came more often by rail.

As a self-sufficient working-class sporting culture emerged, successful outdoor sports began moving to enclosed spaces, where people had to pay to attend. In the case of soccer or rugby sides, increasingly looking to celebrate urban identity, celebrations of cup success provided another form of ritual, the sporting counterpart of the symbolic vitality of popular radicalism or of the ceremonies of the various friendly societies. Cups gave teams a structure to their season and a prize to work towards. Cup matches generated exciting contests that drew upon local allegiances and loyalties. In short, it was the physical and mental stimulation of intense competition and the operation of chance that made football, like many other sports, appealing to players and, more critically, to the crowds that watched matches. Cup finals became major secular festivals with their own rituals. It has been argued that the organisation of football and rugby leagues helped to shatter the social mould of those traditional rituals upon which the communities of work and religion had relied on for sustenance.[22] This was not so. The search for transcendence, ritual order and elements of worship were all to be found in accounts of cup finals in the later nineteenth century. Equally, the welcomes given to successful soccer teams merged the team with the town. Their flags, speeches and parades became both highly stylised rituals of local cohesion and solidarity and manifestations of civic pride. When Blackburn Rovers, the losing FA Cup finalists, returned home in 1882 their welcome by several thousand was still a novelty. When rivals Blackburn Olympic won in 1883 they came back by train like a victorious battalion triumphantly returning from overseas, waving their colours and flag and exhibiting their captured trophy, and celebrating with alcohol. It was reported that 'there was a plentiful supply of whiskey with which "The Cup" was frequently filled. The players were decorated with light blue ribbon and a blue flag was displayed at the carriage window. The Cup was exhibited at every station'.[23] Brass bands and applauding crowds met them at Blackburn station, and they were drawn through the town on a wagonette pulled by six horses. By 1890, when Blackburn's population was 120,000, between 30,000 and 40,000 welcomed them home after their fourth win in seven years.

This celebration of the return, for a very successful hero, team or even a thoroughbred racehorse, was common throughout Britain. It was highly visible, and highly audible, with large welcoming crowds supervised by the police, loud cheers, fireworks set off, music provided by one or more brass bands, shops sometimes bedecked for the occasion with colours or pictures, a procession on wagonette or coach and pub stops for refreshments. The mayor and other political figures would often welcome the team and host a reception.

Belts in wrestling and boxing had been presented as symbolic contest prizes well before the Victorian age, but now they increasingly were given by patrons and the press. An *Illustrated Sporting News* belt was presented to the pugilist Jem Mace in 1866. The Lonsdale Belt became the most famous amateur equivalent. Racing cups were highly expensive works of art for winning owners throughout the period. The best were crafted by top jewellers like Garrard and could be worth several hundred pounds. And they were given to professionals as well as amateur sportsmen. In rowing, the professional Harry Kelley was presented with a massive silver cup, worth upwards of £250. It was thirty-four inches high and its lid was surmounted by a figure of Britannia, while the sides had a view of Putney and a representation of a boat race, symbols which linked Kelley's Thames achievements and his British championship wins to his Putney pub.[24] By contrast the first heavily embossed, eighteen inches high FA Challenge Cup cost only about £20 and rugby's similar Calcutta Cup about £60. Further down the social scale there were competitions for medals or public house mugs.

The newer forms of team sport allowed self-confident middle-class youth to take centre stage, displaying their skills, prestige and status in front of a varied urban audience in the public space of parks, cricket grounds, commons and fields. They made social difference visible, with middle-class muscularity offering a challenge to the mental ability usually more highly prized in middle-class reformist circles. Often the initial act of following a sport was a form of cultural osmosis, passed on through the family, public school, university and the media, allowing participants to learn about their sport's past, its heroes and stars.

The importance of sports clubs both to Victorian sport and to Victorian society is hard to overemphasise, although it should be stressed, too, that club instability was a defining period characteristic. Few clubs had much permanency, especially those further down the social ladder. Many clubs, like many teams, lasted only a short time. We know less than we should about them or their members. In leading clubs, membership could be retained into middle age and beyond, but in most clubs membership was confined to playing members, although generally club officials were largely somewhat older and more literate.

Even in the eighteenth century social clubs of various sorts were becoming central to the spread of pleasurable experience and the making of modern social relationships, but the Victorian period was particularly characterised by its myriad of non-commercialised and unsubsidised voluntary associations. In sport these were impressive in both their numbers and vitality. And numbers grew rapidly. Glasgow alone had twenty private golf courses and more clubs by 1900. In Britain there were more clubs devoted to organised sport than to any other activity. Sports clubs often had their origins in the societies, social organisations and institutions that dominated Victorian life. Where large numbers of young men already associated, in worship for example, sporting activities were a natural progression. Where young men found no club to fulfil their desire to play they often founded one, and there were often local press, police, teacher or music hall sports sides. There was even a Darlington Gardeners Cricket Club. Public houses, the church and the workplace, for example, all played a key role in football club formation. Some clubs were formed to ensure and demonstrate members' social exclusivity; others were formed because they were excluded. The spate of late nineteenth-century golf clubs, with their lower subscriptions, was in part to cater for the unfulfilled ambitious of lower professionals, clerks, shopkeepers, tradesmen and artisans whose membership of more select clubs had been refused. It is worth noting that many Victorian men, and some women too, played a wide range of sports and were members of several clubs. Playing specialisation was not common, so clubs too often became multi-sport. A summer cricket club might spawn a tennis section, or a winter football or harrier cross-country section, which might later split off. Modern soccer club names such as Oldham Athletic (1899) or Kidderminster Harriers (1886) provide reminders of this. Or divisions within a club might lead to a split.

The chronology of British club formation varied from sport to sport and region to region. In early Victorian Britain press coverage was largely confined to the doings of clubs associated with racing, coursing, yachting, cricket and rowing, although in the Stirling area, for example, curling and quoits clubs were already being formed. These were small-scale, often formed from self-selecting urban elites and existing political, social and cultural institutions, with membership limited by high annual subscriptions. More select sports clubs, where membership was controlled, created private social space, offering opportunities for social interaction as well as healthy exercise.

From the 1860s, as they expanded, towns increasingly became sites not just of business and public affairs, but of consumption and private pleasures. As sport came to constitute a larger part of male leisure and sociability there were growing numbers of middle-class urban sports clubs concerned with the amateur sports of rowing, athletics, bowls and football, although football clubs only reached east Northumberland in the 1880s, and lawn bowls clubs in the late 1890s. The last quarter of the century saw the expansion of sports clubs across Britain, catering for more 'modern' sports like cycling, lawn tennis, soccer, rugby, golf and harriers.

Membership of elite and middle-class sports clubs enabled fine degrees of status and playing style to be signalled to the discerning, providing valuable cultural capital. Clubs provided exclusive, select and private domains where business, professional and white-collar members could eat, drink and socialise. Official club positions provided opportunities for administrative and organisational experience.

Sport played a major role in the formation of social relationships in an increasingly urbanised world, providing a key source of friendship, fellowship and fraternal identity. Indeed, Charles Dickens's appreciation of cricket's humane influence once led him to claim that 'more valuable acquaintances, more permanent and faithful friendships, have been made in the cricket field than in any other social rendezvous of the United Kingdom'.[25] Clubs were a masculine sanctuary, part of the wider world of male society, with an absence of women, although a winter ball might sometimes be arranged. Becoming a member was a move away from parents, women and domesticity into urban social life. Sporting voluntary associations fostered convivial sociability and cultural improvement, not of the mind but of the body. Membership initially required a demonstration of social and sporting competence, and an ability to know the written and unwritten rules of the game. In the more high-status sports the more select clubs like Manchester Cricket Club, Newcastle's Gosforth Rugby Union Club, Royal Chester Rowing Club or St Anne's Golf Club were almost always the keenest to follow national governing body rules.

Clubs formed a hierarchy, and club membership marked an individual's progress up the social ladder. The most select and exclusive clubs, such as the Jockey Club, Henley and MCC, all tried to ensure that invitation and recommendation were the only effective means of entry. Committees were extremely powerful bodies, controlling membership policy and subscription levels. These clubs made rules that were often emulated nationally. Social relationships within elite clubs were usually friendly. The new sports clubs, like their literary and professional counterparts, were almost invariably non-political and non-sectarian. The Jockey Club and MCC, for example, contained both Liberals and Tories. There were only rare occasions when political divisions affected clubs, as, for example, when Everton Football Club split in 1892. Its newly-formed rival, Liverpool Football Club and Athletic Grounds Co. Ltd., was formed by a board with a clearly defined identity through the Liverpool Conservative Party, Freemasonry, the West Derby (Poor Law) Union and the drinks trade.[26]

For those amongst the better off who mixed sociability with the pleasures of credit betting, most towns had betting clubs, evidence of the powerful hold betting had in the later nineteenth century. London's Tattersall's, with its upper-class and commission agent clientele, predated the Victorian period, but it was soon joined by the Victoria Club (founded 1860) with a socially mixed membership and an annual subscription of six guineas, and by the more exclusive Turf Club (founded in 1876). A range of others followed, including the Beaufort, the Albert and Junior Tattersall's. Manchester's Post Office Hotel had been its early Victorian betting centre but by 1881–82 Manchester's Derby Club and Salford's Victoria Club had appeared, while Nottingham's Victoria Club in 1882 was 'a place of resort for sporting and other gentlemen'.[27]

The formation of clubs was rarely democratic. It was an expression of self-esteem and identity. Most clubs were dominated by the middle classes. Working-class clubs were relatively rare. Independent sports clubs organised, financed and controlled by the working classes only really emerged in significant numbers in the later 1880s and 1890s. Exclusivity increased middle-class chances of playing and watching others of a similar social status. This sustained 'respectability' and avoided any undignified opportunity of defeat by social inferiors.[28] Membership of select clubs provided young commercial and professional men with pleasant summer exercise, and, by association, affirmed their gentlemanly aspirations and asserted their members' prestige, even if some of them were in reality economically insecure. It offered opportunities for establishing status, identity and political self-interest, helped generate cultural and symbolic capital, and built up useful contacts.[29] Many members saw their club as a social opportunity, as well as an opportunity to play sport. Teams enjoyed occasional competition against other sub-regional clubs of a similar level of ability, and beyond routine sporting contests there were displays, trips, social events, receptions for other clubs and even attendance at the funerals of deceased sportsmen. Membership cost money, so the wealth and often the resulting success of clubs largely depended on the subscriptions of members. In 1899 Bury Cricket Club was only able to attract £119 in subscriptions at a time when the town's population was 51,000, while neighbouring Ramsbotham, with its population of 16,000, generated over £200. Bury's entire season's gate money only amounted to under £8. Even so, it still employed a professional, managed a summer tour of distant Great Yarmouth, attracted a Lancashire county match to its ground, and raised funds to send poor young local children for a seaside trip, partly by holding an amateur dramatic performance.[30]

There were some elite cricket clubs without subscriptions or grounds, touring and playing teams of gentlemen at country house grounds, and composed of university and ex-public school players. Most clubs, however, sought a stable, permanent base. Clubs provided opportunities for the exercise of organisational and business skills. The pooling of resources for purchase and rent of lands or buildings was easier. Socially aspirant clubs wanted their own clubhouses, which soon became an increasingly visible part of the urban fabric. Racing clubs usually leased pub premises for race weeks in the early nineteenth century, and Doncaster's 'Racing Club House' had two large dining rooms, a drawing and breakfast room, seventeen bedrooms, together with many other rooms for offices, storage, cooking and servants' quarters.[31] In the earlier Victorian period yachting and cricket clubs were the most likely to have their own premises year round. In the later nineteenth century these were joined by bowling, angling, tennis and golf clubs. As early as 1881, Lancastrian cricket and yachting clubs had been joined in local directories by numbers of bowling clubs with listed addresses, alongside smaller numbers of other clubhouses for sports as varied as billiards, boxing, cycling or tennis.[32] Of these the Manchester Tennis and Raquets Club (1880) was the most highly select, the Radcliffe Hall Working Men's Bowling and Billiard Club the most clearly working-class.

Although bowling had declined in popularity in the early nineteenth century, as central urban greens in England were sold off to speculative builders, the pot-share variant retained its popularity in the north-east coalfield, and bowling greens survived in Scotland in some numbers. By the 1880s the sport was reviving in the north of England. By the 1890s, largely thanks to the licensing trade, pub greens were again common, encouraging a cross-class involvement in the game. Rink or lawn bowls soon became a fairly exclusive sport for older middle-class men, with bowling greens added to the facilities at elite private sports clubs and the more select resorts. In London however, there was little interest and there were few bowling clubs, though a public green was established at Battersea in London in 1895. English golf clubs were also largely a product of the late Victorian age. Even in the 1870s there were still only about a dozen golf clubs in England.

Clubhouses were built for a variety of reasons. Setting up a clubhouse reduced the costs of middle-class sport in the longer term, by creating shared facilities for storage, reading, meetings and bedrooms, as well as domestic sociability and *cameraderie*. At Sunderland, for example, once its town football club became well established, its clubhouse allowed teams to be 'provided with meals at a much cheaper rate than under the hotel system. Besides this, the place is open daily for the use and recreation of the members'.[33] The Manchester Bicycling Club in 1895 had a clubhouse consisting of a large general room fitted up for billiards, a reading room equipped with cycling and general journals, a committee room, bedrooms for 'country members', a bathroom and space for machine storage; there was a plan for a gymnasium to be added.[34] Billiards assumed an increasing importance as a leisure activity from the 1870s. By the 1880s even non-sporting clubs such as Manchester's Reform Club had recognised the billiard room as the most important club room, and almost all sporting clubs, and many pubs, had billiards tables.

Clubs which could not afford a clubhouse sought other premises. For much of the period the pub played a central role. The Victorian pub not only sold alcohol, it was also a leisure centre and meeting place for business, a bastion of male privilege with drinking seen as proof of masculinity, and an oasis of warmth in the winter, before the advent of central heating. Pubs offered space for committee meetings, refreshment and changing facilities, but were also important to sport in a wider sense. In the early nineteenth century pubs were a focal point for the community, with a vibrant social life, and the importance of sport to patrons of most pubs should not be underestimated. Pubs were a key location of working-class sporting sociability in the 1840s. Publicans sustained the culture of challenges in pugilism, pedestrian and rowing events in the face of attempts to impose changes on working-class sports. Clubs for pugilism, most often in London, were another feature of the early Victorian period, allowing the fraternity to meet together. 'Sporting' pubs often had landlords with particular sporting interests, and significant numbers of licensees were themselves sportsmen or ex-sportsmen, offering drinkers opportunities for nostalgic conversation about past sporting glories, traditions and associations. Even in remote Wastwater, on the edge of the Cumbrian fells, the Huntsman Hotel, frequented by early walkers and rock-climbers, had, as landlord around mid century, Will Ritson, former huntsman, champion wrestler,

mountain guide and raconteur.[35] No less than six Blackburn Rovers soccer players of the early 1880s were also publicans. Breweries were clearly
well aware of their potential for attracting customers.

Pubs, inns and hotels had varied clienteles, and thus different social
tones. This allowed their use by both middle- and working-class sports
clubs. At Lytham and St Annes, for example, its highly select golf club
continued to use the St Anne's Hotel as its headquarters from 1886 to
1897. Cycle clubs would use their pub 'headquarters' to 'stable' their
cycles during meetings. The soccer side Crewe Alexandra was even
named after the Alexandra Hotel, a team base whose recreation ground
they initially played upon in the 1870s. Pubs were also centres for sporting news, a function enhanced by the extension of the electric telegraph,
local newspapers and finally the telephone. In the 1850s news could
include the location of pugilistic encounters. By the 1890s pubs provided
updates on racing results or soccer away games. In 1895 the Scarborough
Hotel in the centre of Leeds advertised match updates every ten minutes
for major games. Even when sports clubs moved to the larger stadiums
of the 1890s, pubs near the ground would still benefit. Most football and
rugby clubs still maintained a pub headquarters that provided, at the
very least, a place to hold meetings or eat after the match.

Such conviviality lay at the heart of much Victorian sport. For the
upper classes, hunting, shooting and fishing, alongside horse racing,
remained as much social activities as sports. The sexes mixed at racing
house parties, and a day at the races might be followed by a visit to the
theatre or race ball, 'ordinaries' (set meals) at local inns or dinner at a
house party. Hunting initially had a more hard-drinking male social culture, although women began to take part in increasing numbers. Hunts
often began at a local pub, with communal imbibing of punch, port or
whisky. Hunting men were notoriously fond of wine, fun and good dinners, although hunt balls were social occasions for the county set. In
hunting and other field sports, a day's sport was often followed by a
night of serious eating and drinking. In the 1860s, at the Spa Hotel,
Hurworth, where many of the Hurworth Hunt stayed, there was a
dinner party every night. Its huntsman recalled that

> Squire Wilkinson and several of the others drank the strongest, blackest port
> and did not stint themselves either. As the evenings advanced, and the dew
> of vintage had fallen pretty heavily, it was a regular practice to see who could

put a champagne or port bottle on his head, and by stages lie down and rise up again with the bottle still in position. The result was that there was a good deal of broken glass on the floor.[36]

Eating and drinking took place at different times in different sports. Fashionable cricket clubs would have a sumptuous lunch and cigar during the midday interval. Elite rugby clubs would dine after the match. The Scottish FA's dinner after the international with England in 1890 cost them over £80, including £30 for champagne.[37] Dining might even be built into the constitution of select clubs. The first Surrey Football Club rules, for example, emphasised that the members should dine together at the end of the season and that any subscription surplus should be applied to the dinner. At such meals some of the aristocracy might celebrate not wisely but too well. In a disturbance on the evening after the Eton versus Harrow game at Lords, the Honourable A. Harbottle and Lord Harry Vane Tempest were charged with disturbance of the peace, but dismissed with a caution.[38]

Elite sporting clubs, like the Victorian music halls, encouraged friendliness and good fellowship in an atmosphere of shared interests.[39] There were a host of clubs whose main purpose was social as much as sporting, with dining, drinking and other activities playing a leading role. This should certainly be qualified with a recognition of the role of temperance in, for example, church clubs, where it was argued that playing and watching sport kept working men out of public houses. Temperance advocates were active in senior positions in the Football League and elsewhere. William MacGregor (the League's founder), C. E. Sutcliffe (its first secretary) and Charles Clegg (chairman of Sheffield Wednesday) were all teetotallers. But it is worth noting that both Methodism and the temperance movement were weak in London.

Alcohol has always been central to sport, sustaining and complementing it.[40] Pubs were significant in the construction, maintenance and celebration of community solidarity and comradeship, and strong drink was part of the attraction, especially after a victory. A north Yorkshireman 'of independent means', charged with drunkenness in 1888, explained that he was 'a little excited in consequence of his two sons having taken part in a football match which was played at Carlin How, and the company were having a little jollification at the inn to celebrate the club's victory ... five gallons of beer were paid for by several gentlemen who felt so pleased with the victory that they stood treat'.[41] Losing could be an excuse for drink too. Aberdare's defeat by rivals Merythr Football Club in 1885 led them to 'drown their sorrow in the flowing bowl', and subsequently 'steer their way' home about midnight.[42]

Sports clubs did not just focus on the playing of sport. They often arranged smoking concerts ('smokers'), annual dinners, socials, bazaars and other fund-raising events. For team sports, many such activities were all-male, with speeches, conviviality, cheers, songs and toasts. These were time-honoured rituals that helped to assert male team spirit, together with a sense of a club's importance and uniqueness. Members even sometimes went to the pantomime or music hall together. To an extent such activities allowed members the fantasy of being members of a gentlemen's club, and to be included in the guest list of a 'smoker' as an invited member representing another club became a matter of ambition. It conveyed an air of respectability, even if behaviour itself was less so. Many early bicycle clubs concentrated on social and recreational activities, such as afternoon 'tea runs'. The press increasingly reported such events, and by 1887 a *Northern Review* cycling correspondent was telling readers 'I will be glad to receive and insert ... notices of club festivities'. Alcohol seems to have flowed freely at such events. One beneficiary of a testimonial dinner 'had to be helped home, and will remember the proceedings for many days to come'.[43] The meet of the West of Scotland Harriers at the Erskine Ferry Hotel in 1887 was followed first by a meal, then a social, with 'poetry', singing and many toasts, a dogfight under one of the tables, and a merry journey back to Glasgow, with the coach driver leaving the road on more than one occasion.[44] By the 1890s lawn tennis, bowling and golf clubs, often now with a mixed membership, were also enjoying a winter social life, with dances and balls, teas and suppers.

For many of those who played and watched, the most frequent reason for participating in sport was its sheer excitement, the fun, pleasure and enjoyment it provided. Sport was a form of pleasurable play. As one observer noted, games like football offered 'all those elements of physical exercise ... There is congenial companionship; there is the stimulus of legitimate and honourable rivalry; there is the stimulus of public applause, in short these sports employ the exuberant animal vigour which remains in strong constitutions after the toil due to bodily labour as means of livelihood has been paid'.[45] The pleasure of watching soccer, for example, became an obsession for some, with tension and joy, physical struggle and pure release combining together in shared vicarious experience. As one Durham miner claimed in 1889, 'witnessing a struggle between two teams worthy of each other ... affords an enjoyment that in this dull, weary, workaday world, I could ill afford to lose'.[46] Away from the covered stands, the main market for gate-money sports in the later nineteenth century was the working class, although cricket crowds were seen by contemporaries as above soccer ones, and rugby league support was most strongly working-class. Although bad weather always affected attendances, many still went even though many outdoor sports had little shelter. In Football League grounds, for example, less than a tenth of their capacity was commonly under cover.

For spectators, curiosity merged with admiration in sports from bareknuckle fighting to pedestrianism where high levels of physical pain, endurance, exhaustion and acute suffering were involved. Some early pugilistic encounters lasted two hours or more. In the 1880s there was a fashion for long-distance pedestrian races, in which foot-blistered, body-punished groups of pedestrians traversed small indoor tracks for six days at a stretch. The Sheffield runner George Littlewood once reportedly covered 531 miles in that time. In a sixty-hour race in Dundee, the winner covered 352 miles.[47]

For some sportsmen, proof of a sport's pleasure lay in the money they paid to play it. In 1899 polo cost an estimated £102 to start up and about £58 a season afterwards. For tennis, entrance to a good club would cost a guinea, plus annual subscriptions of one or two guineas. Rich fishermen could rent Scottish salmon water at about £1500 a season, and even for those unable to rent, the cost of fishing was about £1 a day plus living expenses and the cost of equipment.[48] For others, sport offered opportunities to gamble, and the reports of the sporting press right across the reign provided odds on a variety of sports including bowling, football, pedestrianism, quoiting, racing, rowing and angling. A gambling industry serving all classes grew up round racing from the 1840s.[49] By the same decade racing sweeps were also growing in popularity. The period from the late 1850s saw a growth in working-class betting, often amongst skilled workmen. As racing information became increasing available, there was a rapid expansion of working-class betting in public houses and streets. Local authorities employed by-laws to control it, but only spasmodically, while many middle-class magistrates were reluctant to convict.

As the notion of separate spheres became more widespread, men had a diminishing role in the home and family. For some, the workplace could seem increasingly individualistic and competitive. For others, the industrial process, with separate but highly limited roles, took away individuality. In either case sport could offer opportunities for compensation. It provided an antidote to middle-class domesticity and affluence, and offered something to all participants of whatever level of athletic skill and strength. Taking part in and watching sport provided a release from pressure and tensions in a society where work could be mundane, monotonous and boring.

The cameraderie and companionship sport offered were also major attractions. In the more successful teams values and objectives could be shared, leading to social bonding, emotional satisfaction, group intimacy and self-esteem. At the same time smaller groups of players could retain their own friendships.[50] Even in individualistic pursuits, such as shooting or fishing, mutual respect amongst competent participants produced a close bond. According to Henry Seton-Carr, the big-game hunter, shooting with other men produced a bond unequal in any other social interaction.[51] Sport provided an alternative community, with banter and bonhomie. Soccer and rugger games not only allowed men to play with their equals in friendship, but brought along family, workmates, neighbours and friends to support. Many early games were played on Saturday afternoons in parks, where football was initially a free attraction.

Active participation in sport was also seen as fostering the health of those in sedentary urban occupations, providing physical, mental and moral wellbeing. George Cadbury would rise at five 'so as to be on the ice before dawn and have two hours' exercise before going to business at nine in the city'.[52] Sport could even teach people to come to terms with disappointment, the experience of losing, personal inadequacy and failure. For those in industrial occupations or living in squalid urban areas, sport provided vital mental stimulus and strengthened the body.

For women, sport was much more likely to be social, recreational and casual rather than strongly competitive.[53] Victorian women's participation in sport was always that of a tiny minority, usually upper and middle class, and socially well connected. Archery societies, with largely elite membership, offered young ladies opportunities for gentle competition while displaying the female figure to advantage and providing the opportunity to socialise with gentlemen. Lawn tennis in suburban gardens was likewise a low-skill, social diversion for most playing it, although it could advance a woman's social prospects. For some women the finding of a marriage partner was soon beginning to be seen as an element in tennis club membership, as it had been earlier in hunting or croquet. Indeed, it is worth emphasising that although some male clubs let women in, if at all, only under severely restricted conditions, mixed clubs were understandably an attraction for men. At Nottingham, for example, 'the introduction of lady members' in the 1880s was seen as a main reason for the rapid development of the lawn tennis section of the Nottingham Castle Club.[54] In 1896, most of the sixteen women's golf clubs in Scotland were in coastal resorts, suggesting ladies' golf fitted in with holiday patterns, and North Berwick Club had members from as far away as Liverpool, London and Brighton.

Women enjoyed physical exercise, and in some sports club membership was almost equal by the late nineteenth century Swimming clubs often had ladies' sections with different times, and the opportunities this provided often meant nearly as many women members as men in the Greater Manchester area. In the Cycling Touring Club, 20,000 of the 60,000 members were women by 1890, although they rarely participated in competitive events. Appleby Golf Club had forty-three men and thirty-three women subscribers for a clubhouse with equal but separate accommodation in 1894. By 1900 a small number of women were actively participating in a wider range of sports, seeking healthy enjoyment through new opportunities for competition and more rigorous physical activity.

5

Money

It would be misleading to suggest that making money from sport was ever the norm in Victorian Britain. The upper classes and sporting amateurs who ruled sport had a strong antipathy to commercialism and professionalism and tried to keep both at bay. Most clubs and sports were for amateur sportsmen who just enjoyed the individual or communal pleasures of play. Some of sport's leading administrators and organisers actively disapproved of payment or excess profit and tried to restrict or stop it. Even the more commercial mass sports were influenced by gentlemanly, amateur values. The bulk of money made by sports companies was not distributed to shareholders. From the 1880s the Jockey Club limited profits at the racecourses it controlled to 10 per cent. The FA, from 1896, limited dividends to a maximum of 5 per cent, although clubs often gave extra season tickets to larger shareholders.

Yet less well-off people had grown increasingly used to paying for their entertainment and profits were being sought. Betting was already using the language of Victorian business by the 1840s, exploiting terms like 'remuneration', 'investment' or 'speculation', and presenting Tattersall's as 'the Turf Exchange'.[1] By the 1890s, horseracing was 'more of a business than a sport', Scottish soccer was 'a big business', and cricket had supposedly 'become more or less a gate-money business'.[2] There was even a fresh commercial arrival, the soccer agent, helping players negotiate transfers. In April 1901, for example, E. Higson was seeking 'First Division, Second Division, Southern League players desirous of change, state age, height, weight and probable amount of transfer'.[3]

The emergence of a mass sports industry has been recognised as one of the economic success stories of late Victorian Britain, when spending on sport accounted for perhaps about 3 per cent of the total gross national product.[4] Railways and tram companies, newsagents and tobacconists, printers and publicans all benefited indirectly. There are still insufficient data to allow analysis of its overall impact on the British economy, but the industry had significant financial benefits. Sport had become, according to the London Census Office, part of a wider entertainment industry. The numbers involved professionally were not large, even taking into account the manufacturers of sports equipment. At the century's end, there were still only some 2500 full time sports professionals, although many more part-time ones.[5] The census report of 1891 had no separate category, conflating sports professionals with a humbler group of persons, such as showmen and those 'engaged in exhibitions'. Such numbers were rising, in England and Wales alone from 5043 in 1881 to 9095 in 1891, when there were also 6776 'makers of apparatus for games', and 11,524 bicycle and tricycle makers or dealers.[6] Yet we know less than we should about the profitability of Victorian sport. Soccer, county cricket and horse racing have been more systematically studied, but many other sports, such as cycling, league cricket and golf, have attracted only limited attention.[7]

The development of commercial leisure ran alongside that of the development of nineteenth-century industrial capitalism. The potential audiences for sports were beginning to have sufficient time, money, freedom of movement and transport facilities to indulge sporting interests. Entrepreneurs repackaged popular sports for more widespread consumption, confronting and negotiating reformist suspicions. Profit had always been part of sport's appeal, and there were clear economic preconditions for its Victorian transformation. The question of why people invested is complex, although in part increased consumption was the natural result of increased spending power, urbanisation and new forms of communication, and so deeply embedded in Victorian life. While some sports were already relatively commercialised at the beginning of the nineteenth century, it was the demands of the growing market, the appetites, demands and aspirations of spectators and players, that commercial forces tried to satisfy.

Sport was potentially profitable to several sectors of the embryonic sports industry. First, it was profitable to those individuals and groups who promoted sport, sponsored and backed professionals, or otherwise invested. Secondly, some men and a few women found they could earn a living from a sport they enjoyed. Thirdly, bookmakers, commission agents and tipsters sought profit from sports betting. Fourthly, sport raised money to benefit charities. Finally, the media, too, increasingly exploited sport.

The actual extent and nature of commercialism partly depended on the groups controlling the sport, the size of crowds that could be attracted, a sport's traditions, and the availability of investment. Hoteliers, innkeepers and publicans played a pivotal role in promoting sport even in the eighteenth century.[8] In the first half of the nineteenth century money was often made indirectly from the selling of strong drink, and by providing betting and gaming facilities, although even then some had enclosed grounds. Thomas Lord, at his Marylebone cricket ground, was an early example of an innkeeper sponsoring and promoting sporting events to boost trade, a process that continued throughout the period. Racing was exploited more generally by the middle-class business elite of towns to attract both upper- and middle-class owners and more plebeian crowds to spend their money.

Some towns profited directly. Doncaster race meeting, for example, was one of several run by its corporation, using revenue to reduce rate demands. When a local vicar, Dr Vaughan (a former headmaster of Harrow who had left following hints of a homosexual scandal), complained in January 1869 of the immorality and crime consequent upon the race meeting, councillors pointed out that the races had allowed grants to churches, chapels and schools, including £10,000 towards the rebuilding of his parish church. Brighton Corporation was sufficiently keen to gain revenue to absorb Brighton's Racecourse Trustees in 1894.[9] Races were profitable well beyond direct revenue from the sale of stand tickets or the income from booth, stand and beer tent renters. At Doncaster even opponents of racing admitted that the races had 'a silver lining': 'landlords as well as many of their tenants are apt to regard the races as a perfect God-send'. Rooms could be rented out at a high charge. Houses were cleaned and painted, brokers and furniture dealers sold or let furniture for the week, 'the grocers, the bakers, the butchers, the brewers and publicans' all benefited, and prostitution was rife.[10] Towns catering for other more elite sports likewise created their own tourist industries, encouraging ancillary profit-taking through the provision of accommodation, catering, transport and other services. For example, Lutterworth and Melton Mowbray catered for the hunting set, Edinburgh and Cowes for sailing, and Henley for rowing, despite constant complaints of high prices and local exactions. First coach and then railway companies made significant but occasional profits from transporting the better off to watch and participate in sports, as did trams, cab drivers and the like.

Enclosure of sports grounds is often interpreted as evidence of commercialism. Where pub landlords enclosed land in order to provide sports facilities, and charged entrance, this was clearly so. Cricket and racing began the process of enclosure and the charging of an entrance fee quite early. Racing had separate grandstands even in the eighteenth century, but other areas were being railed round to form enclosures from the 1840s. Middle- and upper-class grandstand share owners felt their main customers were their social equals, so kept out the poorer through pricing. Where that failed, wealthier attenders would sometimes erect private stands. By the 1830s and 1840s, the earlier admission-charging gardens in London and elsewhere were also being used for competitive sport, and joined by new sporting grounds such as Belle Vue in Manchester, or Sheffield's Hyde Park.

In cricket, where the pub was probably the only permanent building initially, as early cricket grounds did not have pavilions, perimeter walls of tall wooden panels or perhaps even just canvas were erected. Tents were used to provide shelter from the rain and for changing. James Dark, the innkeeping cricketer who leased Lord's cricket ground from 1836, provided drink, added a billiards room, tennis court and running track, hired and fired professional staff, and sold cricket equipment. Ex-bricklayer William Clarke enclosed the ground beside his Nottingham Trent Bridge Inn in 1837 to make a cricket ground for his own professional team. It became the county club in 1841.

In more select clubs members had less concern for profitability. Enclosure here was more to keep out the unwashed and unwanted. Some racecourses like Pontefract's Stapleton Park were reserved for gentlemen riders and kept out 'roughs'. Newcastle Cricket Club was still deliberately keeping out working men in the 1850s.

Publicans were almost always amongst the most entrepreneurial members of the Victorian leisure industry. Early musical halls like Weston's Canterbury Inn in London, or Sharples' Star Inn at Bolton, stemmed from their efforts; so did early 'pleasure' grounds like Blackpool's Winter Gardens. Working-class sports, in which one sporting personality or 'champion' could be promoted against another, attracted sufficient crowds for more innkeepers to enclose grounds in the 1830s and 1840s. Sporting activities often began on the grass by a pub. Then publicans began providing facilities such as running tracks, seating and even covered grandstands. In London, for example, John Baum had a sporting pub, the White Lion at Hackney Wick, with a one-acre field attached, which initially staged pugilism and poor-quality 'Victoria Park Races' in the 1840s and early 1850s. His son James made it a leading pedestrian centre from 1857 to the mid 1860s.[11]

Publicans advertised contests and provided drink and food. Up to the 1870s and often thereafter they sponsored and supported plebeian sports from angling, bowling, knur and spell, to quoiting, especially in England. They offered grounds, trophies and cash prizes. They backed pugilists and footracers, 'for the sake of personal advantage of their own house, or for the sums they may risk on the issue'.[12] They were, however, not the only ones involved. Tradesmen, local businessmen, and even professional backers might also risk their money by supporting the professionals as they trained.

Pubs were places of ritual for issuing challenges, meetings of parties and backers, signing of articles, deposit of stakes, appointment of officials and determining of locations. Victors returned to celebrate, the vanquished to drown their sorrows. Those innkeepers and publicans seen by the sporting public as generally honest, honourable and reliable often held the stakes as bankers or acted as referees. Prize fighting was very dependent on sporting landlords for its administration and its staging, and for the provision of stake money. By the 1840s dozens of London pubs were known as sporting pubs.

Not all publicans promoting events had their own enclosures. The publican lessees of Hampton racecourse apparently made 'a small fortune' out of the speculation in 1859.[13] In Sheffield in the 1850s and 1860s a number of different innkeepers near Hyde Park cricket ground sponsored and organised sporting events there. Such events usually included handicap foot races, quoits, pigeon shooting and knur and spell, and proved a way of generating income for the park's proprietors with a lower level of risk. This became a common pattern. James Phoenix, a publican who had began as a beer seller, was perhaps the leading Sheffield entrepreneurial figure at this time, but in spring 1862, for example, there also events sponsored by five other landlords.[14] This pattern could still be seen at the century's end. As late as 1899, at Oldham's Higginshaw grounds, events were arranged both by E. S. Chadwick, the ground's proprietor, and by E. Garside of the Minder's Arms, while the landlord of the Royal Commercial Hotel at Salford organised monthly pedestrian handicaps at Broughton Rangers' football ground.[15] Towards the end of the century music halls and theatres in search of profit laid on indoor spectacles, notably boxing and wrestling.

While pedestrianism was a major driving force in the 1850s and 1860s, dog handicaps were becoming almost as popular by the early 1870s. At a time when demand for beer was falling, and tobacco began to compete for scarce working-class income, landlords redoubled their efforts to attract customers. At the Old Welsh Harp at Hendon, a long-standing venue for a wide variety of sports for a varied clientele, greyhounds were soon following a dummy hare on wheels, pulled by a windlass, on a 400 yard grass track. *The Times* concluded in 1876 that 'the new sport is undoubtedly an exciting and interesting one'.[16]

As illegal ready-money betting became more popular, many publicans with no sports ground available nearby tried to increase profits by providing betting facilities. At Stockton, Thomas Devereux, owner of the White Hart Inn from 1878, built the Victoria Club next door at a cost of £3000 as a betting club. He set up sports events while also managing, matching and backing boxers, scullers, cyclists and pedestrians, as well as racing his own horses all over the north, carrying out betting commissions from leading jockeys and turfites, and taking bets by letter, on racecourses and in his public house.[17]

When a small sports enclosure was attached to a pub owned or rented by a local landlord, the enclosure was almost always impermanent. Potential problems could include economic fluctuations, irregular use, the changes in popularity of particular sports, sale of the land, insufficient custom, police prosecution, a run of bad weather or the ageing of the landlord. Pub land near town centres was also constantly being sold off for residential development. The first enclosed race meeting in London, John Whyte's Hippodrome at Bayswater (opened in 1837), failed because local ratepayers objected and there was insufficient custom.[18] At Newcastle-upon-Tyne an early pub enclosure on the Westgate road was followed by the Victoria Grounds in the west end with purpose-built

1. Fred Archer (1857–1886), drawing by Jane E. Cook.

CRICKET.

A GRAND MATCH!

WILL BE PLAYED AT THE

COPENHAGEN CRICKET GROUND,

Islington,

ON THURSDAY, AUGUST 9, 1849,

BETWEEN ELEVEN GENTLEMEN OF THE

ISLINGTON ALLIANCE CLUB,

AND ELEVEN GENTLEMEN OF THE

WINDSOR & ETON

JUNIOR CLUB.

☞ **WICKETS PITCHED AT HALF-PAST TEN O'CLOCK.**

N.B. Good Stabling.

W. A. WRIGHT, Printer, 9 & 10, Fulwood's Rents, Holborn.

2. Cricket. A Grand Match!

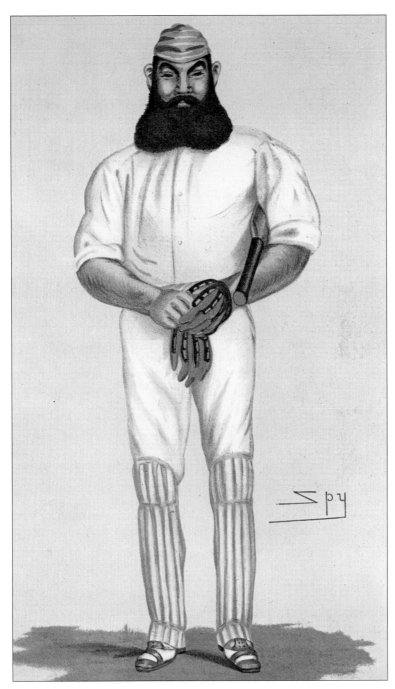

3. W. G. Grace (1848–1915), cartoon by Spy.

BLACKHEATH

Cricket, Football and Lawn Tennis Company,

LIMITED.

Incorporated under the Companies Acts, 1862 to 1883, limiting the liability of Shareholders to the amount of their Shares.

CAPITAL £3,000,

IN 3,000 SHARES OF £1 EACH.

Proposed Issue 2,000 Shares Payable in full on Application, of which promises to the extent of upwards of £1,400 have already been received.

Directors.

The Rev. J. W. MARSHALL, St. John's Vicarage, Blackheath, *Chairman.*

G. W. BURTON, Esq., Lee Park Lodge, Blackheath, Hon. Sec. Blackheath Football Club.

DERMAN CHRISTOPHERSON, Esq., Grove House, Kidbrooke, Blackheath.

M. J. DRUITT, Esq., 9, Eliot Place, Blackheath, Hon. Sec. Blackheath Morden Cricket Club.

G. ROWLAND HILL, Esq., The Circus, Greenwich, Hon. Sec. Rugby Football Union.

S. LEEKE, Esq., Sunfield Terrace, Blackheath.

A. POLAND, Esq., Eliot Vale, Blackheath, Hon. Treasurer, Blackheath Morden Cricket Club.

F. W. PRIOR, Esq., Gordon House, Blackheath Park.

AUBREY SPURLING, Esq., The Nest, Vanbrugh Park, Blackheath, Hon. Treasurer Blackheath Football Club.

FREDK. STOKES, Esq., The Cottage, Love Lane, Blackheath.

LENNARD STOKES, Esq., Eltham Road, Lee.

H. VASSALL, Esq., Wedderlie, East Sheen, Captain Blackheath Football Club.

ROBT. WHYTE, Esq., Pentland House, Old Road, Lee.

Hon. Secretary.

M. J. DRUITT, Esq., 9, Eliot Place, Blackheath.

Bankers.

LONDON AND COUNTY BANKING COMPANY, LIMITED (Blackheath Branch.)

Solicitors.

Messrs. MASON & EDWARDS, 65, Lincoln's Inn Fields, London.

4. Blackheath Cricket, Football and Lawn Tennis Company. Its Honorary Secretary, Montague Druitt, remains a leading Jack the Ripper suspect.

5. Footballers in action. Note the variation in caps and hats.

6. The Guides Race up Little Silverhowe, etching by W. H. Overend, *Illustrated London News*, 28 August 1895.

7. The Colman's football team. Employers such as Colman's in Norwich often supported employees' football teams. (*Unilever Historical Archives, photograph by Terry Burchell*)

8. Members of the Norwich High School hockey team, 1899. (*Norwich High School for Girls*)

9. Sportswear for women. Bicycling made women independently mobile for the first time.

stands. When the land was sold to the North-Eastern Railway it was replaced by the Fenham Park Ground to the north of the city, which closed when fines of £50 for allowing betting on the premises forced it out of business in 1875/6.

Towards the end of the century publicans were no longer the leading sporting entrepreneurs. They continued to be involved in the more working-class sports, including dog handicaps or professional pedestrianism, and there was still money to be made from matched fights and races. More than a few retained their enclosed grounds. The owners of the Builder's Arms Recreational Ground at Wolverhampton and the Black Bull Ground at Sheffield were still supplying a service in 1900. Some rented out grounds or let premises as changing rooms for cricket, rugby and soccer. Even where a nearby ground was used by a successful club, any rise in rent or a personality clash could mean the club would move to find better terms elsewhere. And the profits from drinks sold before and after home matches had to be balanced against lack of custom during away games. The Cardigan Inn almost closed in 1890, despite being directly opposite the ground of St Johns, the leading Leeds rugby club.[19]

Even in the 1860s there were beginning to be greater expectations amongst the better off about the standards of accommodation at sporting events. A letter to *Bell's Life*, for example, in 1862, complained about

the rickety benches and wretched fare at the Oval or Lords, with our feet in the damp, even if fortunate enough to get a sit down ... Give us a fair chance of a comfortable seat, with wholesome food and drink at a moderate price, and many would gladly come to see a match who, as matters are now conducted, stay away in despair.[20]

Sports now needed to be more highly capitalised if they were profitably to draw crowds. Investors increasingly combined to provide the more expensive facilities required. In Merythr, for example, about ten members of the local licensed victuallers association provided organised sporting entertainment, such as sports days, in the town from the 1870s to the 1890s. In 1875 a partnership set up Sandown Park as an enclosed course to exploit London interest in racing.

The more successful sporting organisations increasingly turned to buying, or taking a long lease on, their grounds. Incorporation was generally the best way of raising capital and spreading the risk. The first joint stock limited sports companies, established from the 1860s, were usually racecourse grandstand or racing stud companies such as Manchester Race Course Company (1868) or the Low Field Stud Company (1867). The 1860s also saw some pleasure grounds following the same approach. Gateshead's Redheugh Pleasure Ground unsuccessfully did so in 1867. Enclosure and incorporation was by no means a guarantee of financial success. From football grounds to cycling tracks, profit or loss was often rooted in local economic fluctuations, the extent of unemployment, and the changing popularity of particular sports. Some of the latter can be traced through the records of failed companies.[21] Between 1874 and 1876, when there was a short-lived boom in the popularity of roller- and ice-skating rinks, limited companies were set up throughout Britain. Almost all failed. Some hare-coursing grounds were enclosed, beginning with Plumpton in December 1876, and this received a further boost when the Ground Game Act of 1880 led to a shortage of hares. Through the 1880s there were attempts at gate-money hare coursing at Gosforth, Kempton, Wye and Haydock racecourses, but attendances decreased once the novelty wore off, and even Haydock, near to Manchester and in the middle of a coursing district, 'hardly received that amount of patronage from the public one would naturally expect'.[22] The Doncaster Coursing Company, with a capital of £5000, lasted only two meetings (1882–83). The Four Oaks Park Company near Birmingham was set up with a larger capital to run horse-racing and coursing but went into liquidation in 1890. In the 1890s a number of baseball companies, often linked to professional soccer clubs, achieved only brief success.

There were similar increases in the scale of capital investment which necessitated limited liability as rugby, cricket and soccer clubs grew larger, again mainly in the 1880s and 1890s, though Huddersfield Rugby Club was incorporated as early as 1879. Most sought a properly equipped freehold ground, often with a fully licensed hotel attached, with a good urban position and good transport access, and commonly with a cycle and running track to generate summer revenue. There was a flood of incorporations in the mid 1880s at rugby and some cricket grounds, fuelled by an inflow of capital.[23] Warwickshire Cricket Ground, for example, incorporated in 1886. When Blackheath Cricket, Football and Lawn Tennis Company was formed in 1885, its capital was £3000 and it cost £1500 to lay out the Rectory Field. Its thirteen middle-class directors were headed by the Reverend J. W. Marshall, the local vicar. Leeds Cricket, Football and Athletic Company, founded in 1889 by local businessmen, dignitaries and politicians, erected a splendid sporting complex at Headingley for cricket and rugby union, at a cost of between £25,000 and £30,000. It had lawn tennis, athletics, harriers, cycling and bowling sections and briefly experimented with soccer from 1895 to 1898.

Soccer arrived later. Birmingham's Small Heath club was the first to become a limited company in July 1888, followed by Notts County in 1890. North-east England provides a case study of such development. Sunderland Albion, Middlesbrough Ironopolis, Newcastle East and West End all incorporated in 1890, both Stockton and Middlesbrough in 1892, and Sunderland and Darlington in 1896. In Scotland the dominant clubs acquired limited liability in the 1890s too. Golf clubs were also relatively early entrants into company status, because of the large funds required for land purchase, the laying out of a course and clubhouse construction.

Bicycling's novelty and sensation also attracted and fascinated large crowds, and it was hyped up by the press. An indoor race at Islington Agricultural Hall, renamed the Velocipede Cirque for the occasion, made profits for its promoter as early as 1869. The initial craze had become a sporting habit by 1870, with major events at enclosed grounds in London, Birmingham and especially at Wolverhampton, while purpose-built indoor wooden tracks with banked turns became a winter mainstay of revenue.[24] There were further tracks in London, Coventry or Manchester as cycling boomed in the late 1880s and early 1890s. The increased size of new grounds, the costs of compliance with local authorities and demands of grandstand supporters for shelter and comfort led to a generally upward trend in terms of company capitalisation. In racing Sandown became a limited company with a share issue of £26,000 in 1885; by 1898 Haydock's issue was £34,000. The higher standards and better ground facilities demanded in the later nineteenth century led to stadium improvements, making these sporting cathedrals larger, more appealing, exciting and fashionable, in order to improve revenue. Glasgow Rangers' new steel-structured stand in 1891 cost £1300 and it had its own telegraph office. Even so, the larger amounts of money spent on stadiums tended only to follow on from sporting success and increased gates, and facilities often were still rudimentary, with open banking covering most of the ground. While association football and racing got the largest crowds in the 1880s and 1890s, only a few thousand were sheltered from the weather.

For most clubs and shareholders it was not profit but competitive success, pleasure or prestige which were the key motives in investment. The quest for playing success dominated their thinking. Gate money was first charged to offset costs. The exciting knockout cups attracted larger crowds. Gate money provided the revenue to pay elite sportsmen. Clubs which were relatively successful sucked in turnstile cash and used it to purchase better players and further success, keeping fans happy. Here money talked. Clubs were always keen to increase profits. But this was generally less important than winning as many matches and championships as possible.

If enclosure was the way to make money in the towns, in the countryside enclosure was a way for landowners to gain profit as well as pleasure. On the Yorke estate in Nidderdale for example, renting out of the grouse moors proved more profitable than the mining of ore or the renting out of farms.[25]

By and large, however, sport was commercial but not capitalist, financed largely within the local community, a fairly traditional form of ownership and control, and a clear parallel to other Victorian entertainment industries such as the music hall.[26] Enclosed racecourses and English soccer were more profit conscious than cricket and Scottish football, but most directors strove for glory, not dividends. Just because some of those involved were businessmen did not mean they adopted a business approach. Their pursuit of sporting success was often for reasons of personal vanity rather than financial sanity, for kudos not cash, even though there was some potential for indirect gain through contracts for the provision of equipment and catering or for building work. There might perhaps be free advertising for their business, and there were social gains so long as the team was successful. But rational calculations about risks and costs were often overshadowed by the opportunity to link their destiny with that of their local team or their favourite sport.

Directors favoured a break-even approach, operating at the least cost commensurate with success. Dividends paid to shareholders were not large. Many soccer clubs rarely paid a dividend. Most clubs regularly spent more than their income trying to improve their team. In 1887/8 only four professional soccer teams were a pecuniary success, and Bolton lost £500 on the season.[27] In soccer and rugby few companies promised investors dividends. Fewer still actually paid them. In county cricket, although most counties wanted attractive sides to visit at holiday periods, there was no consistent attempt to maximise gate receipts. Horse racing was only occasionally profitable, despite offering increasing numbers of sprints, handicaps and two-year-old races to attract entries and punters. Although the new enclosed racecourses offered larger prize money, with Sandown putting up £10,000 for a single race in 1876, most courses only opened for a few days a year. Shareholders were content with modest revenues and were primarily motivated by love of racing. Cricket and soccer grounds also stayed shut for part of the year.

That is not to say that there were no attempts to increase revenue by almost all larger organisations, whether incorporated or not. Events were advertised by poster and in the press. Clubs were keen to have their stadiums set up near a railway. Entrance fees were differentially priced, and prices were sometimes reduced to get more turnover. Even the nature of the game might be changed to attract more spectators. County cricket clubs always ensured their main ground was in a population centre. During the summer cricket, rugby and football teams might organise a summer athletic sports meeting to raise funds, while at a lower level friendly societies, bands of hope or even public park committees followed suit, using club grounds. In the winter, Middlesbrough Cricket Club was not alone in raising funds by a 'veterans' soccer match between ex-Middlesbrough and 'District' soccer players in 1888.[28] Most clubs tried to target potential punters and identify particular market segments. Some diversified to offer more sports, extending their range. The Irish Champion Athletic Club's Lansdowne complex had an archery ground, croquet lawns, tennis court, rugby and cricket pitches, and a cinder track. Others refocused on a single core activity. The winter football activities of an 1867 Preston Cricket Club eventually saw the triumph of Preston North End, the 'Invincibles'. In the 1880s Leicester Fosse likewise defined its market by dropping summer cricket and concentrating on soccer.

There were some attempts to maximise profit. In team sports, arranging a series of guaranteed home and away matches against other well-matched sides maximised profit by attracting larger crowds. Competitive leagues were an attempt to do this for top teams but were a relatively late arrival in Britain. In America baseball had a national league in 1876, and the American Football Association created one in 1884. England's Football League was only established in 1888 by William McGregor, a Birmingham draper and Aston Villa committee member. The league comprised twelve successful soccer sides from the Lancashire textile district and the midlands. Its establishment showed a clear shift towards a more economic approach. Although playing records, and geographic and traditional factors played a part, financial stability, crowd potential and ground capacity were of prime importance. So initially was cheapness of travel to keep costs down.[29] The small Lancashire town of Halliwell, and distant Sunderland, were excluded because of such factors, even though they were both highly successful. England's first cricket league, the Birmingham League, was formed in December the same year, and gave workers in factories and heavy industry the opportunity to watch Saturday afternoon cricket.

Leagues took off fast. In soccer the Northern League, created in the spring of 1889, was largely composed of north-eastern professional clubs.[30] Other northern regional leagues followed over the next year. The contemporary Football Alliance was a more direct rival to the League, drawing from across the north and midlands. Most of its clubs joined the Second Division of the Football League on its establishment in 1892, allowing expansion into Sheffield and Manchester. The South Wales and Scottish Leagues began in 1890–91. In cricket, the Lancashire League was formed in 1890, initially under the name of the North-East Lancashire League, changing its name in 1892 and limiting teams to one professional. In rugby union Lancashire and Yorkshire introduced leagues in 1892, while the equally competitive Glamorgan League was founded in 1894.

Voluntary organisations at the higher reaches of racing, football and rugby steadily gave way to companies and boards of directors. Directors dropped men out of form, recruited better players from the midlands, the north and Scotland, and made them train consistently. Even though much of the crowd may have been working-class, all commercialised sports, from racing to football and rugby, sought to attract a crowd which included a significant proportion from the middle classes. The national administrators were also increasingly prepared to modify rules to make the game more appealing. Many top football, rugby and even cricket teams would often only allow a visit if given a guarantee of a certain amount of gate money.

Even so, British sport was commercially oriented only to an extent. No national sports were played on Sundays, the day when almost everyone had free time. Clubs showed little interest in maximising profit, and ground admission charges eventually levelled off at 6d. for ground entry in cricket, soccer and other team sports. English soccer clubs did not even initially charge women for entry, although moves to charge for grandstand admission began in the late 1880s. Middlesbrough, for example, first passed a resolution to charge women '2s. 6d. per season for a seat in the stand, or a special charge for occasional visits' in May 1888.[31] This was then half the cost for men. Scottish clubs didn't charge women even in 1901. Clubs played many unremunerative 'friendly' matches, and didn't try to sell the game or expand it. Few soccer clubs were willing to use their grounds for other purposes.

Neither cricket nor rugby's Northern Union appeared concerned to make substantial profits. The Northern Union, for example, made little effort to expand into Wales, and did not try to ensure equality of playing strength between clubs. If anything, cricket had an even more limited sense of market forces, although touring professional sides had made money from the game in the 1850s. County cricket used a commercial gate-money approach merely as a supplementary means of support to their membership subscription schemes and aristocratic patronage. There were some attempts to raise extra revenue. Trent Bridge, Bramall Lane, Derby County Cricket Ground (itself then part of the racecourse) and Surrey's Oval all staged major soccer matches, including FA cup semi-finals or finals, in the 1880s. Surrey regularly let its ground for rugby internationals, bicycle and amateur athletics events, and less often for skating, lawn tennis and baseball.

The three-day county cricket matches, where the third day often finished early, still started on Mondays and Thursdays, and so did not attract a good Saturday afternoon crowd. The first known first-class match actually to start on Saturday was an England XI v. Australians match, significantly in Yorkshire, in 1882. Although an embryonic cricket county championship was in existence by the 1860s, with published tables by 1870, the championship was only formalised in the 1880s. There were no attempts to equalise playing ability between counties, to change the two-year residence qualification to get closer games and attract larger crowds, or to increase entry charges for attractive games.

Even in the 1890s county championship sides did not have to play more than eight other first-class counties home and away, so while the clubs in most highly urbanised areas, such as Yorkshire or Surrey, would play all other first-class counties, others would reduce costs by playing the minimum number of games, and would demand financial guarantees. In the 1890s Yorkshire raised nearly 70 per cent of its revenue from the gate, Derbyshire less than 40 per cent. Improved standards of play often simply increased costs, and most more rural county sides, such as Derbyshire, Hampshire or Essex, ran a deficit and only survived through donations, appeals for voluntary subscriptions, interest-free loans and fund-raising campaigns.

Worcestershire's experience is illustrative. As a minor county, Worcestershire had a deficit of £309 in 1896 and £328 in 1897, despite its playing success, and made efforts to achieve first-class status in 1898. When the county entered the county championship in 1899, Worcester's first match against Yorkshire drew gate receipts of nearly £86, about half the previous season's total receipts. On the second day of the visit of the London side 1926 people paid £49, record takings at Worcester. The Sussex match attracted even larger crowds, and a new record of £227. The season's match receipts totalled £897. Subscriptions, where club membership cost a guinea, with lady members paying 10s. 6d., rose to 609 full members and 189 ladies, and totalled £839. But the costs of professionals, ground staff and match expenses were now higher. The professionals' bill had risen from £307 to £547, creating a larger budget deficit. Worcester was heavily reliant on donations, and the goodwill and generosity of patrons and members, to stay afloat.[32] By contrast in 1899 Yorkshire's subscriptions were £2512 and Leicester's £1123. Yorkshire, with a large urban population, raised nearly £9000 in gate receipts, and Leicester £1357. Worcestershire's profits were used to improve the ground and strengthen the playing staff. So the next year's deficit was even higher. Yorkshire, like Surrey and the MCC, was a financial success. But most clubs operated at a loss.

Minor counties generally attracted smaller crowds and fewer

subscribers. For smaller counties one strategy was to allow three or four outclubs to affiliate, granting an annual county match in return. This generated revenue of around £5 a club. To increase interest, the Minor Counties Cricket Association was formed in 1895, instituting its own championship. Such counties' revenue was similar to that of leading urban clubs, with annual gate-money of between £100 and £200. A few clubs did well financially. Liverpool Cricket Club managed a profit of £282 in 1894. For most clubs, gates for individual matches were low. In the north east, a £10 gate at the final of the 1887 Cleveland Cup was seen as the 'best thus far'.[33]

Clubs faced running costs, as well as those of site and facility development, especially if regular ground maintenance was necessary. Attempts at profit could easily be affected by outside factors. Bad weather could lead to severe losses. Steeplechases with one annual event found cancellation financially ruinous. Cricket clubs in wetter areas were at a disadvantage. Sports clubs were particularly affected by local considerations. Some members could only afford fees in good times. Headingley Bowling Club membership was 112 in 1873, at the peak of the trade cycle, but the depressed years of 1874 and 1875 saw its membership drop to fifty-four by 1876.[34] Then there would also be unpaid arrears in subscriptions in bad trade years. Drops in revenue often meant less competitive activity. Clubs were often forced to amalgamate to maintain or improve playing strength, or follow their members' interests and diversify, placing more emphasis on a formerly subsidiary sport. Increases in field rent could also mean problems, and loss of a field could be disastrous, at least in the short term.

In horse racing, owners and breeders showed more interest in profit. Realising this interest was quite another matter. Any increase in total prize money brought more owners into racing. Even when prize money was at its peak, between 1881 and 1890, and the average annual prize money per horse was almost £207, the average annual cost of training a horse was over £300. Only the leading owners profited. Most lost money each year unless they could bet effectively. The same held true of breeding. Much publicity was given to successful owners and to the minority of breeders with fashionable stock. They made good profits. But more than half of all breeders lost money on public auction sales of their horses, if all costs are taken into account.

Race meetings generated income, but potential profits were limited by high and ever-increasing setting up and running costs, with constant press pressure for improvements and increased prize money. Up to the 1870s, the Jockey Club devoted the whole of its Newmarket income to racing in the form of prize money, maintenance and the salaries of officials. Even when it moved to augment revenue from the 1870s, increased profits from some meetings were used to cover increased losses on others. Certainly enclosure at some urban courses, such as Gosforth Park or Kempton, was highly successful and profitable. Despite a limitation to 10 per cent dividends, Gosforth's shares tripled in value between 1881 and 1893. But enclosure proved disastrous at many smaller meetings. Subscriptions from the upper classes, local tradesmen and publicans almost always dried up on completion of enclosure. Gate money failed to cover the deficit. Newly enclosed courses set up in areas without a longstanding tradition of race-week absenteeism almost always failed to attract crowds. Very expensive courses at Halifax, Portsmouth and Birmingham all failed in a few years.

Some speculative builders found sporting provision indirectly profitable. The exclusive housing estate at Bedford Park in Ealing had a tennis court as early as 1871. Nottingham's exclusive Park Estate likewise incorporated a bowling green and had tennis courts.[35] By the 1880s most of the more select seaside resorts had private golf and tennis facilities, and tournaments at Exmouth, Hove and Eastbourne became resort attractions. Local authorities first involved themselves in sport through their parks providing some facilities. Crystal Palace, an early Victorian theme park, had a cricket ground by 1857, and a representative of Crystal Palace football ground was present at the meeting forming the FA in 1863. Increased demand forced local authorities by the end of the century to make further provision. In 1890, for example, the London County Council endorsed a popular subscription which allowed the purchase of the Lea or Tottenham marshes, soon a main venue for amateur football in north London. London's Playing Fields Association thereafter became active in seeking better playing facilities for cricket and football. A few municipal tennis courts were appearing by the late 1890s. The first English local authority golf course, Bournemouth's Meyrick Park, was established in 1893/4. St Andrews town council built the Jubilee course in 1897.

The upper classes invested in sport only to a very limited extent, sometimes in racecourse share-ownership or in racing stud farms and more occasionally in county cricket, but almost never in soccer clubs. Their investment in sports facilities at the seaside resorts was largely to help sell land. Lord Scarbrough, for example, laid out golf links at Skegness in 1894. At Eastbourne, the Duke of Devonshire provided facilities for a range of sporting activities. Racehorse and greyhound breeding were both acceptable businesses for the middle classes. Most investors in sports companies were middle-aged, middle-class men, often married, buying for social reasons. In the case of soccer, it was the brewers and shipbuilders at Sunderland and those in the cotton trade at Preston who were major shareholders.[36] Some soccer share-holders, publicans, brewers, bookmakers and sports outfitters benefited indirectly. Others sought prestige, local status, esteem or even votes. Share ownership allowed them to exert community power, and to enjoy the lifestyle, and were a type of psychic capital. Brewers continued to be amongst the leading investors and directors in the new incorporated sporting organisations. They also maintained a direct involvement, perhaps playing cricket and owning racehorses. Some bought shares and financed grounds not just for potential profit but as part of a wider social role, maintaining the traditional relationships of duty and obligation.

Smaller, more amateur sporting organisations showed relatively little interest in profit, although attempting to reduce costs. Golf clubs every-where, for example, especially those at seaside resorts, reduced their costs and got revenue to improve facilities through daily and weekly vis-itor charges. The assets of most golf clubs were controlled by a small committee who decided policy relating to membership, subscriptions, and social relations, and were generally not keen to expand membership and so limit their own dominance.

It was sportsmen, and a very few sportswomen, who were the most likely to profit from sport. We have already seen the ways in which some middle-class 'shamateurs' could make money. But most players who profited from play came from working-class roots. One major effect of commercialism was the increased number of full-time professionals, with more time and incentive to train. Even so, they were a relatively small, select social group.

Most professionals worked part-time, and had another trade outside the season of their sport. Relatively few came from factories and industrial employment. The pedestrians of the 1840s and 1850s, for example, almost all had working-class occupations which allowed them some time off. Some were skilled tradesmen such as tailors or weavers, others were manual labourers such as navvies or shepherds. Semi-professional Cumbrian wrestlers, throughout the century, were from similar backgrounds, walking miles to various wrestling competitions during the summer season, paying their entrance fees and hoping to make a profit by getting past the first rounds against local men. A winter's hunting required huntsmen and whips, a feeder, grooms, second horsemen and stable assistants who all pursued other rural callings in summer.

Numbers involved varied from sport to sport. In flat racing there were over three hundred jockeys riding in the 1850s, but following the licensing of jockeys by the Jockey Club in 1879 numbers dropped, with only 104 flat race jockeys and eighty-four apprentices licensed by 1899.[37] In yachting, an 1868 estimate was that some two hundred owners hired about 5700 men for the summer, paying weekly rates.[38] Professionals in team sports were usually employed only for the season. Cricketers, for example, usually returned to their original trades and occupations during the winter. Even in the 1881 census enumerators' books many professional cricketers still often described themselves in terms of these dual occupations, as both cricketer *and* (for example) miner, mason, weaver, tin plate worker, turf layer, licensed victualler, cotton porter or groundsman.

Being a professional sportsman was very much a working-class dream, an avenue of hope, an escape from relative poverty. It offered the more talented and hard-working both steady employment and the exhilaration of doing something they loved. Notions of play and work overlapped. They were expected to win, and forced to do so even if they enjoyed the sport, because to lose regularly meant loss of their job or earnings. There was pressure from sponsors, gamblers, club owners and the press, who published statistics of their performances – batting and bowling averages, tables of results, or lists of winners ridden. But at the same time sport was different from much other work. It had job satisfaction, a large element of craftsmanship, and demanded skill and the display of talent, freshness and creativity. Leaving skilled work to try and make a regular living in a sport was a high-risk strategy. Most who did so were insufficiently successful. Injury was an ever-present danger. In team games skills were transient and dependent on colleagues. In soccer, despite the large numbers of players registered for the English First Division in 1900–1, only 216 actually appeared for a first team that season.

Conditions of work and pay also varied. Top sportsmen's incomes were very high, although there are insufficient records to make any accurate calculation of the income of top pedestrians, pugilists or quoiters, where their promoters and backers doubtless claimed much of their winnings.[39] The very top jockeys earned most. In 1885 Fred Archer's total income was assessed by the Inland Revenue as £10,000, and by this decade other leading jockeys were earning over £5000 a season. W. G. Grace earned about £120,000 over the course of his career. Most individual sportsmen struggled to get and keep money. Champion pugilist Tom Sayers did not earn most of his money through his championship fights. Personal appearances were an easier and less painful way. At Barnet Fair, for example, he 'was a conspicuous object during the afternoon as he rode up and down the course'. Public subscriptions for 'upholding English pride' and benefit 'sparring' nights at various pubs also helped. Sayers even took over the Great United States Circus in 1861 and gave sparring demonstrations. But it failed in 1862.[40]

Such ways of supplementing sporting income were extremely common. In the 1830s and 1840s boxers were already displaying their skills in booths, pubs, theatres and halls, or earning money as bodyguards. By the 1880s professional boxers could act as 'professors' to amateur clubs. Top swimmers found employment at urban baths, and combined teaching with occasional appearances at theatres and music halls, locally or nationally. James Finney of Oldham was the attraction at the Canterbury Music Hall in 1886, for example, trying to beat the underwater record. At the beginning of the period amateur rowing clubs, such as Leander, still sometimes used professional coxes to steer in competition, and both Oxford and Cambridge used professional coaches for a number of years from the 1840s. But as rowing clubs became increasingly socially differentiated as for 'Gentlemen, Tradesmen or Watermen' professional coaching ceased, and experienced amateurs began to coach crews. By the later nineteenth century most amateur sporting clubs were trying to avoid using professional coaches.

Amongst players of team games, top professional county cricketers were the most successful, gaining bonuses for good performances, appearance money for England at home and abroad, coaching contracts and benefits. Cricket professionals got match fees from the start, but often provided other services. Some had pubs or managed catering on the ground, others did ground-keeping or coaching. Harrow had its first coach in the 1820s. Eton had one by 1840. Professionals were only con-tracted to the MCC until mid August, when members went off to the grouse moors. This left scope for mid century late summer professional tours. These started with William Clarke's All-England XI. It first toured in autumn 1844. Thereafter the side went on tour annually to the larger industrial towns like Newcastle, Manchester, Leeds or Birmingham, with players earning £4 to £6 a match. By 1851 the side was playing thirty-four games. Other professional sides followed Clarke's example over the 1850s and early 1860s.

From then on county sides gained in strength, generally paying pro-fessionals only match fees, not travel, subsistence and accommodation expenses. Even Yorkshire CCC only paid £5 a game initially, but the basic average seasonal earnings of county professionals rose from £100 in 1870 to £275 in 1900, twice that of a skilled worker. In the 1880s top professionals earned about £10 to £12 a week, which included all expenses during the season.[41] Henry Wood, the Surrey player, in con-trast then only received £2 a week, £5 a match and £1 win bonus, and worked in winter turfing at 26s. a week. At Lancashire, almost a third of the twenty-four professionals employed in 1899 earned less than £3 a week, and eleven were only employed through the season. Surrey led the way with winter pay and star contracts; Yorkshire followed.

By contrast at Worcestershire, the leading minor county, the top rate was £5 for a three-day match in the early 1890s, and they paid Albert White, their bowler, £2 10s. a week during the summer in 1896. Club professionals got even less. The better club sides usually had at least one professional player from the mid nineteenth century, often contracted for the whole season, and usually earning 2s. to 3s. a game in the 1860s.

In a minority of cases loyal, hard-working and talented professional cricketers could increase their incomes through benefit matches. These were matches where the beneficiary paid all the expenses and kept all the gate receipts.[42] Benefits were already a common practice in pugilism, pedestrianism, the theatre and the music hall. A benefit was often swelled by the testimonial gifts of subscribers, which reduced the risks of poor crowds or bad weather. The All England Touring XI were arranging benefit matches for themselves from the 1840s. Joseph Guy's benefit, played at Trent Bridge in 1856, raised £165. The MCC first awarded a benefit (to William Lillywhite) in 1853; Surrey followed in 1860. By the 1870s the leading counties were beginning to approve a few benefits, but only for outstanding professionals who had served their clubs well, usually for at least fifteen years. Up to 1886 the six Surrey benefits averaged £332, and the six Yorkshire benefits £435. Between 1887 and 1890 their benefits averaged £732 and £1178 respectively. These leading counties had the largest urban centres, the best rail links, the wealthiest patrons and the biggest ground capacities. Smaller counties awarded far fewer benefits, partly because expenses could exceed revenue. In 1901 Yorkshire's John Brown received £2282 for his benefit, but Thomas Soar of Hampshire had lost £6 the previous year. As they got older, cricketers could earn money plying their trade in the public schools. George Atkinson, who had been a Yorkshire bowler in the 1860s, spent the 1870s and 1880s cricket coaching, teaching and occasionally umpiring at Rossall School, later aided by a younger assistant.

Earnings of professional soccer players were well above those of unskilled labourers, and in excess of skilled workers. Lancashire clubs were the first to import good players, first finding them jobs with friendly employers, and later giving them travelling expenses and providing broken time payments to cover lost wages, Darwen had Fergus Suter and James Love, Scots from Glasgow, in their 1878 team. Blackburn Rovers engaged McIntyre the next season, soon afterwards giving Fergus Suter £100 to come from Darwen. In the mid and later 1880s soccer professionals usually earned from 4s. to 30s. a week through the season, with some part-timers earning perhaps only 2s. 6d.[43] It is hard to tell, since concealed cash payments from gate money or supposed employment in a local firm were difficult to detect. The formation of the Football League in 1888/9 raised wages, but only to about £1 10s. to £2 a week for the top players plus any winning bonus. First-team weekly wages of £3 or even £4 were soon being reported at leading clubs such as Aston Villa, Preston, Newcastle United or Sunderland, plus signing on fees of up to £100. One estimate of the average retained professional's wage in 1893 was £3 a week in the season and £2 in the close season, although this may be a little high. Thereafter wages rose further at the top of the scale, with Beats and Baddeley of Wolverhampton Wanderers earning a reputed £7 a week throughout the year by the end of the decade.[44] Other good players received about £4 a week, though in the late 1890s Tottenham Hotspur paid James Collins £2 when he played, but only £1 when he played as a reserve. Signing-on fees, job sinecures, cheap accommodation and other inducements all helped. Celtic in 1891 brought Doyle from Everton with the offer of a pub tenancy worth £5 a week, plus a fee for each match played.

Support staff were also earning more money. By 1889 the part-time financial secretary of Sunderland FC was receiving £20 per annum. Thomas Watson, the secretary and future manager, was getting 35s. a week to arrange matches and ensure 'that the best team was got on the easiest of terms'.[45] At Surrey, the secretary C. A. Alcock was given £330, a silver inkstand and candlesticks in 1881.

Professional rugby players living in the north in the 1880s may have earned at least as much as soccer players. But where soccer turned to Scotland for good players, it was Welsh players who went to Leeds, Bradford and other Yorkshire and Lancashire rugby clubs. In 1986 six Llanelli players went to Rochdale for £50 down, £3 a week and work for three years. Peripatetic professionals Evan and David James of Swansea eventually signed for Broughton Rangers in 1899 for £200 down, £2 a week and jobs as warehousemen. Inducements to sign were common. By 1899 at least one Union Club was reportedly offering 'a present of £100 and an assured income of over £200 a year' to top Welsh players.[46] Such income was at the upper end of the scale. Most leading players earned between thirty shillings and £4 a week but only during the season.

Like Doyle at Celtic, many sportsmen were given jobs by brewers in order to attract custom, even when still playing. This also could be used as a devious device by amateur sides to disguise illegal payments. It was no coincidence that, of the thirty-five players who played Yorkshire county rugby in the 1892–93 season, ten were publicans. On retirement many more might take up running a pub. Some had saved up, like the professional cricketer 'with some capital' who advertised for a 'beerhouse or pub to get near to a good cricket club ground'.[47] Not all had the requisite skills or the ability to avoid drinking too much alcohol.

Former England rugby captain Dicky Lockwood went bankrupt at his Heckmondwike pub in the 1890s and returned to manual work.

Professional golfers earned less, largely making money from playing rounds with the wealthy and offering advice, ball making, selling clubs and balls, green keeping, acting to control caddies or even caddying themselves by carrying clubs. The leading Scottish professional Tom Morris was only getting fifteen shillings a week as greenkeeper at Prestwick in the 1850s. When he went back to St Andrews as a professional golfer in 1867, he still only received £50 a year. Even this was more than most, and he only got a testimonial in 1895. As golf grew in popularity, laying out courses offered further return. Tom's brother George laid out the Hoylake course in 1869, and, keeping it in the family, Jack Morris became its first professional.[48] Even so, in the 1890s most professional golfers still earned little more than a pound a week. The thousands of caddies got even less, perhaps six or seven shillings a week.

Those sports professionals, such as jockeys, associated with upper-class sporting activities generally did better. Several north Yorkshire trainers left between £30,000 and £40,000 as early as the 1860s, and Thomas Craggs, the clerk of several northern racecourses, died worth £40,000 in 1885. By the 1890s head lads in a racing stable could earn up to £400 or £500 a year. Will Goodall, the huntsman, received a testimonial of nearly £1300 in 1894 after serving as huntsman to the Pytchley hounds for twenty years. Frank Beers, huntsman to the Grafton hounds for nearly thirty years, died worth £15,340 in 1895.[49]

Sporting equivalents to the Victorian friendly societies allowed sportsmen to insure against injury or death, though the Pugilistic Benevolent Society in 1852 catered only for the leading pugilists, and the Cricketers' Fund Friendly Society, founded in 1857, never really attracted the bulk of professional cricketers. Membership of the Players' Union of Association players, formed in 1898 by Wolverhampton Wanderers' W. C. Rose, was limited by a high rate of labour turnover, the geographical dispersal of clubs, and the attitudes of professionals themselves, divided by self-interest, greed and competitiveness. The Professional Golfers Association, founded in 1901, was the first permanent professional body.

Many sports depended on what was often relatively expensive equipment. The manufacture and distribution of sporting equipment such as

cycles, golf clubs and cricket bats created a living for substantial numbers of people.[50] Recreational sport encompassed a large percentage of
sports-related turnover and employment, as people spent money on
sporting goods, equipment, clothing and shoes. Early in the century
the production of sports equipment was largely in small-scale, craft-
orientated workshops, while money could also be made by supplying
animals for hunting or killing, from rats and pigeons to foxes and deer.
Redfern, for example, made a business of supplying most of Lancashire's
pigeons in the 1840s.[51]

Greater spending power helped increase demand, and sports equipment figured in the Great Exhibition of 1851. Equipment slowly became
more standardised and mass produced. By 1901 there was a trend
towards industrialised factory production, alongside a continuing
emphasis (by the wealthier) on higher-quality, hand-made sports goods.
For participants in fishing, shooting and almost all branches of rural
sport their tackle, rifles and other equipment in 1873 were supposedly
'twice as good as they were a generation back', while 'every new sporting invention is in the direction of new luxury'.[52] The new breech
loaders demonstrated at the Great Exhibition increased demands on
London and Birmingham gunmakers. Holland & Holland (founded
1835), who were very successful in competitive trials held by the *Field* in
1883, became a leading firm, opening a larger factory in Harrow Road,
London, in 1898.[53]

Fishing had a large service industry supporting it, producing both bait
and fishing tackle, since both regularly needed replenishment. In London at mid century, dead dogs were being collected by makers of fishing
tackle and covered with bran to rot so as to collect 'gentles' for bait.[54]
Before pollution overtook the Thames, it was well recognised that 'the
Cockney is a fishing animal', and there were tackling and bait shops not
only in the Strand but 'in all the busiest courts from Fetter Lane to London Bridge'.[55] Hardy's, an Alnwick firm, became the leading producer
of quality fly-fishing rods, producing about 800 a year in the mid 1880s
and about 3500 by the mid 1890s, still basically adopting a craft approach
but in a small factory.[56]

Many firms clearly profited from the sports boom. In 1881 Francis
Dark had forty-two employees in St John's Wood, and James Heard
twenty-seven in Surrey, making cricket materials. Dukes of Penshurst

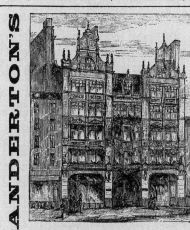
Cricket and Football Times advertisements in 1880. Recreational sport encompassed a large percentage of sports-related employment, turnover and advertising. Richard Daft was an ex-Nottinghamshire cricket captain.

had a two-storey factory by 1880. Across the country were large numbers of small family manufacturing businesses. In Yorkshire alone in
1881 there were thirteen cricket bat manufacturers listed on the census.
There were fewer ball makers, though balls may often have been made
as a sideline to making cricket boots, part of the broader leather trade.
As in America, emergent sporting goods manufacturers expanded
demand for specialised equipment by linking their goods whenever possible to coaches, players, journalists and sports administrators. James
Lilleywhite and John Wisden provided examples of ex-cricketers selling
such sports equipment. Richard Daft, the captain of Nottinghamshire in
the 1860s and 1870s, not only owned a small brewery but maintained a
cricketing outfitters at Radcliffe on Trent. By 1880 he had expanded into
football and tennis. His advertisement called 'the attention of Secretaries
of Clubs, Colleges and Schools to his celebrated Patent Waterproof
Association and Rugby Footballs, which have given such unqualified
satisfaction since their introduction. R.D. has had the honour of supplying most of the principal clubs in the United Kingdom'.[57] Numbers
of such sports shops for sporting equipment and clothes expanded rapidly towards the century's end. There were eight football outfitters in
Glasgow in 1885 and twenty in 1900.

By then the small-scale craft-orientated and hand-made equipment
businesses, still attractive to the better off, had new machine-made
cheaper mass-production rivals. John Jacques & Son produced goods
largely for team games and was incorporated in 1899. Slazengers, originally a mid-Victorian producer of hand-made sports equipment,
exploited the demand for tennis equipment, especially balls, and made
a profit of £26,867 in 1901. Cycling best epitomised this trend, once the
pneumatic tyre became popular in the later 1880s. John Dunlop, whose
first company was formed in 1889, sold it in 1896 for three million
pounds. Raleigh, the bicycle firm, was floated for £200,000 in 1896.
Other technological changes helped profit. Better refining and working
of iron allowed the production of iron-headed golf clubs. Increased sales
of lawnmowers and rollers helped create smoother playing surfaces (and
higher standards) for croquet, bowls, cricket or tennis.

A final source of potential profit was betting on sport, already commonplace in the Georgian period, not just amongst the 'fancy' but also,
though less regularly, right across the class system. It first grew in British

racing regions, like Yorkshire or round Newmarket, with results brought by the mail coaches. The general public lacked detailed and up-to-date knowledge about form. This meant that racing insiders with access to privileged information were able to manipulate the betting market to their advantage. There were also racing sweeps on the major races. These were initially aimed at the upper and middle classes, but by the 1840s they were being organised by publicans in racing towns such as London, York, Doncaster or Leeds, with prices the working classes could afford. Some publicans advertised in the sporting press. Not all were honest. On occasion, according to *Bell's Life*, 'fictitious names were put forward to call attention to schemes equally fictitious'.[58] Home Office alarm at such actions saw prosecutions of newspapers carrying sweep advertisements in 1848.

Early betting on racing was largely between individuals, entered in betting books and based on trust. Debts were paid after the race. The Gaming Act of 1845 made gambling debts irrecoverable at law, and off-course cash betting shops, known as 'listers' or 'list-houses' because they posted up lists of runners, grew up in response. The Betting House Act of 1851 tried to ban these with little success. Despite some police prosecutions, betting was soon well rooted in urban society, and increasingly common amongst the better-off working classes. At a time when income was unreliable, betting could be a successful example of self-help, a risky investment of a temporary small surplus in hopes of winning a significant sum. For a few it proved a path to self-destruction. The invention of the electric telegraph brought news of horses' progress in training, their entries and wins, more quickly to the public. The trains carried press betting information nationwide. By the 1880s betting had become a key part of urban popular culture, while sporting tipsters made their money by exploiting the more gullible. As early as April 1862 some sixteen tipsters were advertising in *Bell's Life*. Firm action by the police against betting houses and pubs simply increased the numbers of street bookmakers. By the late 1890s the *Sporting Chronicle* was even issuing racing coupon competitions, to cash in on betting demand.

Bookmaking had always been found at other sports such as pedestrianism. Bookmakers were present throughout the century at the majority of working-class sports. When formerly 'respectable' sports like rugby began to attract working-class support, betting also emerged there, much to the anxiety of administrators like the RFU's Conservative MP secretary Rowland Hill, who felt that betting was amongst the 'many evils that had crept into the game.'[59] Late century films regularly recorded bookmakers' presence, even at supposedly amateur events. *The Great Glove Fight*, for example, a 1900 film, shows a contest between the Southern English champion and the Sussex champion with a bookmaker paying up his calls.[60]

Increased betting could lead to more corruption: jockeys pulling horses, owners looking for betting coups. There were regular scandals in horse racing, especially in the 1840s and 1850s. In 1844 two older horses masqueraded as three-year-olds in trying to win the Derby, while the favourite was almost certainly held back by its jockey. More generally, professional sportsmen were well aware that money could be made by losing as well as winning. Money was to be made from bookmakers' bribes, or by backing their opponent. Boxers or pedestrians fixed bouts for the same reason. When the athletic star Deerfoot staged exhibitions against other runners in his travelling troupe, who earned about £7 a week, he had always to win, according to one of his team's later memory.[61]

Such greed contrasted with the relative altruism of charity events. Publicans and music-hall entrepreneurs had always run these and they continued to do so in a variety of sports. By the 1880s charity 'friendly' matches were a regular occurrence in football and rugby, usually at the beginning of the season. In working-class communities they were organised for worthy causes such as hospitals, strike funds, disaster funds, or the unemployed. Darlington's St Augustine soccer side played a benefit match for 'the widow and family of the engine driver named Metcalfe, who was killed at the North Road Engine Works' in 1889.[62] Celtic was founded specifically to raise money for a Catholic charity. Charity cups, such as the Cleveland Medical Charities Cup in the 1880s or the Dewar Charity Shield matches between English and Scottish clubs in the 1890s, stimulated much popular interest. Athletic clubs often put on charity sports during the summer, and these usually attracted large crowds.

Music hall artistes also became involved in charity sports, although this was also self-promotion to drum up custom and increase their own fame. Theatrical groups, especially pantomime companies, often engaged in charity matches with local clubs, the press, or rival troupes, especially in the provinces. At Newcastle in 1889 a match between the press and the pantomime companies was for the relief of 'the widow and child of the late James MacDonald, the well-known comedian'.[63] By 1890 such events were becoming annual events in Bradford, Glasgow, Liverpool and other large cities. Even the famous Dan Leno formed a music hall comic cricket eleven in 1898 to raise money for charity, parodying sporting figures on the pitch.[64] Reversing the process, professionals from a range of sports appeared on stage in sketches and melodramas and gave demonstrations of their skills in order to enhance their income. Such music-hall entertainers by now relied for their national success on the media, and charity games were well publicised. But the press had a symbiotic relationship with sport. Sports journalism both helped to create an audience for particular sports and used the audience for sport to increase newspaper circulation and profits.

6

The Media

In 1895 *The Times* claimed that 'all the schoolboys in England read the cricket news', and that sport had become 'a positive passion, thanks to the publicity given by the sporting press'.[1] Certainly it was true that news supply stimulated demand for sport, and demand further stimulated news supply. Before the nineteenth century sport was a mainly orally transmitted part of popular culture.[2] In the Victorian age newspapers became the main means of conveying information. They carried a high level of cultural authority, and a vibrant sports journalism emerged, both responding to and helping create modern sport by reporting it in the national sporting press and in specialised books. Press coverage was a recognition that sport was important and newsworthy. At the same time it provided a stimulus to the growth and popularity of many sports, and supplied the flow of sporting statistics and records of achievement sporting organisations increasingly provided. The 1890s were saturated by sporting print, with mainstream national and local papers playing a full role in what had become a late Victorian obsession.

The media's importance in constructing the Victorian sporting world cannot be overestimated. Many first came across sport not by playing or watching but through media coverage, a combination of factual reportage, viewpoint and promotion which the sporting 'tyro' could appropriate for his own use. Sporting reporters, journalists, local correspondents, novelists, playwrights and finally film-makers all serviced, represented and interpreted an increasingly all-pervasive and voracious appetite for sport, extending their audience and deepening its loyalty in so doing.[3] At the same time they aided the construction of a sporting reality dominated by the interests, values and ideological needs of the middle classes.

The Victorian media changed public views of sport as they refracted them in print. They created new forms of sporting reality, shaping response and direction, while contributing to and reinforcing national, regional and local sporting loyalties to powerful urban teams and players. The press created national sporting celebrities while pre-publicity boosted interest in and crowds at major contests. Press publicity first made the Derby, St Leger or Grand National major betting races, and the FA Cup Final significant in national sporting terms. The media were active in constructing the very meaning of sports, since what people understood of them were largely shaped by the way they were represented. Press powers to determine readers' understanding resided in both the issues they raised (or chose not to) and the ways in which they framed them. The popular press, for example, played a leading part in the rapid emergence of football as a popular spectacle and cultural form in the 1870s and early 1880s, a time when actual crowds were still low but were growing as games were regularly reported and local rivalries fostered. Readers were drawn into this imagined sporting community, becoming part of a larger passive (or active) body of supporters. The free publicity papers provided informed readers what was on when and where.

Sporting journalists provided a running commentary on change, mediating, interpreting and directing the meaning of issues such as professionalism or women's sporting participation in ways which catered to middle-class sensibilities. They both reflected and formed opinion, encouraged or discouraged emerging trends, and suggested changes in the laws. They provided a sporting vocabulary, a language for sporting novices to discuss the skills and achievements of pugilists or pedestrians, rugby players or rowers. Sometimes as in pugilism, this was arcane, redolent with terms like 'phizzog', 'rib roaster', 'nob', 'peeper' or 'drawing the crimson'. They provided hints about how to play the new games. They underlined and reinforced regional rivalries and popular prejudices. Their advertisements promoted the sporting commodities and equipment that helped keep up appearances and style. They created a tradition and a history, often with mythologised references to a sport's origins to endow it with further value and prestige.

The print industry itself expanded and was transformed over the period. The abolition of newspaper Stamp Duty in 1855 and Excise Duty on paper in 1861, growing literacy through the activities of the churches and the English Education Acts of 1870, 1876 and 1880, increased

ILLUSTRATED SPORTING NEWS.

AND THEATRICAL AND MUSICAL REVIEW.

No. 36.   SATURDAY NOVEMBER 15, 1862.   ONE PENNY.

SPECIAL NOTICE.

ON THE DAY OF THE

GREAT FIGHT FOR THE CHAMPIONSHIP

A SPECIAL EDITION

OF

THE ILLUSTRATED SPORTING NEWS

Will be issued, containing

A MOST ELABORATE REPORT

Of this Exciting Event, from the time the Match originated to the termination of the Battle.

.*. As the demand will be tremendous our Agents and Subscribers will oblige by forwarding their Orders immediately.

THE FIGHT FOR THE CHAMPIONSHIP!

The Proprietors have made every available arrangement for producing on the week following the Fight

A GREAT ILLUSTRATION

OF ITS MOST EXCITING INCIDENTS IN A

GRAND DOUBLE NUMBER

OF THE

ILLUSTRATED SPORTING NEWS.

In order to do full justice to this Great Event the services of several Eminent Artists have been retained for the occasion.

ORDER EARLY!!!

AQUATICS.

MATCHES TO COME.

NOVEMBER.

17—Oxford University Boat Club—fours.

—Cambridge University Boat Club—Colquhoun sculls.

22—Cambridge University Boat Club—trial eights.

DECEMBER.

1—Cambridge University Boat Club—scratch fours.

20—Albany Amateur Rowing Club—four-oared races.

THE TWO GREAT SCULLERS' MATCHES ON MONDAY LAST.

KELSBY AND SPENCER FOR £50—GARTEEN AND LOVELL FOR £30.

THE GAME OF KNURR AND SPELL, PLAYED AT WEST BROMPTON, BETWEEN KIRK STABLES AND JOB PEARSON, FOR £100, NOV. 3, 1862.

The game of knurr and spell, 1862. The *Illustrated Sporting News* was the first weekly paper consistently to provide detailed pictures of sporting events.

economic expansion in the late 1860s and early 1870s which led to higher real wages, and shorter working hours, all fuelled reading demand and created an unprecedented level of readership. New print technologies like the rotary press from the 1840s, better reproduction of pictures, and the growing use of new techniques of reporting, were also crucial. So too was the manufacture of paper from cheap wood pulp. Production rose from 11,000 tons in 1800 to 100,000 tons in 1860, and to 652,000 tons in 1900.[4] Pulp-paper books and newspapers became increasingly cheap, while the railways aided distribution. First the electric telegraph, which was increasingly influential from the 1850s onwards, then the telephone, passed on sporting news ever more quickly.

One result was a growing demand from both the expanding middle classes and urban masses to read about sport, the more so from the 1860s as regular fixture lists and seasonal events began to give a firm structure to sports' narratives and running commentaries. A specialised sporting press emerged to meet the needs of the most committed. Circulation figures underestimate the actual readership. Sporting pubs and gentlemen's clubs often took copies of newspapers as a way of retaining or attracting membership, as did the various clubhouses for particular sports. *Cricket* expected that it 'will be filed for reference in the Pavilions of all the principal Clubs'.[5] Country house drawing rooms might have a copy. A mass public, initially less interested, began coming across regular sporting journalism in the mainstream press by the 1890s. Specialist sporting articles guided their readership in sport's meanings, a subtle or not so subtle form of sporting indoctrination. Articles built bridges between a nostalgic 'golden age' and the sporting present, with modern champions measured against those of the past. How readers responded is less clear. No doubt some responded enthusiastically; others turned to more interesting reading. Letters from readers, often written under pseudonyms, offering controversial or humorous opinions, encouraging a club or individual to show courage in a crisis, complaining about dirty play or cheating, offering excuses for poor play and 'correcting' supposedly wrong or biased reports, were a common feature. They kept the paper in touch with its readers. Such cultural conversations are suggestive, but letters generally reflected stronger feelings rather than the views of most readers.

For readers, newspapers provided knowledge and opinions to be exploited. For followers of horseracing, for example, specialised knowledge of form, the going, how horses went in training, or successes of trainers and jockeys provided cultural capital: a rich repertoire for the pub, club or street, and an explanation for betting successes and excuses for betting failures. Football supporters could gain status amongst peers by being up-to-date with the latest news from the club, the latest signings, recent injuries, forthcoming matches and how other teams were doing.

In the first part of Victoria's reign, even though weekly newspapers were expensive, there were already a few devoting much of their columns' space to sport. The elitist sixpenny *Bell's Life in London and Sporting Chronicle* (1822), published on Sundays, dealt largely with field sports, racing, pugilism and pedestrianism, news, police intelligence and entertainments, largely from a metropolitan perspective. The paper's title reminded readers of Pierce Egan's spectacularly successful 1821 novel, *Life in London*, and Egan's 'flash' argot and picaresque, anecdotal style had already built up a cross-class readership for racing and pugilism material through his books and work for the *Weekly Dispatch*. News gathering from the provinces relied on the stage coach, or pigeon-post, so was often late.

The editor of *Bell's* from 1824, Vincent Dowling, became a central figure in such sports, especially pugilism. He created a paper carefully presented as sportingly impartial, reliable and respectably Tory, and he himself gave expert evidence to the 1844 Select Committee of the House of Lords on betting and gaming. He fostered his reputation as a man of integrity, acting as referee or stakeholder, and becoming an arbiter of occasional disputes and a guardian of the interest and honour of the early Victorian sporting world.

The growth of gambling was a major economic focus for the paper. Its early target market was 'the fancy', together with a wider upper-class and provincial audience, a cross-class group with an appetite for vicarious sporting experience: insider accounts of pugilistic contests, doings at the races, the fives court or boxing club, elite cricket, hunting and coursing, or the current betting odds at Tattersall's. The use of knowing references, specialised sporting 'slang' and cant terms, and the regular columns of cryptic replies to readers' letters, settling betting arguments, laying down the law on sporting procedure and explaining rules, helped cater for its audience. The paper claimed to exceed 23,000 copies weekly in 1840, and 27,000 by 1848. Although always far more interested in London and Home Counties sporting life, up to and beyond the 1860s it also made attempts at national coverage, by then coming out in 'town' and 'country' editions, and including the new 'modern' sports. It included significant foreign sporting news, a suggestive indication both of the global spread of sport and of some foreign readers.

Bell's Life first came under threat from other upper- and middle-class weekly sporting papers in the 1850s. The *Racing Times* (1851–68) relied on racing and drama. The *Field* started out in 1853, initially as a struggling sporting, farming and upper-class 'life in London' paper. In late 1857 the editorship was taken over by John Henry Walsh, a former ophthalmic surgeon, who aimed it more directly at a rural readership. It became a socially grand, 'Country Gentleman's Newspaper', covering farming, stock breeding, rural agriculture and country occupational interests as well as field sports. Its circulation was not large, still only 19,000 in 1890. Horse-racing, hunting, shooting, fishing and coursing were its sporting mainstays, although later in the century it began to give ball sports more space. Walsh himself was a keen field sports participant, hunting with the Heythrop and Worcestershire, coursing greyhounds, shooting and hawking. He was also a founder and first secretary of the All-England Croquet Club, and organised the first Lawn Tennis open championships at Wimbledon in 1876. His enthusiasm for amateur, country and outdoor sports turned the paper round and built up reputation amongst middle- and upper-class rural dwellers.

Such papers were economically driven by increased advertising, targeting upper-class readers with items of conspicuous consumption. The *Field* maintained a 'Sporting Registry' for such items as the availability of hunting boxes or fishing waters. The potential of such advertising revenue from sport was a lesson to all other papers. The *Field* was soon itself challenged by other long-lasting high-class papers, such as *Land and Water* (1866), the *Fishing Gazette* (1877) and *Horse and Hound* (1884), and by more ephemeral papers such as the *Country Gentleman, Sporting Gazette and Agricultural Journal* (1862), the Hull-based *Turf Herald and Yorkshire Field* (1881) or *Rod and Gun*, which aimed directly at the wealthy sporting set, claiming in Willing's *Press Guide* of 1891 to be 'a welcome visitor in every country house'.

THE
Midland Sporting News

EDITED BY "ECLIPSE."

No. 112 | Published on Saturdays, and every Race Morning. Registered at the Post Office as a Newspaper. | BIRMINGHAM, SATURDAY, JANUARY 11th, 1873. | Without Afternoon Returns or Weekly Circular, | ONE PENNY.

Midland Sporting News, 11 January 1873.
In the 1870s provincial sporting papers were becoming more common.

The growth of a specialised sporting press had a symbiotic relationship with the spread of sporting participation and spectatorship. By the 1860s *Bell's Life* was under threat from a new breed of penny London papers such as *Sporting Life*, first published in 1859, which claimed initially to cover 'the turf, the chase and the [prize] ring'. It was quickly followed by the *Sporting Telegraph* (1860), *Sporting Gazette* (1862), *Sporting Opinion* (1864), *Sportsman* and *Sporting Times* (both 1865), covering little other than a wide range of sports, still aimed initially at 'the classes' but now also targeting 'the masses'. *Sporting Life* came out twice a week. By May 1859 it was already claiming weekly sales of 150,000 copies, forcing its main rival, the *Sportsman*, into four issues a week. By the 1880s *Sporting Life* had a circulation of 300,000.

Provincial papers were slower to emerge, and early ones like the *Midland Sporting Chronicle* (1852), published in Nottingham, were short-lived, but in 1870/1 Edward Hulton brought out the *Sporting Chronicle* in Manchester, focusing largely on racing. He claimed 30,000 readers for each issue by 1882.[6] The Birmingham-based *Midland Sporting News* followed in 1872, also with four weekly issues. A widening north-western interest in sports other than racing allowed Hulton in 1875 to publish *Athletic News* at 1*d*. Under the editorship of Thomas Sutton it provided full weekly reports of all sports 'leading to promote physical education', stressing initially that it was 'a weekly journal of amateur sports'. It excluded racing and betting, but covered cricket, aquatics, bicycling, and both football codes from its Manchester base. Initially published on a Saturday, it took off once it extended its coverage of professional soccer and moved to Mondays, increasing sales from some 25,000 a week in 1883 to a claimed 100,000 plus copies a decade later. Many leading FA and Football League officials wrote for it, usually pseudonymously, providing description and key interpretations of matches, events and personalities. The London-based *Athletic World* (1878) provided particular coverage of more amateur sport in London and the universities and public schools. In Scotland, the weekly *Scottish Athletic Journal* began in 1882, merging with the *Scottish Umpire* in 1888 to form the penny *Scottish Sport*, appearing twice weekly with a claimed circulation of 43,000.

Racing news dominated most sporting papers. Off-course betting and racing reportage had been invigorated by the electric telegraph. By 1875 no less than 436,603 telegrams were sent in connection with 264 race meetings.[7] Newspapers quickly created and maintained a network of training area correspondents. Their reports allowed the press to provide better information to prospective punters: reports on the progress of horses in training; 'inside' knowledge from the stables; information about horses actually setting out for a meeting; detailed analysis of each horse and its supposed future chances; and more general racing 'tips'. Newspapers' involvement reduced the manipulation of horses in the betting market by unscrupulous owners and trainers.

Newspapers also had the latest betting intelligence, and provided a rapid results service from racecourses, with starting prices. One result was a major expansion of cash betting amongst working-class punters. In turn tipsters, turf commissioners and sweep organisers were soon providing significant newspaper advertising revenue. Competition forced *Bell's Life* temporarily to drop its price and move to two issues a week before reverting back to a larger, costlier weekly. But it was in decline. In 1881 it was still claiming 'the very respectable circulation' of 10,000 copies, albeit circulating 'among the wealthy of the land', but had been sold for £7000, less than its former annual profit, to the proprietor of the *Sporting Chronicle*.[8] By 1886 it was taken over by the *Sportsman*, by now circulating daily, although the *Sporting Life* claimed to possess the largest circulation of any sporting paper in the world.

Differences between the papers mostly reflected their perceived readership. In covering association football, for example, by 1896 the *Athletic News* concentrated on the games of the Football League, with briefer reports on other competitions, especially those in the north and midlands, and weekly regional news columns from almost every part of Britain. Although the *Sportsman* also provided reports of the Football League games, most of its coverage was given to sides such as the Corinthians or Oxford University, and to the amateur game in London and the south-east.

All these papers, especially *Bell's Life*, *Sporting Life* and the *Sportsman*, aided their circulation and promoted sport through an increasingly wide range of ancillary activities. Almost from their inception they moved into the organisation and administration of sport. They printed challenges from pedestrians, pugilists, rowers and other professional athletes. They sponsored and supported contests, and announced forthcoming ones. Their reputation ensured more honest dealing. They were also willing to receive stakes at their offices and act as stakeholders, appointing referees, timekeepers and other officials and presenting prizes and giving the stakes if all was 'fair and square'. All devoted special attention to 'Answers to Correspondents' on sporting matters, ruling on bets, giving information on sporting rules, settling disputes and answering queries authoritatively on past events. Replies could extend to two columns. Even in the 1850s large numbers of reports came in from cricket matches, pedestrian grounds and other venues, few of which the papers' correspondents could have visited in person. Instead papers solicited voluntary reports from organising officials. *Bell's Life* for example, in compiling its cricket reports, stated, 'We earnestly request secretaries of clubs to send their communications plainly written, particularly the names of persons and places, and to draw up the scores in proper form'.[9] As demand for coverage grew, income was generated by charging minor clubs for coverage.

Numerous examples show how newspapers boosted individual sports and their own circulations by offering trophies or contributions to prize money. The *Field* provided the trophy for the first Wimbledon championships at the All England Croquet Club in 1868. By the 1870s, professional rowers were competing for the *Sportsman* Championship of England Challenge Cup, while on Tyneside the *Newcastle Daily Chronicle* tirelessly boosted rowing from the 1860s to the 1880s through donations and cups. In Birmingham the *Midland Sporting News* gave £70 for a 130 yards handicap at Aston Cross Grounds 'in order to give further encouragement to pedestrianism in the Midland district'.[10] In Scotland in the 1890s the *Dundee Evening Telegraph* provided the trophy for the amateur golf championship of Scotland at St Andrews, while the *Glasgow Evening Times* sponsored an open event in Glasgow.

More importantly, even regional papers worked ever harder to be national, if not international, in their sporting coverage. By 1873 the *Midland Sporting News* carried reports on Australian turf, cricket and pedestrianism. Interest in sport now came not just from educated Londoners, but from throughout the country and beyond. Some readers were clearly working-class. North-east England music-hall songs of the 1860s, for example, have several references to the mining readership of London sporting newspapers. In Joe Wilson's 'Fighting Jim', for example, a miner's wife laments on the corrupting effects of the sporting press: 'he was a real decent lad, and dressed just like a draper, until he read *Bell's Life* or some other sporting paper'. 'Bob the Beuk [Book] Traveller' described how the hero tried to sell books at a Northumberland pit village but found they only read *Bell's Life* or the *Sportsman*.[11] This was despite a contemporary view that *Bell's Life* 'had long been notorious for its determined hostility to the sporting affairs of Newcastle-upon-Tyne'.[12]

In the nineteenth century, sporting journalists were rarely dispassionate observers of the sports they reported. Many were deeply involved in such sports themselves as players, as committee members, as secretaries or administrators of clubs. Their reports often had a built-in bias which the unwary could miss. Most, though not all, were educated at public schools, and many had literary aspirations: their reports and comment occasionally included classical allusions, Latin tags and literary quotations, especially from Shakespeare. Sentences were long, convoluted but carefully grammatical. This is how *Bell's* discussed forthcoming discussions between the Scottish and English Football Associations in 1882.

> Should the coming conference only result in arrangement or compromise which shall commend itself to the growing acceptance of the various associations into which the dribbling game is divided, it will to many be less of a surprise than that a difference should have been allowed to exist so long to the obvious detriment of the sport on both sides of the border. 'A plague on both your houses'. A little mutual concession, my very noble and approved good masters in London and Glasgow, and the difficulty of conflicting codes will trouble you no more. It is rumoured indeed that the governing bodies in London and Glasgow have each of their own accord given expression to a desire for an arrangement which shall give rise to a common understanding, and as such a consummation is devoutly to be wished by football players everywhere, I am confident that next session will witness the establishment of closer than mere diplomatic relations between those who have the interests of the game in the two countries.[13]

For those in positions of power in administering the sport, the expansion of the sporting press offered both problems and new possibilities. More literate, usually middle-class, players, officials, patrons, and sporting administrators often became involved as reporters and journalists, usually beginning by contributing match reports to the press on behalf of their club. William Denison, the honorary secretary of Surrey, reported cricket for the London *Times* as early as the 1840s. Harrow-educated Charles Alcock, a former FA Challenge Cup winner and England international and referee, a prolific London sporting journalist, editor and publisher, was also secretary of the Football Association (1870–95) and of Surrey County Cricket Club (1872–1907).[14] Ex-footballer J. J. Bentley, an anti-gambler who stressed football morality, was secretary of Bolton Wanderers from 1885, and on the Lancashire and then the national Football Association committees. From 1893 he was president of the Football League. He edited the *Athletic News* from 1892 to 1900. In Scotland, the writer of the 'Athletic Notes' in the *Glasgow Examiner* in the late 1890s was the leading Celtic official, a publican from Hamilton educated at Stonyhurst.[15]

Sport may have played a major role in the British press by 1901, but this had been a slow process. Published press guides suggest that as late as 1861 there were still less than a dozen publications where sport dominated. In 1881, when there were over thirty, a survey of journalistic London commentated that 'the newspapers devoted to sport and pastimes are many and influential'.[16] By the 1880s and 1890s publishers were finding a sufficient market for papers and magazines devoted to individual sports. Willing's *British and Irish Press Guide* listed ninety-one specialising in sport in 1891 and there were one hundred and fifty-eight in 1901.

The different trajectories of sporting growth can be tracked through this specialist press. Racing news was the first and largest specialist area, with an ever-widening demand for information from the 1850s. The more 'rational', 'improving' and respectable middle-class forms of sport took longer to disseminate, and did not attract the same wider cross-class audience as racing. Only the most popular of recognisedly modern, middle-class sporting activities, such as cricket, cycling, golf and tennis, could sustain their own specialist weekly papers even in the later 1880s and the 1890s. Early ones, like the *Cricket and Football Times* (1878–1881) could not attract sufficient readers, but *Cricket*, subtitled 'A weekly record of the game', was launched in 1882 by C. A. Alcock, and enjoyed conspicuous success. By contrast, his *Football*, launched in 1882, ceased in 1883. There were only two tennis periodicals in 1881 but five in 1891.

With the exception of *Pastime*, all proved short-lived. It was not till 1890 that the earliest golf periodical, *Golf*, published in London, was issued. This ceased in 1899. The Edinburgh-based *Golfer* was next, lasting from 1894 to 1898, but only with *Golf Illustrated*, in 1899, did golf achieve a lasting audience. Less broadly popular sports like swimming had still less chance – the *Swimming (Rowing and Athletic) Record* lasted only from 1873 to 1874. Only a few papers had 'cycling' in the title in the 1870s, but over twenty different ones briefly existed in each of the next two decades. In 1891 at least eight different cycling papers were published in Birmingham, the centre of cycle-building. Even Belfast and Grantham managed three.

Although the dominant sporting reader was male, from the 1880s upper- and middle-class women were showing interest too. By 1881 its editor tried 'every means' to 'make *Land and Water* as attractive to ladies as it is to gentlemen'. The *Illustrated Sporting and Dramatic News* instituted a 'Sportswoman's Page' in the 1890s, apparently written in the first person by a lady correspondent, describing 'society doings', life in 'town' and country, Ireland or the Riviera, with much name-dropping, sporting material on hunting, shooting, yachting, golf and tennis and details of appropriate dress. She focused both on personal appearance and the conspicuous consumption of sport. Her description of a new Humber cycle conveyed the style.

> I ... fell violently in love with it. It had nickel rims, and the handles of ivory are cased at the end in caps of pieced gold. The fittings are, however, not what pleased me so much as the exquisite neatness of the whole machine – the narrowness of the treadles, and the slimness of the gear case. It is rigid yet light and it looks ... imposingly handsome.'[17]

The formula was exploited by the publisher Alfred Harmsworth, who sensed popular trends early. One of his early ventures, *Bicycling News*, had a 'Ladies' Page' with a woman correspondent by the early 1890s.

Specialist sporting newspapers were for the already committed follower of sport. Sport gained a still wider following through the Sunday press, and the ordinary weekly and daily national and regional papers. The first to give significant space to sport, the *Sunday Times* (1822), was by 1851 firmly a 'literary, dramatic and sporting' paper focusing mainly on horseracing, but taking in a great deal of other sporting news. It claimed to be 'exactly the paper for a large proportion of the middle classes', reflecting widespread middle-class interest in racing. Its price dropped from 6*d.* in 1851 to 2*d.* by 1871. Two Sunday papers specialised in results of ball sports, the *Referee* (from 1877) and *Umpire* (from 1884).

By contrast the leading paper *Reynolds's News*, like its close rival *Lloyds Weekly Newspaper*, had little sporting coverage until the 1870s and 1880s.[18] The former's strongly artisan and unskilled working-class reading public were provided with material on gambling, professionalised sports like horse-racing, pugilism and pedestrianism and not on 'respectable' amateur sports. The same held for the *News of the World*, whose 'Sporting World' was less than a single column in length in the 1840s. In the early 1870s it still had only a single column focusing largely on racing and betting information, with limited material on a few other sports such as pigeon shooting, cricket, or quoits.

Sports coverage expanded only slowly in the London Sunday press, except for national events like the Boat Race. In 1886 coverage still occupied just less than 3 per cent in both *Reynolds's* and *Lloyd's*.[19] Even in 1890 the *People* had less than 4 per cent. By contrast, Hulton's Manchester *Sunday Chronicle* (founded 1886) had about a third of its columns devoted to sport, with very full coverage of Saturday association and rugby football results. Most London papers regularly devoted almost half their sporting coverage to racing, giving tacit support to the illegal working-class cash betting market, and providing reports, tips and predictions about forthcoming races. Condemnatory attacks on other forms of gambling, on rich speculators or dishonest bookmakers, were commonplace, but working-class gambling was defended as a form of relaxation, recreation and intellectual challenge. Cricket still received only limited coverage in the early 1880s but then increased significantly (except in the *People*). Interest in football accelerated rapidly in *Lloyd's* from the mid 1880s when it came to dominate winter sports coverage, but was still poorly covered in *Reynolds's*, and the *Weekly Dispatch* in the early 1890s, suggesting more lower middle-class than working-class interest in the game at this stage. The 1890s proved the key decade. In 1891 the *News of the World* had 7 per cent sporting news coverage and this reached 14 per cent by 1895. Racing and betting still dominated, but a wide variety of professional and amateur sports were now also covered. By 1893 the Retail Newsagents and Booksellers' Union felt that

'ninety-nine out of a hundred people' bought the Sunday paper primarily for the sporting news.[20] *Lloyd's* improved its circulation alongside its
sports coverage, selling a million copies weekly by 1896.

At the end of the nineteenth century Sunday papers were a leading
cultural product, significantly outstripping the audience for music halls
or soccer crowds, even though still not seen as respectable. They were
perceived (incorrectly) as working-class and offending sabbatarian
opinion. Their sale was universal. There were even 'lads shouting at the
top of their voices "The *Humpire* and the *Sunday Chron'kle*"' outside
Hartlepool's church in 1888.[21]

Most national dailies gave relatively little coverage to sport for much
of the century. Those with more reformist editors were known to
'delight in deprecating all things of a sporting nature'.[22] The *Daily Telegraph*, with its predominantly middle-class readership, first began giving
more than nominal coverage to sports, usually racing and cricket, in the
1880s. Most dailies really responded to demand only in the 1890s. In 1897
sports content in the *Telegraph* had reached about 8 per cent, when the
Daily Mail had about 12 per cent. The daily halfpenny *Morning Star*,
edited by an American, Chester Ives, even gave over its front page to
sport in 1892.

There were major differences between regional and local papers in
their sports coverage. Yorkshire papers led the way, perhaps reflecting
their racing interests. In 1851, for example, the *Doncaster Gazette* claimed
'particular attention is devoted ... to obtaining the latest and best
authenticated sporting intelligence'. The *Yorkshire Gazette* was 'an excellent sporting journal, being second to none for accurate and early
information' and the *York Herald* was 'in the first rank of provincial
sporting journals'.[23] All three were relatively expensive weeklies. By 1861
the *Nottingham Telegraph*, selling at a penny, was also incorporating a
great variety of 'sporting intelligence'. Daily papers like the *Birmingham
Daily Post* began carrying more sporting news from the 1870s, starting
often with racing news, and then widening their remit slowly. Papers in
rural counties like Lincolnshire only expanded coverage at the end of
the century, orientating sports coverage towards the supposed demands
of their readers. In the case of the Tory-inclined, county-orientated
Lincolnshire Chronicle, this meant significant attention was paid mainly
to hunting and shooting, with only occasional race results. Sport was

usually less than 4 per cent of its coverage even in the 1890s, and it was the more plebeian, urban *Lincolnshire Echo* which first began to focus largely upon football and cricket.[24]

Occasional racing tipster papers or 'tissues' like Liverpool's *McCall's Turf Register* (1861) were published in the 1860s and 1870s, some like the *Middleham Opinion* (1876) implying to readers that they were assembled in training areas, but it was the 1880s when they became more widely produced and circulated. About the same time, especially in England, evening papers began providing various 'editions' from mid-afternoon, often differing only in the amount of 'stop press' racing and betting news drawn from the telegraph. Saturday evening football 'specials', began in the same decade, first in Birmingham and the north west, and then spreading to other football areas.[25] Most were printed on coloured paper. By 1888 Sunderland's *Football Pink* had a first issue of 5000 on the streets straight after the main local match, and subsequent editions thereafter containing away results 'bought up with alacrity'.[26]

Middle- and upper-class readers were better catered for. The monthly *Sporting Magazine* had provided broad coverage of gentry sporting interests from the late eighteenth century, with racing and hunting as a mainstay. The equally solid *Bailey's Magazine of Sports and Pastimes* (1860) also covered these. Articles were highly literate, but chatty, undemanding and written largely in the first person. The level of critical analysis and numbers of sports covered expanded in the 1890s, largely due to competition from the *Badminton Magazine of Sports and Pastimes* (1895).

Organisations like the Royal Statistical Society or the Manchester Statistical Society testified that the Victorians liked facts and statistics as much as more entertaining reading. Growing demand for sporting minutiae was affirmed by press summaries at the end of a sports season, and by annual guides to major sports. Racing and cricket dominated the first half of the reign, and were soon followed by sports like football. Racing already had Weatherby's *Racing Calendar*, with northern rivals like Johnson's *Racing Calendar*. More detailed analysis began from the 1840s with *Ruff's Guide to the Turf*, compiled by the *Bell's Life* racing editor, which soon listed jockeys' success tables alongside the initial lists of horses, races, trainers, successful owners and prize money won.

In cricket published score-cards, biographies, averages and other statistical data were popular, and former cricketer, scorer, cricketing entrepreneur and printer Frederick Lillywhite began his *Guide to Cricketers* in 1848/9. The family were soon leading figures. John Lillywhite's *Cricketers' Companion* was first issued in 1865 and lasted in various forms till 1882, while James Lillywhite's *Cricketers' Annual* was first published in 1872, providing hints about the game, and leading match results, including club and public schools cricket. *Wisden's Cricketers' Almanack*, written by former professional cricketer, Leamington ground developer and London cricket and cigar shop owner John Wisden, began in 1864, selling at a shilling. Initially it covered a miscellany of general information, not only cricket accounts of ancient matches and a few contemporary ones, but it soon focused more tightly on county and MCC cricket. Counties began publishing their own county cricket annuals in the 1860s and 1870s. Shropshire CCC brought out the first in 1865. Publishers, including the sporting press, eventually began publishing a wide range of sporting annuals under their own imprint, such as the *Athletic News Cricket Annual*. The football equivalent was the *Football Annual*, first published in 1868, initially covering both codes, and drawing advertising largely from sports warehouses and publishers.

It was in non-fiction book production between 1880 and 1900 that an increasingly discerning market for sport was most marked. By then cycling and fishing were by far the most popular topics, although much of this was purely recreational information.[27] Over a hundred books were also written on cricket, where writers like James Pyecroft or Charles Box had begun consciously constructing a canon of literary cricket writing, and from the 1860s, if not before, cricket had been rearticulated and defined in terms of its impeccable Englishness, prestige and respectability, marketing itself ever more to the cultural needs of the middle classes. Although writers on cricket tried to ignore the continued existence, at the edges, of gambling, books on betting, gambling and horse racing came next in popularity over the last two decades of the century. This suggests that at least some with literate interests found the topics of interest, and over sixty books were also written on football (soccer and rugby). There were over forty books on hunting, golf and tennis, and boxing, rowing, and shooting sports each had over twenty. References to sportswomen were beginning to appear occasionally by the century's end. Horace Hutchinson's *The Book of Golf and Golfers* (Longmans Green, 1899), for example, contained a chapter by Amy Pascoe on 'Women Golfers'. Publishers also developed the concept of the 'Sportsman's Library', a device to increase sales amongst the more lucrative gentry and upper-middle-class market. The *Badminton* series was produced by Longmans from 1885. F. G. Afalo, one of the most prolific contemporary journalists, edited the *Encyclopaedia of Sport* with the Earl of Suffolk and Berkshire in 1897. T. Fisher Unwin offered the cheaper 'Sports Library' series from 1899.

Creative literature linked sport with recreational reading. There were a few books with authentic 'realism', rooting the narrative in a clearly sporting setting, and depending for their dramatic effect on a sport's situations and tensions, as in the case of the hunting novels of R. S. Surtees in the 1840s, still essential to the student of sporting life of the period.[28] There were more numerous books using sporting metaphors and characters, such as H. G. Wells's *The Wheels of Chance* (1898), centred round a bicycle mishap which allows an attractive young lady to come to a cyclist's aid. But few leading Victorian novelists or poets took much notice of sport. Their social world and interests largely bypassed it. Dickens, for example, makes little mention of it.[29] His only visit to the St Leger caused him to describe punters and bookmakers as 'Lunatics' and their 'Keepers'. For most, sport was something they saw at a distance, and for which they had little personal appetite. Tennyson's 'In Memoriam', mourning the passing of youth, recalled the 'measured pace of oars amongst the willows' at Trinity College, but Tennyson saw himself as an intellectual. So did Carlyle, dismissing most of the upper- and middle-class elite, with their sporting interests, as 'Barbarians' and 'Philistines', although commending toughness of muscle as well as heart. Disraeli in *Coningsby* (1844) praised England as 'unrivalled for two things – sport and politics', but referred only to hunting, shooting and racing. Trollope's novels used sporting contexts more consistently, stressing 'gentlemanly' behaviour, codes of dress and manners, and looking down on those who did not know how to ride to hounds, or were ignorant of sporting rules, although privately he disliked upper-class hypocrisy. While his sight was poor, and he was never a good horseman, he owned several hunters and hunted three days a week, often in Essex.[30] There were also religiously-inclined writers who found physical prowess exciting, if dedicated to the service of God. Thomas Hughes was one, believing in games for social reasons as well as a means of developing manliness, chivalry and purity. The clergyman and novelist, Charles Kingsley, whose book *Two Years Ago* (1857) first attracted the term 'muscular Christianity', was another.

Despite modern attempts to validate sport aesthetically by stressing its links with 'high' literature, it is clear that most leading Victorian writers felt uncomfortable with sport. Even Conan Doyle, who enjoyed cricket and played it seriously in the 1880s and 1890s, rarely mentioned cricket in his stories, although wittily including the names of some four hundred real cricketers amongst his characters. Despite occasional references to hunting, racehorse ownership and cricket, neither male nor female novelists exhibited much taste for 'modern' commercial or proletarian sports. The villain of Wilkie Collins's *Man and Wife* is a champion pedestrian, brutalised and debased by energetic cultivation of athletic exercise. George Eliot in *Daniel Deronda* (1876) praises an archery contest for being 'free from those noisy, crowded conditions which spoil most modern pleasures'. Archery, she claimed, 'breaks nobody's shins, breeds no athletic monsters', and had prizes of 'a symbolic kind, not property ... degrading honour into gain'.[31] Paradoxically, such sporting behaviour was too serious.

There were some minor Victorian novels which exploited sporting contexts for universalistic human themes. Most were formulaic, set in the shires, with country house settings, good-looking upper-class heroes and youthful heroines, and with content appealing to both sexes. Racing and hunting novels were particularly common. The anonymously written *Derby Day: or Won by a Neck* (1864) was a romantic novel in which 'handsome', 'polished' Sir Bridges Sinclair, an old Etonian with 'an estate of over £10,000 per annum', finally marries his nineteen-year-old sweetheart Edith, a 'charming girl from one of the oldest families in the country', with an 'absolutely faultless' form, only after an initial misunderstanding which leads him to break off his engagement. He stakes the best part of his fortune upon his Derby horse, and there are attempts to nobble his horse and jockey before his horse wins, and the couple are reunited.

The bulk of surviving sporting novels date from the last decades of the century. Many made their subject explicit through the subheading

'A Sporting Novel' (or 'Tale' or 'Story'). Many, such as Frank Hudson's *The Last Hurdle: A Story of Sporting and Courting* (1888) or John Gilbert's *Across Country: A Sporting Romance* (1898), had a romantic focus. By the century's end several married women novelists were drawing on their own hunting experience for realistic context. Mrs Robert Jocelyn wrote a series of novels during the early 1890s which have hunting scenes described with breezy, spirited confidence, and a detailed knowledge of the social complexities of hunting, horse dealing and racing. They usually have a woman as the main character. In *Run to Ground* (1894), for example, Violet Clifford is 'a good rider' with 'excellent seat, beautiful hands, and is utterly without fear'. Readers knew that sporting contexts were not always respectable, and reading about the scandalous disreputability of the country house shooting party was undoubtedly part of their appeal. Mrs Edward Kinnard's *Morals of the Midlands: A Sporting Tale* (1899) introduced Rory McGregor, who 'shoots, fishes, hunts, rides, plays golf and cricket better than ninety-nine men out of a hundred'. He marries Rhoda Markham, niece of Lady Pilkington, to get a legacy, but is 'fast', 'pleasure-loving', an amateur jockey with 'a reputation for his successes with smart ladies'. Rhoda believes firmly in the sanctity of marriage, and in 'religion, morality and conventionality'. Although they have a child together, she is jealous of his flirtations and they quarrel. On a fishing trip to Norway he is seduced by Daisy Dacre, and they live together for some time, but his public misbehaviour brings his downfall. He loses caste and face. His former friends 'cut' him. The novel ends conventionally, as Daisy returns disgraced to her father and he, appropriately penitent, goes to his wife.

Children's fiction also exploited the growing interest in sports. Their major impact on social attitudes perhaps began with the mythic images of Thomas Hughes's *Tom Brown's Schooldays* (1857), which sold 11,000 copies in its first year, and its less-circulated sequel, *Tom Brown at Oxford*. Brown is shown in the former playing an early form of rugby, is involved in horse-racing indirectly by drawing a favourite in the Derby lottery, goes fishing and bird-nesting, takes part in hare and hounds, cricket, running, and uses an old wrestling hold in a fist fight. His schooldays, and the book, end when he plays against the MCC as captain of cricket. The book was widely read, not least abroad, and helped to legitimate sporting leisure. The philosopher Hippolyte Taine used it as a key source. De Coubertin, the founder of the modern Olympics, was even more influenced by its amateurist ideals, and by his own visits to public schools. He wanted to take 'la pedagogie sportive', 'athletic education and muscular Christianity', with its system of school sports and postgraduate athletic clubs to France, and refresh its vigour and moral fibre.[32]

Later books used public school and increasingly imperialistic sporting themes.[33] These provided heroic sporting role models for boys. The absence of female heroines reinforced existing gender roles. W. H. G. Kingston published over a hundred books between 1850 and 1880, in which sport, and especially sport in the colonies, was placed alongside adventure, exploration and conquest. In the last two decades of the century, R. M. Ballantyne, R. L. Stevenson and Manville Fenn had schoolboy heroes, with whom readers could identify. As doers and participants, they also exemplified middle-class, public school sporting ideals. The great apostle of imperial manliness, G. A. Henty, was a dominant figure for sales, output (eighty-two books) and influence. He had learnt to box, was a member of the London Rowing Club, and his boy heroes, of stories usually set in the past, were upper-middle-class lovers of boxing, as he was himself.

In the more 'disreputable 'penny dreadful' serials, sold to a less well-educated teenage audience, attracted to sensation, crime and melodramatic content, sport was initially less a theme. But their increasing sales from the 1870s reflected growing literacy, and a growing taste for sport, if, as seems likely, their content reflected the interests of their readers. Leading sports personalities were soon lending their name to articles to boost sales. The first series to cover sport in any major way was *Boys of England*, produced by former radical E. J. Brett in 1866, and lasting till 1899. Its cover described it as 'a Young Gentleman's Journal of sport, sensation, fun and instruction', and sport took a leading role from the start. By its eighteenth number it claimed a weekly circulation of 150,000, and its sales soon climbed.[34] Typical examples focus on the public school sports story, or those set in the context of a more national sporting event. The first, W. Thompson Townsend's well-liked serial 'The Captain of the School', which started its run on 20 July 1867, featured a vital school cricket match whose outcome was delayed by skulduggery, a stock ingredient of subsequent public school fiction.

The same firm's *The Oxford and Cambridge Eights: or The Young Coxswain's Career,* originally serialised in 1875, opens the day before the annual university boat race, when Cecil Barrington, the young Oxford coxswain, discovers an anonymous note at the riverside: 'Private and v. confidential. Drug the C's; I have a heavy bet on the O's. If you fail I can hedge at the last moment'. This incriminating missive is intended for haggard-looking 'Shuffling Jemmy', otherwise dishonoured ruffian Harold Mainwaring, 'evidently a long way down in the social scale', who soon attempts to garrotte and then drown young Cecil. 'He'll pay for this Quixotic interference', Mainwaring mutters, 'curse him, he belongs to a family I hate. His mother jilted me; in desperation I took to horse racing, gambling – worse. I'll be even with her yet though, through him'. Harold, a vicious and unmanly gambler, makes a neat contrast with gentlemanly hero Cecil, who recovers sufficiently to warn the Cambridge boat crew of the dastardly plot. Further melodramatic developments take place before and after the famous boat race, revealing a familiarity with gaming vocabulary, until Harold is finally exposed and receives his just deserts.

Another leading publisher was the Religious Tract Society, which published the *Boys' Own Paper* from 1879, selling 200,000 copies in 1880 and over a million of each issue sold by the end of the century as literacy increased.[35] It aimed initially predominantly at middle-class readers. Respectable middle-class sports (like cricket, rugby and hunting) with middle-class heroes were its mainstay. School stories were always set in public schools, about which readers were assumed to have some knowledge. Advertisements for relatively expensive sports equipment and cycles featured prominently. Sportsmen such as W. G. Grace occasionally wrote for it.

Its very first article, entitled 'My First Football Match', described the sporting experiences of a new boy at a public school, learning the sporting code of an elite. Its author, Talbot Baines Reed, who had a major impact on the heroes and ethics of boys' school stories of the period, wrote early articles on the boat race, a football match, a paper chase, a cricket match and an athletics meeting. The paper appealed to both boys and parents, subtly stressing the virtues of manliness, honesty, courage, determination, teamwork and muscular Christianity alongside good stories and a substantial matter of information and stories about sport.

Reed's leading characters conformed to a not overly intellectual but sporting type, with moral grit, and an honesty and coolness of purpose. Jim Halliday in *The Adventures of a Three Guinea Watch* was 'a good bat, a famous boxer, a desperate man in a football scrimmage, and a splendid oar'. Reed was negative about gambling and racing, which he portrayed here as 'low' and corrupting, with crowds of 'blackguards' and 'cads', a 'yelling, blaspheming, drunken multitude'. Later papers for boys came to be dominated by the publisher Alfred Harmsworth whose cheap but modern periodicals *Marvel* (1893), *Union Jack* (1894), *Pluck* (1894) and the *Boy's Friend* (1895) were all imperialistic, jingoistic and full of well-born, strong, courageous and heroic sporting boys. The first edition of the comic *Chums* (1892) contained advice on 'how to train for the football season'.

The importance of the visual in the Victorian period has recently been restressed, and certainly the visual was as important as the printed word in promoting sport.[36] The audience for sports, especially but not exclusively in London, was often also the 'man about town' audience of 'swells', 'bohemians' and the 'fancy', interested in actresses and jockeys, and watching performances at the theatre, music hall and sports ground. Newspaper subtitles like *Sporting Opinion: and Theatrical Review* (1864) or the *Referee: A Journal of Sport and the Drama* (1877) illustrate this visual connection clearly. The picaresque accounts of sporting journalists, especially those involved in racing, likewise reveal their own fondness for the bohemian pleasures of betting, drinking, girls, sport and entertainment.[37]

Richer readers with sporting and theatrical interests seem to have been the first to demand illustrations for their sports. Most papers provided columns of densely-packed print, and in the 1840s illustrations were confined to more expensive magazines. Visual representations of sport were being shown in the *Illustrated London News* from 1842. Sport here focused less on details of the events and more on the social context of sport, with general pictures of the sports ground, the grandstand and the 'society' spectators, often with the event itself somewhere in the background, and the participants fairly difficult to identify. Stock pictures were sometimes recycled with altered captions.

The first weekly to provide more detailed sporting repertoires of pictures, the *Illustrated Sporting and Theatrical News* (1862), first retailed at

2*d*., but was reduced to 1*d*. before its 1869 demise. It was followed by *The Illustrated Sporting and Dramatic News* (1874), which described itself as 'a high-class weekly journal of sports, art, literature, music and the drama'. Both papers provided good provincial sporting coverage, creating a visual vocabulary of sporting experience, often stuck up on public house walls. Sporting engravings of sports stars were sometimes copied from photographs, and photographs themselves were introduced into newspapers in the 1880s in the form of team and individual studio portraits. Cameras were too impractical for outdoor use. Pictures capturing motion were invariably blurred. The development of faster photographic emulsions, and better lenses and shutters, eventually led to improvements, and by 1896 sporting action photographs were occasionally appearing in the illustrated magazines and the daily press, though artists were still more commonly used. In 1897 *Sporting Sketches*, which led the visual field, began using a cameraman on the sidelines for action pictures. Picture postcards began to realise the attractions of sport, as did cigarette cards, from the late 1890s, well after American or Australian equivalents.

The regional press began providing semi-humorous sketches of local sports in the 1880s. Sporting cartoons provided a running commentary on sport, featuring, albeit only occasionally, in popular magazines. *Punch* found sport a fruitful source of satirical commentary from the 1840s, and sporting cartoons were taken up more widely in the last decades of the century by magazines like *Ally Sloper's Half Holiday*, as a way of poking fun at pretension and social class attitudes.

Music halls and theatres sometimes gave a stage to sport. Professional entertainers exploited sports' popularity. Their stage acts relied heavily on topicality and local references. Reference to important recent matches, races and results, often using humour, parodies or the skits, helped to grab and sustain fickle audiences. Analysis of the music hall songs of north-east England shows the popularity of songs featuring commercial, betting sports like racing, rowing or pedestrianism even in the 1860s.[38]

Theatrical performances occasionally covered upper-class sports like racing or hunting, which featured heavily in Boucicault's 1841 comedy *London Assurance*. Tom Taylor's *Handsome is as Handsome Does*, at London's Olympic Theatre, was a north-country comedy drama with wrestling as a novelty feature.[39] Football began to appear from the 1880s, with set-piece scenes often set at Kennington Oval, home of the FA Cup Final. *Football, or Life as It Is,* was probably the earliest, produced in 1883 and performed in London, Liverpool and elsewhere. In 1896 George Gray's four act 'sensational' musical drama, *The Football King,* toured towns and cities including Sunderland, Bradford, Nottingham, Leicester Cardiff, Portsmouth and London, featuring the 'celebrated Preston North End Player, Dave Russell'.[40]

Film was still in its infancy at the end of the nineteenth century, and the variety, sensation and novelty of early films were designed to appeal to a predominantly male audience. The elite topical sporting event had great appeal and stirred audience emotions. As early as 1895 the very short films which the leading British film makers Robert Paul and Bert Acres produced included the 1895 Boat Race and the Derby. The music hall dominated the entertainment market, so early sports films were first shown in the London West End music halls, with their upper- and upper middle-class audience of officers, students, tourists and others. They were then taken round the major syndicated provincial variety halls. The 1896 film of the Derby, won by the Prince of Wales's horse Persimmon, was significant here. Following rapid processing, it was shown the next day to crowds at the Alhambra and Canterbury Music Halls. The enthusiastic Alhambra audience demanded three repetitions of the film, and sang 'God Bless the Prince of Wales!'. Many stood on their seats and cheered.[41] Six months later, Paul's 'Animatograph', then showing in Newport, still included the Derby, despite its poor film quality. A critic claimed that 'the horses went past at such a rate it was impossible to identify them'.[42]

In 1897 about 14 per cent of commercial films had a sporting title. Horse racing dominated, and at least four different film-makers shot the Derby. Three filmed Henley Regatta, two the Boat Race, while football and cricket, and a meeting of Lord Rothschild's staghounds at Aylesbury, were also seen as fit subjects. Elitist sports were reshaped by metropolitan producers and aimed at a metropolitan music hall audience. New techniques added to the spectacle. In March 1897, for example, Acres showed a film of the Cambridge University boat crew practising on the Thames, filmed from the moving stern of a following boat. Cycling provided a popular sporting subject because of its potential for humorous (if clearly painful) accidents and for ridiculing women's cycling. These two themes merged with social class and slap-stick in a Northern Photographic Works film of 1900, in which an attractive young lady cyclist freewheeling down a steep hill knocks over a 'country yokel', who spills the milk he is carrying over the road. He gets up, tries to bring the girl round and tidies up. Just as he succeeds he is 'floored' once again by her 'maiden aunt', who has been riding behind her.

Public appetite for film was increased by interest in the Boer War, with film audiences watching films in municipal halls, pleasure grounds and fairgrounds became more working-class. Four per cent of films still had a sporting content, but with more cross-class appeal. The carnival atmosphere and large crowds at popular sporting events were filmed by several producers. The Warwick Trading Company showed a film of the road to Epsom, which its catalogue described as 'showing brakes, vans, tally-hos and vehicles of every description, including the coster's cart, the people all loaded up with enthusiasm and otherwise, blowing horns, waving flags etc.' Films about Henley, Cowes and Carnarvon regattas, fencing, polo at Hurlingham, gymkanas, lawn tennis and a meeting of the Devon and Somerset Staghounds mixed with football, boxing, badger-digging and tug-of-war. Such representations may have reshaped middle-class attitudes towards sports formerly seen as too unrespectable, too cruel or too working class. One viewer of a boxing film, for example, claimed that 'one's imaginations of a prize fight are completely corrected. Instead of the savage and repulsive butchery, the mighty blows, and the liberal supply of gore which fancy depicts, the unscientific spectator sees an agreeable display of skill and activity'.[43] Sport film coverage had become cross-class in content, and was being viewed increasingly across the class structure, as was indeed sport itself. Like other media, film provided the publicity to ensure sport took firm hold on British minds. By the century's end papers such as the *Scottish Referee* were holding readers' polls to elect the country's most popular player, helping to foster the cult of celebrity and stardom. Sport had become embedded in the fabric of everyday life.

7

Stars

Films, newsreel and more recently television have created the celebrity, famous for being famous, with talent an optional extra.[1] The great figures the Victorians admired gained their status through action and achievement, and they were celebrated in sculpture, paintings and print. The writer Thomas Carlyle accepted that his compatriots were prepared to 'love, venerate and bow down submissive before great men', and saw hero-worship as a feature of his age.[2] His heroes were not sportsmen. They were prophets, poets, priests and men of letters; or, like Napoleon, winning battles and conquering territory, emblematic figures of the period. By the end of the century imperial glory, grandeur and jingoism ensured that the greatest British heroes of all were men of action, soldiers or explorers, men who knew how to live (and die) with honour. Such heroes were often 'gentlemen', members of the dominant social class, with a public school education and polite manners.

Sport was different. Even in 1901 there were still relatively few sportsmen whose names were widely known outside the confines of their particular sport, but their numbers were growing. Many came from the working classes. There had been a few elite performers, enjoying a wide public esteem spread by oral transmission, even before the Victorian period. In the 1790s the pugilist Daniel Mendoza was celebrated in the press and with books, plates and mugs. The *Sporting Magazine* was producing pictures of famous jockeys like Sam Chifney at about the same time. The early nineteenth-century pugilist Tom Cribb was famous all over Britain for his fighting skills; even when not himself fighting, his appearance was calculated to create interest. He was commemorated not only in the Tom Cribb pub, in central London, but in Staffordshire pottery figures.

In the Victorian period, as sport was raised to an activity of even higher national importance and significance, sporting heroes provided opportunities for reworking traditional images of the heroic, emphasising both British national superiority and hegemonic masculinity. The ways in which the Victorians saw and portrayed such men reflected the way they perceived their society and their country. Heroes were successful at sport just as Britain itself was successful on the world stage. Heroes showed courage in adversity, in facing and overcoming challenges. They had a desire to succeed, and great mental strength. They could cope with stress and pressure. Heroes behaved in manly ways, and most followed the rules of good sportmanship. Their image and personalities were attractive to the public. They created their own legends, and their sporting rivalry was often crucial to the popularity and appeal of sporting events.

They were a construct of what Victorians wanted and needed, able to transcend their time, and to exceed expected mental and physical limits. Through their contests the sporting public derived concentrated vicarious excitement which sometimes provided blessed relief from the long-drawn out monotony, mediocrity and uncertainty of everyday life.[3] As more and more played and watched sport, reading about talented sportsmen provided the stuff of their dreams. It satisfied that frustrated desire to play at the top level or to possess that elusive yet yearned for talent. Ordinary people, who would never reach a high standard of performance, could watch, read and dream about the achievements of those who could. Their heroes grew, flourished and changed as part of the wider transformation of British life during the period. Sporting heroes were important to those Victorians who watched them play, wrote about or read about them. They caught both individual imaginations and the collective consciousness. More than mere entertainers, they embodied the hopes and dreams of their communities in dramatic and often epic contests. To understand Victorian heroes we have to look at stories told about them, set them in their cultural context, and explain their significance.

Through the period there was still enough sense of place to create regional heroes for both national and regional sports. The crews of the more amateur university boat race were largely unknown to the huge crowds who watched from the banks of the Thames each year. It was the fun of the event, the excuse for a day's holiday, the result that mattered, not the individuals. By contrast on Tyneside, where regional pride in rowing and pedestrianism was strong, the names of their heroes were widely known, and portrayed as key representatives of local values. An 1860s music hall song celebrated 'the defeat of the Cocknies' by 'coally Tyne heroes' at the Thames Regatta as 'wor pride an' wor glory', making locals 'se prood of thor river'. Another song about 'Wor Tyneside Champions' listed by name rowers, bowlers, quoits players and 'champion peds, bangs a' the lot for racing'.[4] Cumbria's famous wrestlers were constantly referred to in the regional press. When, for example, Henry Hall Dixon (alias The Druid) gave his account of summer rambles looking at cattle, horse and sheep breeding, and coursing, racing and foxhunting in different parts of the Britain in 1870, his chapter on Cumberland included a section on 'Cumberland wrestling champions'.[5] Here too, printed songs in 'Come all ye ...' traditional style were still regularly celebrated these 'bold undaunted heroes' through the 1860s and 1870s. Later, cycling champions were widely known in the Birmingham and Coventry areas.

While sporting heroes were famous in their regional communities, London press domination ensured that those most highly profiled nationally were usually southern men. Men further from London or from non-Anglo-Saxon ethnic groups, and women in general, were far less likely to catch the attention of the British public. Appearance in major events where large crowds attended also helped create fame. In racing, success in the Epsom Derby, the Doncaster St Leger and the Aintree Grand National stood out. In cricket, playing in London-based matches, such as the South versus North matches, leading county matches or the internationals aided press coverage.

Over the period, most sporting heroes were involved in individualistic rather than team sports. This was reflected in their earnings, since top professional pugilists, jockeys and scullers were already being well paid for sport even in the early nineteenth century. In racing the names of Bill and John Scott, or the Day family, were already known to sporting men before the advent of the mass press. Such men were by no means all morally virtuous. Later in the century, as professional sportsmen were employed in cricket or football, their fixed wages meant far lower economic reward, the more so since trade unionism had little impact. Even top players could be submerged in the team's fame. Of team sport players, cricketers were the best known at national level, and some names were being brought to public attention in the press quite regularly by the mid nineteenth century. These included Alfred Mynn, the large, genial and apparently unflappable all-rounder who became perhaps the first popular professional cricketer, William Clarke, wily and determined, who created the first professional All-England Eleven in 1846 and toured England playing exhibition matches, and George Parr, the son of a Nottingham yeoman farmer, the leading English batsman of the period, who took over All-England in 1856 and led the first overseas tour to USA and Canada.

Top stars were often adept at self-advertisement but their fame was created and presented by the press. There was already a clear but relatively small market for books about the leading sports competitors in the early nineteenth century. Most were London-focused, being often linked to the leading sporting papers like *Bell's Life* or the *Sporting Magazine*. By the 1840s the media were more clearly helping construct sports stars, influencing public perceptions and encouraging their admiration. The sporting press and sporting personalities increasingly fed off each other in mutual symbiosis. The Victorians liked to read about their heroes. Sports journalists played a key role in creating, narrating and signifying their images, the uniqueness and power of sporting performance, and embellishing and dramatising sporting deeds, in order to fit heroes with the appropriate personae to meet the needs of the public. They became both gatekeepers and guardians of the heroic tradition. Writers, from ex-players and jobbing journalists to enthusiasts who admired great performances and loved the leading figures most of all, transformed great performances and exceptional displays of prowess into heroic myths. A great event, a particular outstanding moment or consistent high achievement could all mean great copy. Moments of individual excellence, in the broader context of gripping, brilliant performances, could be almost as emotionally draining for the involved spectator, and were long remembered. The year of the Sayers-Heenan fight, or the 1851 York match between the two leading horses of the period, Voltigeur and the Flying Dutchman, became fixed points of reference.

There was sufficient interest from upper- and middle-class sporting men for top sportsmen increasingly to produce, or have ghosted, their own books. There had been rare earlier examples, like the jockey Sam Chifney's *Genius Genuine*, produced in 1795 at a price of £5, and early

OUR PORTRAITS.

MR. H. J. BARRON.

FOREMOST amongst Metropolitan Swimming Clubs stands the "Otter," whose headquarters are at the Marylebone Baths, Edgeware Road. Our portrait this week is that of one of its most prominent members—Mr. H. J. Barron, who was born in London on March 31, 1857. Although able to swim at the early age of seven years, and *facile princeps* amongst his school chums at Charterhouse, he did not make his *debut* in public until the year 1874, when as a member of the Otter Club he won a Novice Race on May 22. This success he followed up by gaining the contest for the Ladies' Challenge Cup, on the occasion of its inauguration on July 3. During the following year, Mr. Barron was engaged in study, and, therefore, had but little time to devote to his favourite pastime. However, he placed to his credit the Open Six Lengths Amateur Handicap at Professor C. Whyte's entertainment at the Paddington Baths, on Oct. 18. On this occasion he was in receipt of 20 sec. start from the scratch man, T. Robinson. He won third prize for Egg Diving at the Surrey Entertainment, and first at the opening gala of his own club. In 1876, on May 25, at David M'Garrick's Benefit he carried off the Egg Diving (twelve eggs thrown in, two dives allowed); first dive, 9; second dive, 10; total, 19; and the following day, May 26, he met Mr. Charles O'Malley on level terms in a 150 Yards Otter Handicap. Barron got the best of the dive, and defeated, perhaps, some of the best all-round men of the day by a yard. On Sept. 9 he competed in the Amateur Championship at the Welsh Harp, but was outclassed. He met Mr. Charles O'Malley once again on level terms, on Sept. 13, at the Surrey Entertainment, in a 500 Yards Scratch Race, when O'Malley turned the tables on his former conqueror, and won in the excellent time of 7 min. 36 sec., beating Mr. Horace Davenport, ex-Amateur Champion, by a yard. (The last-named, however, had previously competed in another race.) On Oct. 13, at the Otter Entertainment, Mr. Barron again won the Egg Diving competition, bringing up eighteen eggs in two dives. A severe illness during the spring of 1877 incapacitated Mr. Barron from engaging in many races, though he started for the Lords and Commons' Prize, contested in the Thames from Putney to Westminster; but he relinquished the undertaking after covering a trifle over five miles. At the Otter entertainment, on Oct. 12, he was again successful in the Egg Diving, bringing up seventeen eggs in two dives; and his feats of ornamental swimming, comprising eating, drinking, and smoking under water, together with the Monto Christo Sack Feat, &c., fairly "brought down the house." On May 31, 1878, Mr. Barron won the 98 yards Gold Badge of the Otter Club, in 1 min. 14½ sec.; time allowed, 1 min. 15 sec. On August 9 he gained the Captaincy for the Year of the Otter S.C.; distance, 1,000 yards, in the Serpentine, after an exciting finish with Mr. James Rope. On August 26 he won the Amateur Swimming Race at Shanklin (Isle of Wight) Regatta; but at Ryde Royal Regatta sustained defeat, after a desperate race (distance 600 yards), at the hands of M. White, of the Portsmouth S.C., who won by a few yards. On Sept. 20, he competed for the 485 Yards Gold Badge of the Otter Club; time allowed being 8 minutes; he won it in 7 min. 48 sec. Mr. Barron then turned his attention

to the cinder-path, and carried off second honours in the race for the Mile Challenge Cup, at the United Hospital Sports at Lillie Bridge. He next engaged in a long walk from London to Portsmouth, starting at 10 p.m., Aug. 9, and reaching Portsmouth at 9 p.m., Saturday, 10th; the distance traversed from "door to door" being 72 miles, and the roads in a bad state, owing to rain. In June, 1879, he won both the Short and Long Distance Races at the Edinburgh University Swimming Meeting, voluntarily conceding his fellow-students 20 sec. start in the 165 yards. At the Whitehall S.C. Entertainment, held at the Floating Baths, on July 31, 1879, he won the swimming under water with 68 *yards 6 in.*; and was defeated in the Otter Captaincy Race by Mr. Charles O'Malley, and again at Ryde Royal Regatta by Mr. Geo. D. M. White; the distances in each case being too far for a quick stroke. He also competed successfully at Sandown and Ventnor Regattas, Isle of Wight. At the Otter entertainment, Oct. 7 (Marylebone), he swam a splendid race in the Open 98 Yards Scratch contest with Mr. Geo. Ellis, defeating him by a yard. At the Cadogan S.C. Meeting at Chelsea Baths, he proved best man in another "swim under water," with 67 yards 18 in.

The Swimming Association being in a weak and critical condition, the Otter S.C. joined it in the early part of the season, with a view to renovating it and making it the strong and representative body it should be. Their efforts have proved very successful. Of their delegates, Mr. H. Davenport was unanimously elected to the office of president, and Mr. Barron as hon. sec. On July 27, Mr. Barron again met Mr. George Ellis in the Otter 98 Yards Scratch Race, and getting a bad start was defeated by "the touch." On August 2 he won the Swimming Race at the Bath Amateur Regatta, and five days later swam in the Floating Baths Company's Long Distance Thames Race, from Putney to Charing Cross, distance, 5¼ miles; he was, however, compelled to retire at the Albert Bridge, Battersea Park, owing to an attack of cramp. On August 28, at the Swimming Races of the Bangor (County Down), Ireland, S.C., Mr. Barron defeated Mr. W. R. C. Richardson, of Portrush, in the 440 Yards Race, and also secured the 100 Yards Race, swimming on the back only; and at Portrush (County Antrim), on Aug. 3, he won the 100 Yards Open Scratch Race, but was beaten after a grand race by W. R. C. Richardson in the 880 Yards Handicap, both starting from scratch.

Unquestionably the gentleman whose prowess has been so lightly touched upon is in the first flight as a "sprint" swimmer, but staying is *not* his forte. As an exponent of some of the most difficult feats in ornamental natation, Mr. Barron has few, if any equals. Both "by land and water" he has striven hard to encourage and give a healthy tone to his favourite pastime, and recently lectured in its favour before the boys at Fettes College, Edinburgh. Not by any means has Mr. Barron permitted his infatuation for the art to interfere with the duties of his profession, in which he has taken high honours, both at his hospital and Edinburgh University. He is not only an exceedingly popular "Otter," but a universal favourite in the swimming world.

The Sunny South.—A gentleman writes to us as follows from Braunton, Devonshire: "I see snow has fallen heavily of late, but Braunton has escaped the visitation. Neither was there any snow here last winter. Only yesterday (Oct. 30) swallows were flitting merrily to and fro."

Mr H. J. Barron, a local amateur, 1880.
He was one of the many local middle-class, public-school educated sportsmen whose deeds were celebrated in the sporting press.

Victorian examples included *Felix on the Bat* (1845), but they appeared in larger numbers in the second half of the century. Sports stars also boosted their names with the public by writing shorter pieces for magazines. The fifth item in the first edition of the *Boys' Own Paper*, for example, was 'How I Swam the Channel' by Captain Webb, whose feat in swimming the Channel in 1875 had made him hugely famous. His picture was everywhere, even on sheet music covers, where the 'Channel Quadrilles' cashed in on his fame.

Press coverage of sport combined notions of modernity, such as discussion of new technology or new rules, organisation and timekeeping, with older, more traditional ideas which also gave increased emphasis on the leading sportsmen. The image of the champion retained its use in sports like boxing, wrestling and sculling, and received new emphasis as national and international competitions became more common. This helped to establish sporting reputation. Athletic celebrity was enhanced by the growing use of titles such as 'Champion of the Tyne' (or Thames), of 'England', or of 'the World'. The creation of special contests, and the introduction of advertisements which highlighted celebrity, helped raise status and fame. So did the increased use by the papers of statistical tables, which clearly identified the jockey with the most wins or the cricketer with the leading batting or bowling average. The language of quantity, of apparently objective figures, helped create a ladder of achievement. As time passed reference to previous sporting performances and performers also became part of the cumulative history of sport.

The period saw increased numbers of sporting biographies and general books about the sporting famous. There were early ones for cricket, such as Fred Lillywhite's *Cricket Scores and Biographies of Celebrated Cricketers* (1862), which combined statistical data with lives of the 'great men' of their day. Later ones abounded for many sports. Amongst several racing examples, 'Thormanby' produced both *Famous Racing Men* (1882) and *Kings of The Turf* (1898), which was a series of 'anecdotal sketches' of celebrities in the racing world, 'owners, trainers, jockeys and backers', with portraits.[6] In wrestling, *Wrestling and Wrestlers* (1893) combined a history of wrestling with details of the leading wrestlers of the past.[7] Coverage by the written press created heroes in the eyes of fans. With no television, and with few opportunities for many actually to see sports stars, fame was in part a matter of name recognition.

But we should not underestimate the importance of pictures to the Victorians. In the eighteenth century coffee houses and pubs were already plastered with newspapers and prints. Broadsheet songs and ballads about sporting events attracted customers. Sporting picture galleries, like art galleries, became a feature of urban life. Even in the 1850s and 1860s sporting pubs were putting up pictures on the walls to add to atmosphere. The Rising Sun, in Manchester, whose landlord George Hardy was a sponsor of events, a referee and stakeholder, went to the length of claiming that its 'portrait gallery of pedestrians, pugilists, watermen etc. is the most complete out of London'.[8] Pubs visually flaunted their association with a particular sport. Liverpool's most prominent betting pub, for example, had its betting room 'decorated with portraits of racehorses and celebrated jockeys'.[9]

Boxers have been enduring national symbols thanks to their strength and resilience. As in Darwinism, only the fittest survived. Amongst the first great national sporting heroes of the Victorian age was the pugilist Tom Sayers, who lost only once, to Nat Langham, before his retirement in 1860. His final fight, with the American Jack Heenan, attracted huge interest in Britain and abroad. Even anti-prize fight papers covered the build-up in detail, though the fight was supposedly illegal and reformist magistrates did their best to stop it. About 12,000 people travelled to Farnborough to witness the contest. After two and a half hours Sayers's arm was broken and Heenan could hardly see. The crowd broke into the ring, probably to ensure Sayers did not lose, and the fight was soon abandoned as a draw. Despite pugilism's falling support Sayers was proudly seen by high and low as the representative of Britain. He was easy to recognise because his picture regularly featured in the illustrated sporting press. As a result, even the Protestant bank clerk William Allingham, a respectable poet, a friend of Tennyson and Carlyle, knew both Sayers and Heenan by sight.[10] Pictures of such famous sportsmen aided newspaper circulation and provided revenue for printers who specialised in this field. Prior to the Sayers versus Heenan fight the *Illustrated Sporting News* announced:

> Special notice. On the day of the great fight for the championship a special edition of the *Illustrated Sporting News* will be issued, containing a most elaborate report of the exciting event from the time the Match originated until the termination of the battle. As the demand will be tremendous our Agents

and Subscribers will oblige us by forwarding their Orders immediately ... the Proprietors have made every available arrangement for producing on the week following the fight a great illustration of its most exciting incidents in a grand double number.[11]

There were better-quality pictures for the wealthier. The publisher George Newbold was a main producer, offering 'a grand representation of the GREAT INTERNATIONAL CONTEST INCLUDING MANY NEW AND INTERESTING PORTRAITS price 21s. tinted or 12s. coloured'. About the same time he also sold 'fine coloured lithographs' of some twenty pedestrians and pugilists at 5s. each. He was also the exclusive seller of portraits of Heenan.[12] Even after pugilism's final decline its former fans looked back on its stars fondly. As late as 1895 the *Grasshopper*, a Birmingham sports paper, was producing a series on 'Memorable Battles of the Prize Ring'.

As well as one-off pictures of major events, the press were soon producing series of the famous, and this became common by the 1880s. *Cricket and Football Times*, for example, ran a series of 'Our Portraits' of sporting celebrities in 1880, linked to photographs, and encouraged the collection of these. The W. G. Grace portrait was advertised as

a perfect likeness, Everyone desiring to possess in a convenient form, a record of the great performances of the champion cricketer, should send at once for the beautifully illuminated four page card, containing a photograph and category of the batting and bowling performances of this Leviathan cricketer.[13]

It should also be remembered that such stars were far more accessible to the public, and thus regularly seen, especially round London. There was a clear public dimension to their fame. They travelled on the same trains, trams and coaches as everyone else. They could be seen in the stations *en route* to places of sport. Late in the century footballers played practice games in late summer on public parks, before the start of the season.

The press portrayed the public virtues of such men, not the private reality. So there was little if any hint about sportsmen's attractions to women, or their private lives. Sporting heroes reflected the values, ambitions and aspirations of Victorian society, and had to meet both class and patriotic expectations. They were portrayed as larger than life, inspirational, strong, tough and competitive. They had to be admirable and distinctive, and the most admired reflected beliefs about honour and individual worth. But the weighting of such values varied from community to community, group to group and from individual to individual. By the 1870s, as the Victorians created new rules and codes of conduct, there were both amateur and professional heroes, but the working classes most admired professional heroes. To working-class communities, working-class heroes could be a source of collective identity, status and pride.[14] But stars also had to appeal to the middle classes if they were to achieve wider success.

Most commonly they embodied working-class characteristics. Almost all were cast in a traditionally masculine mould, like their fans. As in much manual work and on the streets, so in sport physical hardness and toughness were central. Sportsmen were easy to transform into heroes when they broke physical barriers, endured adverse conditions, overcame apparently impossible obstacles, risked death, drove their body further or, increasingly, beat existing barriers of time. Sport was fascinating to the Victorians not just because it built character but because it revealed character. Huge natural talent and athleticism had to be coupled with aggression and bravery, endeavour and struggle, courage in face of adversity, muscular exertion and tension. At its extreme such masculinity could involve indifference to the pain of one's own and other bodies, a win at all costs philosophy, and an inability to form intimate relationships with women. Sporting achievements often glorified some level of violence or acute physicality. But there was clear distaste for too much violence. It discredited the idea of the sporting hero as a common man with uncommon gifts.[15]

Sporting excellence also showed other key Victorian values, such as determination to succeed, being able to cope with pressure, and showing grit, resolution, character, valour and fortitude in making progress over time to reach the top. At the psychological level leading sportsmen might have fears and self-doubts, but these had to be overcome. Hard work and study of their sport were also stressed. Success, like wages, had to be earned through effort, toil, sweat and tears, mental discipline and strenuous training.

Honesty was also important, especially when betting on contests was common across all classes, and it was unsurprising therefore that many descriptions of top sportsmen include specific reference to their honesty. They had to be reliable and honourable, with an irreproachable character, if they were to be backed. When the sculler 'Honest Bob' Chambers died at thirty-seven, his local paper suggested that 'honesty, gentleness, faithfulness were the grand characteristics of his career. Physically and morally he was a model athlete ... He was a genuine type of Englishman'.[16] A sportsman who was prepared to 'sell' contests was despised. There was nothing wrong in being well paid, but being mercenary, like the champion jockey Fred Archer (1857–1886), could be a drawback, although it was permissible that stars backed themselves. They were expected to be driven more by pride in performance, and by a quest for the greater glory and fame of themselves, their community and their country.

Working-class sportsmen were not expected to be either clever or complex. The British wanted their heroes to be good, decent, honourable, unexceptional people, modest, respectable and rather ordinary off the field, but calm and courageous with an aristocratic sense of command and grace when playing, combining the democratic and aristocratic principles which ran widely through English life.[17] Egotism, temperamental outbursts and arrogance had little appeal. Descriptions chimed with working-class respectability and allowed a degree of privacy. Stars were portrayed as common men made good, proletarian heroes. For Tom King, the pugilist, his 'manly fairness' in the ring in 1862 was 'only equalled by his civil and retiring behaviour with those he is brought into contact'.[18] The descriptions applied to Henry Kelley, the Fulham champion sculler, in reports of his rowing race with the American James Hamill in 1866, included 'unassuming', 'gentlemanly', 'civil', and 'a man respected in every circle'.[19] Later on most footballers were presented as modest, ordinary men, with extraordinary ball skills.

Personal charisma was also important, though more difficult to define. Such qualities, catching the historical moment and creating a sense of identification, some imaginary relationship between spectator and hero, were drawn from a combination of factors. These could include stars' exceptional sporting skills, the extent of their success, the size of their network of supporters, and the level of their winnings. Where men were too quiet, lacking sufficient charisma, fame was more elusive. Mere sporting ability was not enough for sporting stardom. The jockey John Charlton, who won several classic events in the 1850s, despite being 'kind and liberal minded' was 'never a very showy jockey, but rather to be known by a careful quiet manner, and ... not a very marked man with the general public', except when he won.[20]

Combined with sufficient reputation, an heroic failure could aid sporting status. Winners could be superhuman, but sporting winners who eventually lost courageously or sacrificed themselves could, through their final frailty, have huge appeal to sporting fans. The sacrificial or tragic hero, whose untimely death showed the price of success, was a powerful archetypal symbol in nineteenth-century imagery. Examples stretch from Nelson or Franklin to General Gordon of Khartoum. There were sporting examples too where the spirit and nature of the enterprise, and the personal qualities and heroic characterisics were more important than the outcome. The rower James Renforth had a brief but brilliant career. He left Newcastle as 'the foremost sculler of his time and nation', carrying the 'hopes and expectations of Tyneside' with him, to compete in the August 1871 world rowing championship in Canada, in a four-man English crew.[21] The build-up to the race was well covered in the national sporting press, and news of his tragic death during the race, at a time when his crew were in the lead, was received with shock not just on Tyneside but throughout Britain. There were leading articles in the London national and sporting papers, as well as in the northern regional press, with poignant eulogies heaped upon his character. He had been cut down 'in the prime of manhood, at the full zenith of his career ... far away from the banks of his native river'.[22] He was praised for his achievements, approach and bearing, and for being a 'model which it would be well for all to adopt'. He had shown himself as honest, straightforward and respectable, and had grown into his high sporting status with gratifying rapidity. From being utterly uncouth, he became softened in manner and speech. Prosperity had made him prudent, and he had been able to save, showing caution, diligence and self-denial in his approach.[23] In fact this public image was part of the myth. Renforth's death was caused by congested lungs. He had continued to compete, despite being an epileptic, in order to better provide for his family.

For some stars it was their excesses coupled with their singular talent that brought them to wider attention. A number of famous jockeys had major problems with alcohol. Will Scott (1797–1848) was incapable of keeping sober for any length of time and was almost certainly an alcoholic by the early 1840s, yet was still the outstanding northern jockey of the first half of the nineteenth century, with nineteen Classic wins. In the 1846 Derby he was so drunk that he was left at the start indulging in an altercation with the starter, yet was only narrowly beaten by a neck. His drinking increasingly undermined his health, but he won the 1846 St Leger when his friends managed to stop him drinking for the few days before the race.

Jem Snowden (1844–1889) as a young stable jockey at Richmond in 1861 was described as a dishonest 'worthless lad', who was prepared to make horses 'safe'. Some owners were not prepared to use him, but he was soon widely regarded by northern trainers as the leading jockey of his day.[24] Another alcoholic, he once said he would have given £5000 to be free of the bottle, and lost many potentially winning rides because of it. He had four Classic successes, but used to indulge in binge drinking which prevented him riding at all. Stories about him were told again and again, in numerous versions. The most often-repeated one involved him arriving at Chester to ride for the Duke of Westminster after a bender only to find that the meeting had been the previous week.[25] He could be wryly humorous. Once when drunk, and finding his horse wearing blinkers, he told his trainer 'Naay, naay, tak it away, tak it away, a blinnd horse and a blinnd jockey'll nivver deea'.[26]

Such men struggled with their own inner demons and were prone to self-destruction, but they were also oddly vulnerable and appealing. They were not portrayed as inspirational. They had weaknesses, their behaviour was not of high morality and they competed for money rather than love of the game, alienating those espousing amateur ideals. Will Scott, for example, stood to win a large amount if his mount Launcelot won the 1840 Derby. Challenged in the run in by Little Wonder, he desperately offered its young jockey MacDonald 'A thousand pounds for a pull', only to be told 'Too late, Mr Scott, too late!' Such men had temper tantrums, showed dishonesty and had a dark side. Yet these fallen heroes picked up those feelings of frailty and the hardships in the lives of working men and sometimes found a place in their hearts.

Middle-class sporting heroes were somewhat differently presented by the press. They provided examples to follow. They were expected (or just assumed) to espouse the principles of virtuous sportsmanship, and to win or lose courageously, with style, fluency, elegance and vigour. Batting in cricket, the national game, best encapsulated such values, most especially for the amateur. Batsmen had to face attacking bowling on difficult pitches and score runs against a keen fielding side. Batting called for bravery and concentration. By the 1890s the cricketing 'quality' press were fostering the myths of cricket's Golden Age. Cricket, dominated by flamboyant gentlemen amateurs, created amateur heroes par excellence. Luminaries included C. B. Fry, Archie Maclaren, and the Indian prince Ranjitsinjhi, who revolutionalised cricket with his elegant leg glances. These were public school, imperial sportmen, espousing the values of fair play. They were reassuring role models for the leisured elite and educated middle classes, supporting their belief that they maintained their rightful places in society and sport. Amateurs, supposedly, were taller, more handsome and more virile. They had natural ability, not vulgar, hard-won expertise. One result of the belief that work was a significant part of manhood (and professionals clearly worked) was that amateurs had to be portrayed as playing and enjoying recreation, an attitude more associated with boyhood and immaturity. So amateurs were often seen as boyish.

They played spontaneously and elegantly, for love not money, while energetically and supposedly successfully pursuing their careers alongside their play. In reality careers were difficult to sustain. A. E. Stoddard, the Hampstead stockbroker, who captained both the English cricket and rugby teams in 1894–95, was idolised for much of the decade, but by 1900 his health and business were both failing and he fell quickly from public view. Another of this gifted band, Arthur Shrewsbury, the Nottinghamshire scholar-batsman, did almost as much as Grace to glamorise the image of cricket, capturing the imagination of thousands of spectators with his graceful, accomplished play. A prince of cutters, with a flawless defence, he led the first-class averages seven times and captained England. His extrovert playing style hid a private bachelor introspection which in 1903 led him to kill himself when he feared he was losing his eyesight and would no longer see the ball.[27]

Breadth of talent was always highly appreciated, praised and respected by the Victorian public, and most especially amongst amateurs. C. B. Fry, a supercilious classical scholar, was deified by the public. He played cricket for England, with a classically correct technique, and scored 3147 runs in 1901 including six successive hundreds. He captained Oxford at cricket, soccer and athletics, then played as an international at both association and rugby football, while building a career as a journalist. Descriptions of leading amateur sportmen produced in the regional press by the 1890s have a similar emphasis on breadth. In Birmingham, for example, E. B. Holmes enjoyed 'sports of all sorts with a penchant for the rugby game and amateur athletics, and now turns his attention to whistle wielding. A genuine amateur, he abhors anything shady. He hates playing for money like the devil does holy water'.[28] Even in later life Sir Claude de Crespigny was described as 'one of the hardest and pluckiest men in England ... ready to box, ride, walk, run, shoot ... fence, sail or swim with anyone over fifty years on equal terms'.[29] Literature further fostered the qualities of such idealised middle-class heroes. G. A. Henty's public-school educated, genteel heroes, for example, regularly showed coolness, courage, modesty, self-possession, pluck and resolution. They manifested good conduct and sound character, gentlemanliness and manliness, coupled with a sense of duty and discipline.[30]

One man defied such over-simplistic categorisation in class terms. The public heroes of cricket rivalled politicians, actors or writers. W. G. Grace (1848–1915) was the most eminent of many eminent Victorian sportsmen, the first sporting superstar, hero-worshipped, admired or envied, a sporting legend.[31] He dominated the international game with his explosive talent, and became the first imperial sporting hero. A *Sunday Chronicle* poem boasted how

> Once again o'er Australia we see him prevail
> Till their fielding gets flurried, their bowling quite stale,
> And all England its gratitude freely accords
> To the man who took down the colonials at Lords.[32]

By the 1890s his hold on the popular imagination was greater than any contemporary sportsman. His mere presence had a major impact on attendance. Cricket was the leading summer game and he was its leading exponent, far transcending existing levels of achievement, the best batsman and one of the best bowlers of his age. A folk hero who first became famous when Victoria had withdrawn into privacy, his

W. G. Grace in action, sketched by Harry Furniss in 1896. The first sporting superstar, hero-worshipped, admired and envied, but also the godfather of gamesmanship and a celebrated shamateur.

achievements were phenomenal. According to *Wisden* he scored 51,545 runs in first-class cricket, often on difficult pitches, and took 2876 wickets.[33] His batting was especially prodigious. In 1871, his best year, he hit ten centuries, including 268 runs for South v. North, and made 2379 runs at an average of seventy-nine. He hit 126 centuries in first-class matches, and ninety-one in minor games. He was technically outstanding, with great hand-eye coordination, and one of the few with both the temperament and technique to build an innings on a poor pitch. In appearance he stood out as picturesque, visually easy to identify, with his long beard and increasing girth. He had the indispensible attribute of longevity, first playing against the All-England XI in 1863 when still only fourteen, but was still opening the England batting at fifty, and played first-class cricket up to his sixtieth year. He was a great cricketer and great character, a man who thoroughly enjoyed his sport, but a dominant presence and legendary figure despite his squeaky voice.

He was a man of sharp contrasts, and far from the heroic amateur ideal, since he was the godfather of gamesmanship.[34] His hugely powerful personality, temper, sharp practice, trickery, bullying and questioning of umpires were well known, the focus of a hundred anecdotes. His treatment of sportsmanship could be cavalier. He may not have deliberately broken the rules but he was out to win at almost all costs. Using his detailed knowledge of the laws, he manipulated and pushed them as far as possible in his favour, arguing the point with socially inferior umpires. He was always newsworthy, but so popular that accounts of his gamesmanship merely added to the fund of humorous stories.

Grace, the son of a Gloucestershire doctor, trained as a doctor himself, although he found studying difficult. He fitted his training round his cricket rather than vice-versa, taking until 1879 to qualify, and was supposedly desultory about his patients thereafter, especially in the cricket season. Nevertheless, the *British Medical Journal* was happy to praise its famous fellow practitioner as 'the Champion Cricketer of the World'.[35] He clashed with the amateur ethos in financial ways too, as he rarely missed opportunities to make money or promote himself. Advertisements, such as the 1890s 'Colman's Mustard, like Grace, Heads the Field', cashed in on his fame. He was well aware of his own value, and the way his sheer presence in a side could add to the gate money. He was a member of the MCC, playing for the 'Gentlemen', presented himself as an amateur, and enjoyed its benefits in terms of status, first-class expenses and treatment. But he was really a 'shamateur', one of a number of supposed amateurs who because of their sporting status expected and often obtained lavish expenses and appearance money for playing. He was so powerful a figure that in 1879, shortly after the Gloucestershire committee tried unsuccessfully to curb the 'sums of money which are ridiculously in excess of any expenses' he and his brothers expected, and after he had been accused by *John Lillywhite's Companion* of having made larger profits from playing cricket than any professional, he was still given a testimonial by the MCC.[36] It raised £1458, and was presented by Lord Fitzhardinge and Lord Charles Russell. A second testimonial, in 1895, raised over £9000 in total. Although no writer himself, he cashed in on fame through the publication of a ghosted autobiography in 1891 and another in 1899.

His supportive treatment by the British amateur cricket establishment can be contrasted with the British RFU's attitude to another less wealthy, and socially inferior, amateur, Arthur Gould (1864–1919), the first superstar of Welsh rugby. He was an athlete, 'the greatest centre three-quarter that has ever played' and 'the finest footballer of the age' according to contemporaries.[37] But he came from a working-class background. His father was a brass founder. Gould became a public works contractor, and played for a number of top southern amateur sides while working away, but also won some £1000 in athletics prizes. He was a key figure in getting Wales to their first triple crown in 1893, playing with flair and opportunism, strengthening national support for rugby. By January 1896 he had played in more top matches and scored more tries than any other player. When a public subscription was opened in his honour after twenty-seven international caps, even the Welsh Football Union contributed £50, and £500 was raised to buy him a house in Newport. But the English RFU saw this as professionalism, and its committee banned him from association with the game, although this was rescinded at a later general meeting. Ultra-puritan, ultra-amateur Scotland and Ireland took the matter still further, cancelling fixtures with Wales. But Wales united behind their hero, and the top amateur clubs needed to play the Welsh. Gould got his detached villa. Scotland and Ireland soon resumed relations.

Increasingly, like Grace, top Victorian sportsmen had their own measure of celebrity, becoming courted by an adoring public. Even by the 1860s the word 'celebrated' was one being frequently applied to top pedestrians, pugilists, cricketers and jockeys. They drew fans and casual spectators to attend various sporting venues. Their names in themselves could be advertised as attractions. One correspondent remembered seeing 'five thousand people collected before eleven o'clock at Town Malling in 1838, literally in a mad state of excitement, to get a glimpse of Dearman, the Sheffield player, who had dared to challenge our great Alfred Wynn at single wicket'.[38] When Fred Archer made his one and only appearance at Thirsk racecourse in the early 1880s, the bellman was sent round to announce it and 'even the pum-Puritan chapel folks ... found the racecourse an irresistible draw and thither they flocked to see Fred ride'.[39] Whilst their private lives were largely still ignored, crowds would turn out for their marriages. When Archer married in January 1883, special trains were run to bring his adoring fans to Newmarket and Cambridge.[40]

Readily identifiable single-name status or use of nickname alone in the press perhaps represented the zenith of celebrity, fame or affection. Based on such criteria, there were few such stars in Victorian sport. In mid century racing reports, while other jockeys were given their surnames, as befitted professionals, Elnathan Flatman, the leading jockey each year from 1846 to 1852, was sufficiently well known to be given by an abbreviated version of his Christian name, 'Nat', and no surname, even in some records of results. 'The Doctor' or 'W.G.' was likewise instantly recognisable. Fred Archer was known as 'Fred' to some, but was also known as 'the Tinman', because of his keenness for 'the tin' (money).

Entrepreneurial publicans with enclosed grounds exploited top names as attractions, helping both boost attendances and make stars even more celebrated in public consciousness by the 1850s and 1860s. When the famous Canadian part-Indian pedestrian Deerfoot toured the country with a travelling troupe of runners, 'celebrated men, who have had the distinguished honour of appearing before his Royal Highness the Prince of Wales', it was their names which were blazed at running tracks at Stockport, Stockton and elsewhere.[41] The unique drama of sport also permeated and was influenced by other dramatic forms, and sports stars also appeared in music halls and circuses. Pugilists usually toured in circuses, but jockeys, scullers and even footballers and cricketers often appeared on stage as attractions. The first English cricket team to tour Australia appeared in their cricket flannels at Weston's Grand Music Hall at the end of May 1862, and Jem Snowden appeared there after his Derby win of 1864. Foreign touring teams or individuals were given free tickets by promoters because their presence even as members of the audience could be exploited. The Australian cricket team, for example, watched the Alhambra ballet in 1893 and the Pavilion acrobats in 1897. They would be introduced from the stage, and acclaimed and cheered by the audience.

In many sports the top sportsmen could continue to compete for a long time, providing they retained their health and eyesight. But they carried with them the hopes, wishes and dreams of their fans. This was a two-edged sword. Fans' adulation, prejudices, pride and loyalty spurred sportsmen on, but it could also be a heavy burden and responsibility. Pressure forced stars to compete more often. Champion jockeys usually got far more rides. Champions in wrestling or other elimination contests had to get through several rounds each competition. Donald Dinnie, the Scottish Highland Games competitor, had won well over 10,000 contests by the time he retired in the 1880s.

Some cracked under the strain and retired early, others went on competing when past their best, too old or too ill to do so. Celebrity was difficult to grasp and even harder to keep over time. Heroes became 'has beens', and crowds drifted away even from the most famous, some caring little and others less. Being friends with stars conferred surrogate status, but such friends could be exploitative. When a star eventually retired, friends could be few. George Fordham (1837–1887), champion jockey from 1855 to 1863, was grateful on his deathbed for his few friends, given that 'all others gave me up'.[42] Sporting celebrity by its very nature was ephemeral. If sufficient money had been saved a comfortable old age was possible, but few top Victorian working-class sportsmen made provision for the future.[43] Generosity and openhandedness was expected of all celebrities, from music hall artistes to sportsmen, and this reduced opportunities of saving.

Most had to turn to other ways of earning money. Taking public houses was a common practice. A few stayed in their sport in other capacities after retirement. Many lesser professionals certainly did so.

Cricketers might become umpires, wrestlers become judges. Fuller Pilch, a publican and the outstanding batting star of the period from 1830 to 1850, turned to umpiring after he retired. Tom Morris (1821–1908), the 'Grand Old Man' of golf, who won the Open Championship four times in the 1860s, held office as Keeper of the Green at St Andrews until 1903. He also acted as consultant to clubs elsewhere about course design.

Several leading cricket professionals set up sports equipment shops. William Lillywhite did so with his two sons in London in the 1840s. Alfred Shaw was one of several Nottingham players who established sports goods businesses, though he also organised tours, published books and coached. Later he joined forces with Arthur Shrewbury, who became involved in the setting up of the Midland Cricket and Football, Lawn Tennis and General Athletic Sports Warehouse at Nottingham. Having gained the patronage of the MCC, he offered estimates for 'the making of new cricket and lawn tennis grounds', stating that clubs, colleges and schools could be 'supplied on advantageous terms' with equipment.[44]

Respect for their past achievements soon faded amongst the public, for whom the next win was all-important. Heroes were meant to be young. As sports stars got older, they were almost embarrassedly trundled out at later events, though over time a mythical element took over. Only the most nostalgic remembered them. Those heroes who had not saved enough, or were unable to keep their money, sank back to the poverty into which many had been born. Sport could be a harsh mistress, and many one-time sporting celebrities died forgotten.

For those that died while still at the top, rituals of death illuminated their status in Victorian society. The period saw an increased enthusiasm for public commemoration of heroes, and the process of mourning became more formalised and commercial, a theme picked up not only in the work of novelists and painters but in sport. Ceremonies, pomp and processions associated with dynastic death had long been associated with royalty, dukes, earls and other illustrious figures. But in the Victorian age the funerals of the most celebrated sports heroes became major public occasions for lavish ceremonial display, theatrical and collective events which were melodramatically and sensationally reported, and where grief, religion and pride in British sporting prowess came together.[45] People travelled long distances to attend. Crowds packed the streets and viewed from windows, sometimes dressed in mourning, in ostentatious displays of respect and grief. Expense was seldom spared. Shops were closed for sportsmen as they were for the aristocracy, and stylised rituals and symbols showed just how important sportmen were, as well as providing opportunities for sporting reunions of friends, sporting opponents, patrons and associates.

Tom Sayers died of tuberculosis, relatively young, in 1865. Reputedly he was one against whose honesty there never was a shade of suspicion. Although fighting only in the south east, and dominating the British championship from 1849 to 1859, he was widely seen as the bravest and truest of pugilists, the great champion of his day. His funeral was heavily symbolic. Publicans and shopkeepers along the route closed, some private houses lowered their window blinds. Huge crowds lined the streets. Crepe flags were displayed, Union Jacks were flown at half-mast and a large sign read 'Peace to England's Champion'. His dog rode on a leopard-skin covered trap, and funeral music was provided by the professionals of various music halls. Ballad singers sold songs, others sold his photograph. The day of the funeral was an excuse for a local public holiday to mark his passing, although marred by crowds breaking into Highgate cemetery to see him laid to rest.[46] A massive marble monument was erected in the form of a Graeco-Roman tomb, with the powerful symbol of his bulldog, another potent national symbol, carved in front, life size. His fame was so obvious that all his tomb stated was 'Tom Sayers: born 1826, died 1865'.[47]

Traditional British hero stories usually ended with the hero attaining his goal and living happily ever after, but early death was the purest form of heroism. So the tragic death of some still youthful Victorian sporting heroes created shock, a sense of personal loss and grief, while allowing them to remain young for ever in the memory of their fans. Their deaths created a powerful mythic image for later writers. Fred Archer's suicide at the age of twenty-nine, not long after his wife's death, came, according to *The Times*, with a sense of shock and almost personal loss to millions.[48] His funeral, held in the public gaze, with much pomp, attracted hundreds of wreaths, crosses and other floral tributes, a clear precursor to more modern symbolic grief displays. These tributes came not just from local residents, but from across Victorian society, including the Prince of Wales, aristocrats and gentry, military men, newspaper correspondents and proprietors, gentlemen's clubs, hotel owners, trainers, jockeys, and racing officials, and from as far afield as America and France. Most tributes were highly symbolic – some associated with the horse like horseshoes or horse-collars, and others, like the broken column, a reminder of a life cut short. His funeral was led by his private carriage carrying wreaths, a second carriage with mourners, a special carriage draped in black with further wreaths, and the funeral car, containing his coffin, totally hidden with floral tributes. His funeral procession aligned him with the racing community, the town and the racing elite. A large number of employees of the different Newmarket stables followed the cortège, with almost forty further carriages behind. Those at the cemetery included Lord Grosvenor, Lord Alington and representatives of other titled mourners, five clergy, at least five doctors, and other middle-class mourners. A vast crowd outside the cemetery were initially held back by police, but the pressure was so great that eventually the gates had to be thrown open. Even so, the local paper used this as evidence of the essential orderliness of the working classes, recording that 'the utmost decorum was observed'.[49]

Local pride ensured regional heroes were similarly recognised. On Tyneside the funerals of leading rowers like Bob Chambers (d. 1868), Harry Clasper (d. 1870) and James Renforth (d. 1871) were major occasions, all watched by huge crowds, with estimates of their size varying from 50,000 up to 150,000. Each received a splendid monument erected by public subscription. Chambers's monument carried masonic symbols, a reflection of the involvement of the local lodge in the sport. Clasper's funeral was described as the largest funeral ever held in Newcastle, and mourning cards of the hero were retailed in the town's streets at a penny each. The funeral was held on a Sunday in order to 'more effectively meet the convenience of the numerous bodies of working men with whom he had for years past been on terms of the greatest friendship'. The *Newcastle Daily Chronicle* used the mining imagery of the region to boast how 'he took his tools, and his strong arm and honest heart, and hewed for himself a pathway to fame and a sepulchre kings might envy'.[50] Renforth had a funeral redolent with symbolism, with a Freemasons apron and Free Gardeners scarf placed on the Union Jack which adorned his coffin, and his friendly society colleagues playing a prominent part.[51] In Scotland the golfer Tom Morris junior (1851–1875), who dominated the Open between 1868 and 1872, lost his wife and child in September 1875. He played six rounds of golf in three days in snow and frost in December, and died of a burst artery in his lung on Christmas Day. He too was commemorated by a major funeral and large tombstone.

The potent power of sporting memory did not just apply to sports stars. As sport grew by the last decades of the century, sporting journalists and racehorse trainers also began to receive funereal and memorial recognition. It is unsurprising that racehorse trainers, like John Scott (1794–1871), the 'Wizard of the North', or Mat Dawson (1820–1898), the leading Newmarket trainer of his time, received such plaudits. After all they were highly successful in winning large sums of money for their owners.[52] But in other, less commercial fields of sport, those who owed their success to training began to recognise trainers' contribution too. Two old Harrovians, the Hon. Robert Grimson and the Earl of Bessborough, who had spent much time to coaching Harrow boys at cricket, were commemorated by a joint Harrow Chapel memorial, stating 'While teaching skill in cricket, they taught manliness and honour'.

But in comparison with modern forms of sporting celebrity, certain groups were conspicuously absent. Both rugby and association footballers had very little national recognition. The problem for footballers was that they existed in a local world, often playing for one club for a long time. They were simply more gifted members of their community, providing a sense of identity and pride. Both rugby and soccer developed a significant spectator following from the early 1880s. Local stars were lionised, and those of rival clubs ignored. Opposing fans might even abuse, heckle or even attack or stone them following a 'forceful' display. At cup finals, their pictures might be seen on cards displayed on hats, but they were not nationally famous and were valued only by their own clubs' supporters. They earned little in comparison to the earnings of jockeys. It took huge talent to be noticed. In the 1890s stars like John Goodall, the Preston North End and Derby County player who was so exemplary in his approach he was known as John Allgood, Ernest 'Nudger' Needham, the Sheffield United captain and full back, or Billy Meredith, a Manchester City and Wales winger, began to stand out. But even the first nationally prominent soccer superstar, Steve Bloomer

(b. 1874), famous for his goalscoring feats, and also an excellent cricketer and basketball player, supposedly never earned more than £5 10s. a
week, even at his peak in the Edwardian period.[53]

The qualities the public admired conveyed powerful images of masculinity. So famous sporting women were conspicuous by their absence.
Indeed top racehorses and greyhounds received far more column inches
of coverage and certainly got more sporting plaudits. Newspaper
journalists largely came from a heterosexual, male hegemonic background. They played down top women's achievements. In Victorian
novels, women heroes embodied 'feminine' qualities of caring, kindness,
motherliness and morality, and were often superior, exemplary or
tragic. Women in sport faced barriers of role expectation. Women's
sporting participation was likely to be upper or middle class, and appropriate to social station. The first outstanding sportswoman, judging by
press coverage, was the prodigious Charlotte 'Lottie' Dodd, first famous
as a fifteen-year-old 'Little Wonder' in 1887. In many respects she
mirrored typical male amateur qualities, being an all-rounder and coming from a solid middle-class Liverpool background. She became British
ladies' golf champion, won Wimbledon singles titles, played international hockey, and also enjoyed archery, skating and Alpine climbing,
though the crowd interest she attracted was relatively small.

Lottie Dodd was an amateur, but most male Victorian sports stars
were professionals, earning money for doing an athletic activity which
they loved. Their competitive involvement, most especially in cups and
leagues, helped the development of local and regional loyalties and
sporting identities.

8

Loyalties

In mid-Victorian Liverpool at the Aintree race meeting, the rows of tents were laid out so that almost every 'class or profession' could 'meet with congenial spirits or old familiar faces'. Tents were divided by tastes: for drink, food, or even the 'indecorous and unbecoming' conduct enjoyed by an 'aristocratic and fashionable' company. There were tents devoted to pugilism and pedestrianism, where the champion ostentatiously displayed his belt on the bar and young men went to buy drink and inspect it. Regional loyalties were catered for, with publicans from the region pursuing their customers with signs showing 'where they hail from'. For the Liverpool Irish, another tent had a representation of the green immortal shamrock, and in large letters the motto 'Faugh-a-ballagh'.[1] Sport clearly provided another way of ordering the social and cultural world of the Victorians. It catered for people drawn from a range of classes and communities, and played a part at local, regional and national levels.

For modern historians too, sport has provided yet another key to the different communities that made up the Victorian world, a world in which individuals carried with them multiple layers of collective identity, loyalty, affection and rivalry, and in which sport in turn shaped social consciousness.[2] Sport could play out tensions, include or exclude, create both in-groups and out-groups. We have already seen how middle-class values and attitudes played a major role in shaping Victorian sporting loyalty, while working-class lives and sporting experiences were inevitably shaped by their lowly economic position. Sport played a important role for middle-class urban men. Their games, their amateur clubs and their rules allowed opportunities of mixing with like-minded young men of similar background. But in many contexts Victorian society, with its rapid urban growth, increased migration and expansion of the railway system and the mass media, put pressure on social relationships. The new cities were unlike the more homogeneous rural villages and towns from which many of the migrants came. The role of the parish was less strong. Even though cities were still small, capable of being walked across, urban anomie, overcrowding and differences in wealth all contributed to a loss of that sense of village, town and regional community so many had previously valued. Sporting subcultures, even if often divided by class, provided one way of facilitating and renewing strong community allegiances and loyalties.

Sport was an integral part of the mainstream of Victorian culture. Its capacity for emotional stimulation, and to evoke a keen sense of occasion and place, meant that it was a powerful vehicle through which loyalties were forged, albeit partially and intermittently and in contention with other factors. Communities of whatever size seemed more real as a named sporting representative or even a team of eleven named people. Sport was bound up with place, and spatial factors and loyalties helped social groups give meaning to their lives.

Sporting frameworks and loyalties, of course, could be complex, contested, contradictory or overlapping. They included real or imagined communities associated with school, workplace, street, town, region or nation, as well as class, religion or ethnic group. Sporting identity became part of a complex and often shifting web of territorial allegiances, in which feelings of loyalty to the locality were part of a wider network of loyalties. So local loyalties could significantly affect regional ones, while regional loyalties could be encompassed within local ones. As such, sport could be used by both minority and majority groups to assert social identity and articulate a sense of belonging. Sports had their past glories, with frequently recalled memories and myths of earlier sporting defeats, great victories and sporting giants of old. Traditional village and town rivalry could be given further focus through sport.

Sport's multiple opportunities to bind supporters together in a common cause were constrained by the quest for success. Sport inspired emotion and loyalty, but in the case of a relatively new sports club, where patterns of support were still weak, crowds were fickle and success could prove elusive. Early loyalties were shifting, changing and sometimes transient. When Middlesbrough's still amateur town club was unsuccessful in the Northern League season of 1889/90, a new professional side, Middlesbrough Ironopolis, to which working-class support transferred, was formed in opposition. Middlesbrough's eventual resurgence following professionalism brought support back.

For most working-class Victorians, sporting identity was shaped either within the family, with father and brothers as role models, or within the peer group, with attitudes to sport acquired in the neighbourly solidarity of the streets and pubs of the locality. There were other forms of identity which had a major impact. Amongst the middle-classes education, with its key role in socialisation, had more major impact on identity formation, since sport drew school pupils together. By 1901 almost all public schools had established magazines which included reports on sporting activities, with articles by pupils and staff expressing a strong sense of sporting ethos. Public school emphasis on games created a sense of conformity, of being a member of an exclusive sporting group, and aided reputation. As early as 1858 the *Tonbridgian* was recognising how, once its games were conducted 'on a scale that brings reputation to the school, and develops the physical and mental energies of the scholars', the school could acquire a reputation 'by the remarkable deeds of the old boys' at the universities.[3] Pupils were proud that their names were found in the school eleven and their achievements displayed on its walls. Nostalgia, team spirit and a belief that life was an extension of the games field permeated their thinking. Sporting rituals, such as being capped, getting one's colours or being blooded, aided the development of loyalty.

Public school rivalries also played a further role in the development of modern games like rugby, soccer and athletics. Eton's identity as the leading public school was threatened by the emergence of Rugby and its handling football game in the 1840s. Eton stressed minimal handling and prohibited carrying in its field game. Tension was carried over into the universities, especially at Cambridge, where representatives from a variety of public schools loyally championed their own school's versions. Compromise rules needed to be developed. Early attempts at codification were informal and have not survived, but in 1856 the Cambridge rules for the University Foot Ball Club were developed. These were dominated by Trinity College men, many from Eton, as were later sets of compromise rules in 1863.[4] Thus modern soccer does owe something to Eton, as does rugby to its rival.

The freemasonry of the public school was strong, the more so since numbers were extremely limited, making the old school tie a powerful symbol of comradeship. Ex-public schoolboys, especially from the older public schools like Eton, Harrow or Winchester, often had a fierce sense of identity, forming old boy teams to compete against pupils from their former schools or against others of similar background. By the 1860s cricket, for example, had the Harrow Wanderers, the Old Harrovians and the Eton Ramblers. The Pantaloons was composed of old boys who had represented Rugby at cricket, while the Butterflies was for those who had not, although the teams later merged.

Other less famous schools showed a similar pattern. The Edinburgh Academicals Rugby Club was founded by old boys of the Edinburgh Academy, York Football Club by former pupils of St Peters School, York, and Darlington Football Club by old boys of its grammar school. Right through the 1870s and 1880s many soccer-playing ex-public schoolboys moved on to play for their old boys' side. Old Etonians won the FA Cup final in 1881/2; the weaker Etonian Ramblers also competed in 1882/3. At this time the Old Carthusians were still strong enough to defeat most provincial sides. Through the 1880s they, along with Old Harrovians, Old Westminsters and Old Wykehamists, still participated regularly in the FA Cup, with less regular appearances from lower-status old boy clubs like Old Foresters, Old St Marks, Old Brightonians and Lancing Old Boys.

For the middle classes, club membership was a major form of loyalty, and in rugby, cricket and football, even when not actually playing, club colours often allowed members to show off their status. As at public schools, where caps, scarves, stockings, ties, badges, braid and blazers all symbolised sporting achievements, appearance was important to the assumption of middle-class adult sporting position. Some sports clubs had uniforms, worn with pride at the hunt club meet or at the cycle club jaunt. Nottingham's Dresden Boat club members wore plain blue flannel jackets and broad brimmed straw hats. In team sports, distinctive playing strips promoted team identification, loyalty and solidarity. Uniform or special kit functioned as a badge of belonging as well as a way of exclusion. Windermere Yacht Club was one of many yacht clubs with a series of ranks, often from Commodore downward, each with its distinctive uniform and badge. Caps awarded by counties and countries in cricket, rugby and soccer had the same symbolic function, and the stress on appearance, dress and behaviour in match reports showed a clear sense of social positioning.

By contrast much adult working-class sporting loyalty was locally rooted. In the 1880s and 1890s many local soccer teams were regularly named after streets, churches and public houses as well as towns. Residential solidarities meant street and neighbourhood names for minor cricket and soccer sides were relatively common. In the Stirling region, over half the football teams formed between 1876 and 1895 were named after specific neighbourhoods. As already suggested, works teams and churches offered their members opportunities of belonging through sporting identity. In Birmingham between 1876 and 1884 about 9 per cent of reported soccer teams were named after workplaces. The soccer sides of Lockwood Brothers in Sheffield, Mellors Ltd in Nottingham, Crosswell's Brewery at Oldbury and Mitchell's Brewery in Birmingham all had regional reputations in the 1870s and 1880s, while industrial sides like Eckington Works had strong cricket teams, although it is unclear how much active involvement the firms had. Despite the place of religion in popular culture, the churches struggled harder to develop sporting loyalty in their members. Church sports clubs were relatively successful in terms of participatory sporting activity at a lower level of performance, but allegiance was less strong than it appeared. Once church clubs began to be more successful, in the vast majority of cases they first began to seek recruits from outside and then separated from the church that had begun them. A club formed at Christ Church, Bolton, by scholars and teachers renamed itself Bolton Wanderers in 1877, after a quarrel with the vicar, while Aston Villa likewise soon outgrew its religious origins.[5] Religious identity may have had more impact at the school level once inter-school contests added another dimension to school rivalries. Here success on the playing field could be seen as a demonstration of the superiority of a religious denomination.

Through their social functions, pubs had a long and important history in shaping loyalties to locality. They were places where fields were provided, sports sponsored, pedestrian challenges agreed, bets were laid and teams changed. Frequenters of 'sporting houses' often had their own allegiances, and lent general support to a particular rower, pugilist or pedestrian before a match. In pugilism for example, sporting pubs nearly always had strong loyalty to particular fighters. In 1866, around

London's East and West End before the Jem Mace versus Joe Goss fight, it was 'to be discerned immediately upon entering, from the expressed convictions, who was the representative man of the particular house where we happened to be. At Richardson's there was no possibility of the gallant Jem being beaten, while at Nat Langham's the greatest reliance was placed on Goss's great pluck, endurance and thorough bottom'.[6]

At a level above the very local came urban communities. Here it was generally sports teams, rather than individuals, who provided the most significant expressions of community support. In the early 1880s dog handicaps were the most popular weekend working-class spectator sport in Middlesbrough. But soccer was just beginning to create a sense of town identity. According to the *Cleveland News*, when a dog fancier learned 'whey [who] had won' a recent match, he 'exclaimed emphatically "The best darned lads in *England*" and on being told by ten goals to nil exclaimed "The best darned lads in the *world*. Only bring on those Sheffielders who licked us last year and I'm blest if we don't put off a handicap"'.[7]

During a period of major industrial upheaval, and of migration from the countryside, sport helped enhance the status of urban areas, providing a new focus for old rivalries between towns and regions. In urban Victorian Britain a strong local sense of place, of 'our town' and our 'roots', of 'our team' and 'our boys', was often the most powerful and overriding form of sporting loyalty. Such towns were potentially anonymous, their inhabitants being drawn from a mixture of backgrounds. A successful local team provided a territorial symbol and a collective metaphor. For the working classes such loyalties often overrode regional ones, or the ties of work or nationality. Support for a local team compensated for a harsh working life, the troubles of home and work, and uncongenial surroundings.

By the 1880s football and rugby were becoming the games that came most to articulate civic pride in provincial towns and cities, while cricket performed a similar function in villages and at county level, as well as for some Lancashire league cricket sides. Sport brought what were often in reality diverse communities together in temporary but fierce local pride, despite differences of class usually perpetuated by different levels of accommodation on stands and terraces. Sport was promoted precisely because of this ability to create what has been called an 'idealised community', helping to paper over tensions, or maybe even temporarily heal them.[8] Popular sports became a source of pride and passion, representative in some way of the soul of the community, offering a densely compelling world of alternative public and private loyalties to those of class, work or politics.

In Britain's provincial towns, especially in the north and midlands, players were far less anonymous than in London. Sides were socially mixed, but players increasingly came from the factories and surrounding areas, and faced more pressure to play well. In most cities several teams, usually bitter rivals based in different locations, would vie for success. Some like Liverpool and Everton, or Sheffield Wednesday and Sheffield United, survive to the present day. Others like Sunderland Albion had brief success and then faded. Such rivalries meant that by 1896 Small Heath (later Birmingham City) supporters cheered when they received news by telegram of Aston Villa's FA Cup defeat at Derby. In most towns fans ended up following the most successful club, which became the town's representative. At the very top, local teams could compete in a national arena, playing out an episodic weekly drama from autumn to spring. As businessmen and other commercial interests increasingly became involved in the running of clubs, and local stadiums expanded as success came, civic pride was increasingly reflected not only in town halls, libraries, museums and parks but in the sporting achievements of what was seen as the town's team. Grounds and stadiums became central focal points, new 'dream houses' where leading teams displayed their skills, calling into being increasing numbers of fans, and difficult to ignore even for those who did not like sport. Clubs held medal competitions on their grounds for recreational and works sides, and held sports days for charity, patronage which emphasised the club's local roots. Local politicians were keen to associate themselves, recognising sport's role in gaining votes and tipping the electorate in their support. Many councillors showed a keen interest, kicking off games, speaking at official dinners and welcoming successful teams home.

It was the introduction of the various soccer cups introduced at national and regional level from the 1870s, and the advent of the Yorkshire Challenge Cup in rugby in 1887/8, which really began to create sporting loyalty. Attendances soared when cups were introduced. Local pride became linked to a crude desire for cup success. Ties which took

The Sheffield Football Team.
Professional football teams became strong focuses of local loyalties.

place against bitter industrial and commercial rivals nearby, especially when teams were of similar standing, made the joy of winning far greater. High crowds were always attracted to such games. For staunch fans, in the company of hundreds if not thousands of friends, neighbours and fellow citizens, it created a new and powerful physical and emotional tie to their town or city for a brief few hours. Recollections of events, rare away trips or great goals came to represent for those involved a loyalty both to the team and to the brotherhood of fellow supporters, and to being part of their own history.

Alongside the increased regularity of matches and the growth of cups and leagues, local and provincial press coverage buttressed urban identity still further. Reports were read by many who never attended games. Several key words ran through reports. 'Pride', 'glory' and 'credit' all surfaced regularly. So did 'honour', when applied to the 'reputation' of the team and the town.[9] In Wales, for example, beating the other rugby teams in the area played a part in 'vindicating the honour of Llanelli against her many detractors'.[10] Blackburn Rover's 1884 FA Cup win 'had brought ... honour to the town'.[11] Such views linked honour with success. For elite sportsmen 'honour' had been associated with a perfectionist code of fairness in play, but this new meaning suggested that honourable play, or defeat with honour, was less important than winning.

Identity soon became linked to the issue of professionalism, and debates about whether local players or better outsiders should represent the town's leading club. Sometimes there was antagonism towards Scottish professionals. In Lincolnshire, for example, it was claimed that 'there has been a big demand in England for Scotch players, but football enthusiasts are now beginning to question the wisdom of going across the border for new blood whilst we have promising young players of English manufacture'. Many correspondents believed Lincoln City should not only select English players but preferably play those born locally. As one correspondent noted, in contrast to 'uncertain foreigners', 'local men would try their very hardest as Lincoln lads to uphold the honour of Lincoln City'.[12] City did not respond to such complaints. The reality was different. In Sunderland, following similar pressures, an attempt was made to build a side composed of local players to represent the town. It got poor crowds compared with the recently professional town side. It was not strong enough, although most Sunderland supporters would rather have had a team of local players, and certainly where local men played well they were particular crowd favourites. Success weighed even more strongly. One correspondent denied any ill-feeling whatsoever amongst spectators against the 'canny Scots', claiming that 'but for our judicious mixture we would not hold the proud position we hold today'. Another claimed that opposition to importation of Scots was 'sentimental rubbish and bigoted nonsense'. What fans wanted, according to yet another, was 'as good a team was there is in England', no matter how composed.[13] But opposing spectators whose clubs could not afford the professionals required for success often took a different and more bitter view. When the Sunderland team scored at South Bank, Darlington or elsewhere in the north east, there were sarcastic shouts of 'Go on Scotland!', 'Play up Scotland!' or 'Well done imported goods!'.[14]

For many more working-class supporters, identification with team and town became fanatical. Watching and supporting offered fun, escape and a sense of belonging. The soccer stadium became a field of dreams, with the sights, the companionship, the match itself long discussed afterwards, building up over time a keen sense of tradition and historical memory. By the mid 1880s northern soccer and rugby supporters were regularly described as being 'partisan'. The success or failure of a team provided symbolic and practical manifestations of local pride and disappointment, happiness and sorrow. Myths developed about supposedly local ways of playing. West Brom were praised for their 'daring dash, a never-say-die, don't-give-a-button for anybody else, go-ahead style'.[15] Yet the criticism levelled at Birmingham supporters in general, of 'narrow minded and prejudiced views upon anything related to sport ... bigotry and prejudice ... ignorance of the game ... blind partisanship and adulatory sycophancy', could have been made of many supporters elsewhere.[16] Local allegiance could lead to aggression, anger and prejudice. Rivalry allowed the vicarious expression of hostility and other strong emotions, as the triumph of one's team came to mean a triumph over another town. Coupled with cup-tie fervour it often meant yelling, shouting and booing, hooting at the opposition's poor shooting, demanding that any over-firm tackle by an opposing player should lead to a sending off, and threats against and verbal abuse of players. Swearing with frustration at the opposing team, the home team or the referee was common, despite the display of notices at grounds saying 'No Swearing: No Betting Allowed'. Ribald jesting, profanity, swearing and cursing permeated many working-class activities and provided social glue at games. The Football League, like the FA, was faced with regular reports from referees like that of Mr J. Lewis of Blackburn, who reported the 'most foul and opprobious language' levelled at him by Derby County spectators.[17] Betting was also commonplace: between optimists and pessimists amongst local supporters; between rival fans; or simply taking attractive offered odds in hope of profit.

Sport was most important for its role in construction of local male identities. Women's identification with sport is less easy to locate, not least since contemporary male Victorian writers often derided women's knowledge and understanding. There are very occasional references to female behaviour at matches which may be suggestive. At the Sheffield Cup Final of 1888, for example, female supporters from Ecclesfield gave abusive nicknames both to the players of Sheffield Wednesday and to those applauding them.[18] Cup Final success was an event of huge local significance. Few could afford to travel to the actual match, but many thousands would flock to see the team's triumphant return. This was a ritualised form of street theatre, but also an expression of communal solidarity and civic ceremonial which helped to enhance social stability, and masked underlying tensions and disharmonies.

In the later nineteenth century, working-class support for urban soccer teams emerged earliest where towns had relatively settled populations and had already experienced their most rapid period of industrial and population growth. The large and expanding cities of Bristol, Leeds, Liverpool, Manchester and Newcastle all came relatively late to any degree of popular soccer success, despite their industrial modernity. Their rapid rate of expansion meant that wider civic pride came in fits and starts in the later nineteenth century, despite their growing industrial strength and self-confidence. Only in well-governed Birmingham, where civic pride was the driving force, and there was an adventurous, experimental and diverse approach to local economics, society and politics was adopted from the 1870s onwards, were there strong soccer sides like Aston Villa and West Brom in the 1880s and early 1890s. Birmingham's diversity of occupations, its multiplicity of small workshops, good relationships between masters and men, its high proportion of skilled workers and high social mobility, all created a strong basis for sporting developments. By contrast, Manchester's large-scale factory production and lower male incomes provided less fertile ground.

The largest city of all, London, was extremely slow to develop working-class support for soccer. Its professional teams came late. London had no rivals in the south. It was a powerful and prosperous commercial and financial centre, the richest city in the world as well as the political and cultural capital. It attracted the very wealthy, many of whom maintained London residences for the season; but 'society' and parliamentary circles were linked with the countryside and county seats, not soccer. More certainly, it had more of the middle classes than any other city simply because of its size. Views vary about the proportion of the British middle classes living there, but it may have been almost 40 per cent. Their disproportionate wealth and free time meant that opportunities for sporting leisure were extremely high, but London was too vast and too heterogeneous to support a single 'London' soccer club, despite its proliferation of sporting teams. Over-rapid growth was another factor. The suburbs of Leyton, West Ham, Tottenham and Willesden had the highest rates of population growth in England between 1881 and 1891. In 1891, *Pastime* still saw London as a region 'destitute of local partisanship'.[19] Londoners had little sense of civic consciousness, and very few had learnt to feel and think primarily as citizens of their borough.[20] Despite being the location of many ruling bodies, London had less sporting dynamism and innovation than the provinces during this period.

In apparently anonymous London, with its dangerous classes, natives and outsiders, creating multiple cultural conflicts and anxieties, sportsmen bound themselves together by other criteria. Old boy teams were one example, but London also saw many sports clubs and organisations based on players' regional roots or national origins. The identities of minorities were forged in part by the attitudes, perceptions and reactions of the majority. London immigrants may well have faced prejudices against religion, region, race or accent which limited the choice and so had to set up their own clubs. Once of the earliest sports to do this was wrestling, which promoted a sense of regional cultural heritage by seeking status through London championship winning.

The Devonshire and Cornwall Society and Cumberland and Westmoreland Wrestling Society both had grand annual contests and championships in London at Easter or Whitsuntide from early in the century, with committees of management holding regular meetings, and subscription lists to collect prize money. For the men from amongst the valleys and mountains of the northern counties this was about £100 in the 1860s, and nearly £140 by the 1880s. Some competitions were for north-country men who had resided in London since the previous 1 January; others were for all-comers from the north. Wrestlers from Cumbria would travel down to compete in these.[21] Like the Scottish Caledonian Clubs overseas, London wrestling served important social functions, helping those who had come to London to remember their origins and heritage, and to pass them on to subsequent generations.[22] Exiles from the other British countries also formed sports clubs. There was a London Scottish golf club at Wimbledon in 1865. The London Scottish RFC were founded in April 1878. London Welsh, founded in 1885 for upwardly mobile teachers, officers and medical students, was initially a nomadic club with no permanent base.[23] Middle-class Irish Protestant politicians, lawyers and businessmen set up London Irish RFC in 1898 to provide hospitality and a base for those with Irish roots, and the Scottish soccer sides United London Scottish and London Caledonians entered the FA Cup in the 1880s. Throughout Britain, exiles remembered their roots. In west Cumbria, for example, the Cornish miners in tiny Moor Row had their own cricket team in the 1870s.[24] Irish migrants established a Gaelic Athletic Association club in Wallsend in February 1885.

Above the local and urban came the regional. Distinctive regional differentiation was most clearly expressed in notions of north and south, but it could be found in other forms too, from the county upwards. Regional culture long predated the advent of organised sport, but even in the nineteenth century leisure and sport were experienced differently by people in different regions. The mental maps of sporting writers and the regional stereotypes which they promoted confirm this, while the numbers of reports on particular sports in the sporting press of each region clearly differed, even taking into account the willingness of correspondents to report, and the sales of the newspapers concerned.

The power of local and regional identity sustained a diverse popular sporting culture in the face of modernising pressures from the state, the mass media and more firmly amateur or commercial forms of sport. Regions created their own stereotypes. Even in the 1840s Nottingham was perceived as prominent in 'sporting celebrity', with 'a prominent distinction in racing, boxing (Caunt and Bendigo), cricket and hunting'.[25] From the 1840s to the 1880s Newcastle was the 'northern hotbed of professional oarsmen', with 'a deep-rooted love ... for contests that bring out courage, skill and endurance', and good knowledge of rowing 'racing lore'.[26] Here soccer belatedly attracted popular support, and by 1901, in nearby east Northumberland, mining village and town rivalries and continued antagonism to the urban dominance of Newcastle in other sporting contexts were temporarily laid aside as mining communities began to support Newcastle United.[27] Lancashire became well known as a leading area for commercialised working-class leisure. Blackpool pioneered the working-class seaside holiday, and the county also saw the development of enclosed sports grounds like Belle Vue in the 1840s, gate-money racing at Manchester in the 1860s, six of the initial Football League clubs, the Lancashire League in cricket, and early members of the Northern Rugby Union.

Where regions had reputations for particular traditional sports, or long-standing non-elitist regional ones, they were regularly forced to reinvent and relaunch them as support waned, in order to make them once again appeal to the public. Cumbrian wrestling, for example, tightened up its rules and improved its presentation in the 1860s, limiting the time taken by wrestlers to get to grips and even offering prizes for the best embroidered costume to make the sport visually appealing.

Sports were unevenly distributed across Britain. Curling, not soccer, was the 'national game' of Scotland.[28] Professional soccer was particularly concentrated in the lowlands of Scotland, northern and midland England and later also the London region. By contrast, in south Wales, soccer was overshadowed by rugby and the South Wales League, formed in 1890, attracted few gates above 1000. Professional quoits was most common in the north east, followed by Yorkshire, Lancashire and central Scotland. It was specially popular in mining areas everywhere, but was also found in the countryside in more amateur forms. By the 1860s, press reports on wrestling largely came from Cumbria,

Lancashire, Durham and Northumberland with very occasional references to London or the west country. Elsewhere there was little interest. Professional cricket, by contrast, was most significant in Nottinghamshire, Middlesex, Surrey, Lancashire and Yorkshire, lessening the further north and west one went. The 1881 census contained no full-time cricket professionals in Durham, Northumberland or Cumberland, two in Wales, and only six in the whole of Scotland. Bowling was strongest in Scotland and northern England. The first Welsh club was only founded in 1860, the second Irish club not until the 1870s.

Yorkshiremen were the most prone to claims of sporting leadership, a view the early development of a sporting press there might support. They supposedly had the most interest in horseracing, although southerners often ascribed this to the north in general. Certainly by the 1870s it was becoming an accepted axiom that Yorkshire was synonymous with sport. Sheffield was celebrated from around mid century for its pedestrianism, 'its splendid sprint courses and its phenomenal footraces'. By the 1870s it was still well known for its large pedestrian handicaps, but also increasingly for its cricket, followed even by the working classes at its Bramall Lane ground (opened 1855), where it was claimed 'men of rough exterior ... who know when a bowler can trowl, a batter can play with his stick straight and whether a colt can field as well or even better than some who lay claim to be the oracles of cricket at Lord's', while 'football nowhere thrives more rapidly'.[29] Their middle-class exiles perpetuated county loyalties. In Cardiff a group of Yorkshiremen founded the White Rose Cricket Club.

Despite support for Yorkshire county cricket, county loyalties across Britain seem to have had little weight amongst the working classes. A sense of county identity, with its late medieval 'county gentry' roots, was stronger amongst the middle and upper classes. County towns had traditionally been venues for assizes and other important social occasions, including race meetings and cockfights between the gentlemen of rival counties. It is unsurprising that such upper-class activities lasted throughout the Victorian period. Cricket provided an early example, and early county teams were often composed of 'gentlemen' playing against rival local counties. In the 1850s there were a number of teams such as the Gentlemen of Surrey, and some counties, such as Montgomeryshire (1855) actually restricted membership to 'gentlemen' for some time. Even when a formal county system emerged from 1875, with more professional players, many matches were attended largely by middle-class members, and *The Times* commented that 'the pitch of interest felt in county matches by all except the players is far from high'.[30] Regional papers, with their middle-class reporters, looked to their local county cricket clubs for success, to beat the opposition, and providing booster copy when they did so. When Warwickshire's cricket team began to improve one Birmingham paper reported that 'drooping hopes are reviving and the folks who were in the habit of wagging their heads are holding them a bit higher'.[31] Yorkshire cricket teams became a way of projecting positive affirmation of Yorkshire talent. Its sides, composed of the best players, represented Yorkshire beliefs in merit, regardless of class.

The notion of the county received a further middle-class lease of life when individual rugby teams began to form county associations and organise inter-county matches, which were well attended by middle-class supporters. The northern rivals Lancashire and Yorkshire first played at Leeds in 1870. Lancashire dominated early matches until the impact of the Yorkshire Cup raised Yorkshire standards in the early 1880s. But by then crowds for county matches were becoming disappointing, 'the gate being anything but up to expectations' in 1882, as growing working-class support followed the successful urban sides instead.[32] Although southern counties, except for Middlesex, were less well organised and weaker, an official county championship was introduced by the RFU in 1888/9 to increase appeal. It was quickly regionally zoned, and these competitions increased attendances, especially in Yorkshire, which won for seven of the first eight seasons.

Soccer county games between associations began with matches between Sheffield and London in the 1860s. But here again this was largely a middle-class phenomenon. It was concerned to perpetuate amateur ideals, with fulfilling two-year qualificatory rules and the demands of social status. Occasionally strong local rivalry overrode this. In north-east England, both Durham and Northumberland fielded teams which 'rigidly adhered' to the FA rules only in late 1888.[33] Crowds for county matches were lower and more middle class than for major inter-town matches. Working-class county loyalty was weaker.

London's growth, and Londoners' claims to the superiority of metropolitan over provincial life, did, however, have an impact on the provinces, where even early in the Victorian period the defining other which created sporting rivalry and ambition was often London. On Tyneside, the connections of work and trade with London aided the frequency of rowing and athletic contests between professionals from the two places. So Tyneside sporting loyalty was in part defined by conscious opposition to Londoners (those 'queer cockney folk'), and by a sometimes defensive provincial pride and self-consciousness. There were regular matches between the 'pride of the Thames' and Tyne scullers, transporting their boats by rail or ship. Londoners founded a special competition, the Championship of the Thames, with top scullers from the two rivers competing for prizes of about £200 a side. The hopes and ambitions of Tyneside were projected onto its rowers, and the victories of Clasper, Chambers or Renforth were all celebrated in Tyneside music hall songs. Top London oarsmen like Robert Coombes and Harry Kelley were well supported in London, where 'the pride of the Thames was not to be entirely subdued without great efforts to wrest the laurels from the Tyne man'. While the names of the rowers came first in newspaper headings, subtitles read 'The Thames against the Tyne'.[34] By the 1870s this led to separate northern and southern schools of oarsmen.[35]

The London press played an important role in constructing images of the provinces, and most especially the north. As sport became one of London's cultural characteristics, the capital became ever more attractive to those who liked sport, further reinforcing its position in the British urban hierarchy. London, as the capital, exerted a powerful pull on the location of regulating bodies, becoming the most common centre for national finals and other major sporting events. Only a few organisations were based elsewhere. Horse-racing's Jockey Club, which was based at Newmarket, despite having a subsidiary London meeting place, and golf's St Andrews in Scotland provided a rare combination of high status and long-standing existence which aided their extra-metropolitan regulatory dominance.

Others, like the Football League at Preston, deliberately based themselves in the north to distance themselves from London dominance. The provinces, and especially northern England, had begun to assert their political, social and economic claims as the industrial revolution

developed, fostering resistance towards London's metropolitan dominance and arrogance, and to the rule of national organising governing
bodies. Sometimes this meant that organisations split, perhaps over the
very different way amateurism was approached in some of the provinces,
and perhaps because of perceived lack of support from London. The
Northern Cross-Country Association was formed because northern
clubs were prepared to accept some limited payment of contestants in
harrier and other events. The Northern Counties Athletic Association
was set up as a counter-weight to the dominance of the London-based
Amateur Athletic Association, though confining itself to amateurs
elected by application, nomination and ballot. In 1889 the Northern
Counties Amateur Swimming Assocation was formed by twenty-seven
northern clubs because the Amateur Swimming Association would not
support northern events. They claimed that 'they could do very well
without the south and hoped that the Northern members will treat the
Southern with silent contempt'.[36] In wider British society there were
always bitter complaints that London knew next to nothing about the
provincial cities, with their supposed lack of cultivation and polish, and
such complaints were echoed in sport. Clashes between northern and
southern factions were endemic in cricket in the 1860s. English cricket
teams appeared to be picked more from southern players. In both soccer
and rugby, perceptions that London treated the provinces unfairly
generated ill-feeling. English team selection was a constant issue, with
the selection committee often portrayed as a 'southern clique' with a
'hatred of northerners'. The occasional northerners included in national
sides, or as representatives of northern clubs on national committees,
could find themselves marginalised. Dr Morley of Blackburn Rovers
protested to the FA against 'the studied discourtesies and lack of
consideration shown toward the northern members' in 1886.[37]

The northern association clubs stayed with the FA, but in rugby the
Northern Union's formation in 1895 marked a divide not just of professionalism but of regional resentment. By the late nineteenth century
there was antagonism in Yorkshire and Lancashire towards the southern 'other', the place where football's ruling bodies were based. In
contrast, in north-east England, teams saw their rivals as being in the
main those based in Yorkshire and Lancashire, and felt less rivalry to
distant London.[38]

In a sense, therefore, sport helped to construct new notions of 'northernness'. The north-south divide long predated the industrial revolution, being rooted in enduring differences and inequalities of power, political influence, lifestyle, material conditions and opportunity. It was consciously felt both in the provinces, where Mrs Gaskell's novel *North and South* neatly made the point, and in London, where what were sometimes believed to be sporting 'missionary' links with the provinces began. Sport both reflected existing divides and developed them further. In cricket the first North versus South match at Lords in 1836 institutionalised existing attitudes, with a return match at Leicester illustrating London geographical perceptions. The matches were leading seasonal fixtures for many years, although by 1882 they evoked less enthusiasm.[39] With the impetus again coming from London, the first North versus South soccer game was played at the Oval in December 1870, and the first rugby equivalent at Rugby in January 1874. Both got much press interest initially, with the North versus South rugby matches in the 1870s being described as 'important and interesting', 'great' matches of the day. In the 1850s and 1860s there were also separate northern and southern professional cricket touring sides, including the United South of England XI in 1865.

In the north there were complex, multi-layered beliefs about inequality of power, political influence and material opportunities compared to London. Resulting differences of perception and understanding made people both sensitive about their treatment and keen to defeat southerners, while aiding the development of stereotypical northern identities. There was a clear sense of being different from the south, making the south the rejected 'other', the opponent to be defeated.

Through sport images developed about what were the perceived qualities of the north, although there was disagreement over its geographical definition, so its boundaries changed over time and with the point of vision. Londoners usually included much of the midlands; for many in the north it stopped with Yorkshire and Lancashire. Cheshire, for example, was debatable ground. The North was therefore essentially an imagined community, a perceived region created by self-vision, literature and the press, something which was as much a state of mind as a place. Northern consciousness was a slippery entity, a product of cultural traditions, assumptions and memories.[40]

The north was itself composed of fragmented regions. Tyneside was different from the West Riding and different again from the Lancashire cotton region. Towns in the north also had a more local sense of rivalry which London lacked, although the east–west axis of economic activity from Liverpool to Hull created a major population cluster that was central to industrialisation and ensured continued economic, social and sporting rivalry after it. No consistent image of northernness can or could be constructed. In popular imagination, where reality mixed with myth, there were stereotypical northern virtues such as hard graft or physical hardness. Northern men were white, 'masculine' and more likely to be working in an industrial context, being recognisable through their speech and appearance. Northern identity became linked to working-class identity, even though they were not synonymous. Northerners saw themselves as supposedly and variously fair, friendly, hard-working, honest, blunt, outspoken, highly competitive and dour, and more oriented towards 't'brass' and professionalism, so more anti-amateur.[41] Tensions over professionalism were papered over in the press.

The north took rugby or soccer to its heart, especially in the rapidly developing industrial areas, where a passion for them developed from the 1870s. Here the local support given to the more successful rugby and soccer sides was linked to images of aggressive working-class masculinity, valuing the 'hard' man. Northerners supposedly had a different, more aggressive style of play, even if there were many southern sides who matched it. When Yorkshire played Lancashire in 1872 at Huddersfield, as an exhibition to boost rugby, it was still a novelty, with 'a wondering, gaping populace who thronged their doors and windows to get a glimpse of the strange beings' en route to the ground, but a crowd of six thousand attended the match. Shouts could be heard from the spectators cheering on the Yorkshiremen, such as 'ger into it wi' thy' or 'punce him o'er', and they were 'evidently delighted at the rough usage of the combatants'.[42] Northern players were represented as highly competitive, tough, with a strong work ethic, not necessarily great stylists but very effective, while northern crowds were more fanatical.[43] As the *Field* noted in 1882, 'in the North of England ... the game is often played in a very different spirit, and at times the desire to win leads to much unpleasantness'.[44]

By 1890 one commentator noted the 'joyous thrill of enthusiasm that passes through the community ... football in the north is more than a game. It excites more emotion than art, politics or the drama, and it awakes local patriotism to the highest pitch'.[45] The key word here was 'local'. Regional identity in the north of England was contained within the locality; it was neither a separate nor distinctive identity. There was little real sense of any shared integrative regional identity.

The north was not the south. To many northerners the south was a place apart, a source of snobbishness, exploitation, marginalisation and lack of understanding. These unflattering stereotypes may or may not have had some basis in experience. Charles Clegg, a Sheffield lawyer and later president of the FA, later recalled that on his first English international in 1872 he never received the ball from the 'snobs from the south'.[46] Southerners supposedly looked down on northerners, were from a different background, soft and aloof, lacking concentration and grit. The 'swells' with their top hats, 'southern amateurs' playing for the game's sake, were compared with competitive 'northern professionals'. In cricket, the late Victorian north had leagues, the south had friendlies and country house games with sides from similar backgrounds.

Such myths took little account of more complex realities. London's Clapton FC side, the first to charge 3d. gate money for their FA cup matches, was composed of 'northerners and Scots' as early as 1888.[47] Tottenham Hotspur, London's FA Cup winners of 1901, was a professional side containing five Scots, three northerners, two Welshmen and an Irishman. The London crowd that welcomed its return blew horns, threw confetti and made up new words to popular songs to celebrate. There had always been plenty of support for professionals, whether rowers, runners or soccer players, in some sections of London society.

The fight for various championships, whether in pugilism, county cricket or the FA Cup, was a reminder of a wider national dimension, attaching the individual to the nation. Most top sportsmen professed loyalty to their country. The pugilist Tom Sayers, for example, claimed 'I did my best for the land of my birth and dearest affections'.[48] The Victorian period saw a revival of the historic nationalism of the United Kingdom countries, and in turn sport came to be a force to be reckoned with as a touchstone of national identity, a test of national worth.

Success was important here. In England the key sport was cricket: its distinctive links with the colonies, and its external moral vocabulary of principled fair play peculiar to the upper and middle classes, provided England with a formidable form of imperialistic sporting nationalism. In Scotland the key sport was soccer. In Wales it slowly became rugby. The banal nationalism purveyed by the press pontificating on British sporting triumphs soon helped to enhance nationalistic self-esteem. Winning enhanced a sense of national achievement. Sporting success was a measure of national virility and power, and international contests became associated with symbols from flags and songs to national strips. Media coverage, with its nationalist talk of pride and status, strongly emphatic and striking images, shared myths and memories of earlier encounters, did much to regularly express and foster such collective ideas of nationhood.[49]

None of the four nations was characterised by cultural or ethnic homogeneity. The British nation was at best 'an imagined political community' as historically speaking, the countries which make up Britain have been culturally and ethnically diverse, problematic and artificial constructs shaped and reshaped over time, creating separate traditions.[50] Sport divided them as well as united them, yet in sport the terms 'British' and 'English' were often used synonymously. The national cricket team was known as England, no matter where in Britain its players were recruited. By the early Victorian period some sports were already introducing terms like 'national', or 'English' in competition titles to foster interest, marking a more modern approach. In 1844, for example, the first Grand National Archery meeting was held at York. Sport thus helped identification with the nation, and the ties of history, culture and ancestry. In part it fostered a unified Britain, a modern industrial state with increasingly shared sporting culture. Chauvinistic pride in sporting achievements helped to hold Britain together, and became part of a conservative and somewhat John Bullish self-image. As a sense of sporting continuity developed, and the press articulated dominant views of key sporting events, a collective view emerged of Britain as being sportingly unique, a world leader. More debatably, it helped provide a safety valve for strong feelings and physical aggression. It has even been claimed that sport may have helped avoid political revolution.[51]

Englishness was difficult to define but useful as a vehicle to foster imperial loyalties. Much middle-class writing constructed a relatively limited set of simplistic beliefs about what it was to be English, emphasising imperial qualities of commitment and fighting spirit. Writers on cricket, the national game, stressed a ruralised, ritualised, pastoral and highly distinctive form of Anglo-British national character, deeply rooted in the past, which helped to ensure that middle-class amateur values were represented as the interests of Victorian society as a whole, foregrounding the values of fair play, tolerance and good behaviour.

Such writing often conflated the English and the British, obscuring geographical, linguistic and ethnic divisions. But the Irish, Scottish or Welsh saw themselves as distinct from England. Much of nationalist Ireland, outside the Protestant enclaves of Dublin and the north, saw 'foreign games' such as rugby or soccer as attacks on Irish culture. The Gaelic Athletic Association, founded in 1884, led strong cultural resistance.

In Scotland, history, material and cultural roots and dislike of the English meant sport was exploited to present an image of Scotland to the wider world. Being Scottish was bound up with myth, legend and caricature.[52] Sport, and beating England, were both important to the Scots. Scottish exiles' success abroad integrated Scotland into the empire and Britishness, but at home beating England was a way of showing national superiority. Sport reinforced a separate Scottish identity and became a way of asserting Scottishness. Sport united Scottish teams and their followers against England, overcoming Scotland's internal divisions and ensuring that for the duration of a match fans and players shared a brief pan-Scottish identity. In soccer the Scots established a long period of dominance against England between 1872 and 1890, losing only twice. Cutting their larger southern neighbour down to size compensated for lack of political independence. The year after the first 1872 international the Scottish FA was founded and the Scottish Cup instituted, a cup significantly costing more than twice its English equivalent.

Home internationals provided an acceptable outlet for nationalistic feelings. The first rugby match between the English RFU and the Scotland team on 27 March 1871 at Edinburgh attracted about four thousand spectators, as did the return match at the Oval in February 1872, far more than any contemporary non-internationals. From 1878 England and Scotland fought for the Calcutta Cup, a cup made from silver rupees donated by Calcutta-based old-Rugbeians in the early 1870s. In soccer there were unofficial matches between Scotland and England between 1870 and 1872 before the first formal international took place, symbolically on St Andrew's Day, in 1872. Scottish players taking the road south to play professionally in England were mistrusted heroes, a symbolic reminder of Scottish economic inferiority, even if feelings were mixed with some pride. Such 'disloyal' Scots who thus 'betrayed' Scotland were not picked for the national side until a run of defeats in the 1890s forced the selection of five English-based players in 1896.

It is difficult to describe succinctly the complexities of Scottish identity, with its regional and historical tensions, and social, cultural and regional diversity. Scotland was internally divided by class, religion, region and gender. Scotland could be Highland or Lowland, Protestant or Catholic, Gaelic or Anglicised, male or female, yet the thistle was symbolically incorporated into club titles both in Scotland and abroad. Middle-class Edinburgh, the legal and administrative capital, devoted itself more to rugby than soccer, and was Unionist, Presbyterian, and imperialist. The industrial working classes in Glasgow and Lanarkshire generally preferred soccer.

Some sports like the Highland Games or shinty (played with ball and curved stick, with taller goals than hockey) looked back to an imagined past. Exiles played shinty in England and the Lowlands through the nineteenth century, usually around Christmas or at Easter, as a way of preserving their Highland identity.

> Amongst the many schemes which the members of the Glasgow Highland Association have originated, the Shinty Club is certainly not the least successful. New members are flocking in every week ... Indeed, the sight of the Queen's Park on a Saturday afternoon would cheer the heart of the most desponding Celt: whilst the cheerful ring of the bagpipes would almost convince him that he was back at his native glens again.[53]

Shinty in the Highlands and west of Scotland became linked to a more radical view of Scottish land politics alongside a desire to raise Scottish national consciousness. Yet Scottish culture was simultaneously becoming anglicised. The Braemar Gathering's relocation to Balmoral in September 1859 helped popularise the monarchy and fostered a more loyalist Anglo-British view. By 1899 the Queen was chief of chiefs and patron, a further example of invented tradition. The sporting culture on Scottish sporting estates was often that of landowners from outside Scotland, and it is noteworthy that amateur cricket spread rapidly across Scotland from the 1850s.

From the post-famine years of the mid nineteenth century, many immigrant Catholic Irish entered Scotland, attracting anti-Irish feeling and increasing anti-Catholicism amongst dominant Protestant groups. By 1901 there were over 205,000 Irish-born people in Scotland. Many underplayed their identity, although a few migrants played some Gaelic sports, including hurling, in the later nineteenth century. Their chief form of sporting identity came with the founding of soccer sides. Tensions of inclusion and exclusion rose out of the religious and ethnic problems faced by Irish-Scots and Catholics. In Scotland, where the Protestant Kirk had deep roots, the arrival of large numbers of Irish immigrants in the years around 1850 caused problems. When football became popular, some Irish were unable to join established clubs, others were keen to form their own. Names like Hibernian, Harp, Shamrock, Emerald or Celtic became potent symbols of identity. When the first successful Catholic team, Hibernian, were founded in Edinburgh as part of St Patrick's Church Catholic Young Men's Society in 1875, it was written into the constitution that all players should be Catholic. Its links with Ireland, and its fostering of Irish Scottish identity, led to the Scottish FA originally refusing to grant it membership.

Glasgow Celtic Football and Athletic Club was founded in 1888 to raise money for the poor in the East End of Glasgow. Its early good organisation, apt location and football dominance soon attracted fervent support from Irish immigrants. By 1893 it had won the Scottish Cup, the Glasgow Cup and the Scottish League Championship. In part it aided Irish integration into wider Scottish society, since the crowds it attracted included many non-Catholic supporters. Irish nationalist politics were to an extent non-sectarian and the community had a dual social identity: holding on in part to cultural, Catholic and Irish identity, yet also proclaiming its Scottishness and wanting to play a part in Scottish life. Scottish Protestant attitudes to the presence, practices or attitudes of the Irish Catholics were commonly negative, so the Irish found opposition, and were convinced they were unfavourably treated by referees and the Scottish FA.

In Edinburgh John Hope, who had founded the 3rd Edinburgh Rifle Volunteers Football Club in 1874, was strongly anti-Catholic and a temperance advocate. Glasgow Rangers, formed even earlier, in 1872, slowly acquired a Protestant-Unionist identity, partly through the role of John Ure Primrose, an active Unionist and freemason. As it began to achieve success in the 1890s, it began to challenge 'the Irishmen', winning the Scottish and Glasgow cups in 1893/4, playing a key role in focusing Protestant identity and drawing in supporters from other teams, while gradually attracting a more anti-Catholic element.[54]

In Wales, since emerging sporting identity was linked to sporting success, Welsh national pride was always best associated with defeats of the English. When the successful Welsh pedestrian John Davies (1822–c. 1904) won a rematch against the Sheffield coal carrier Tom Maxwell in February 1845 at Lansdown, near Bath, the symbolism of returning home to Cardiff on the *Prince of Wales* steamer could have been lost to few. A ballad writer proudly boasted, in the Welsh language, that 'it is no use for an Englishman, Scot or Irishman, to attempt to challenge him'.[55] Late on in the century the Aberdare Workmen's Bicycle Club (founded 1894) quickly provided champions who dominated British and European cycling, becoming widely admired in Wales.[56]

South Wales was transformed by the later nineteenth century industrial expansion of the coalfields. Collieries sprang up everywhere. The population rose rapidly. New industrial South Wales was characterised by in-migration, coming largely from Cornwall and Devon, where rugby was the dominant local sport. Middle-class schools in South Wales tended to play rugby, partly so they could play against the nearest British rugby-playing public schools. Their old boys established rugby clubs; but, although all the leading sides were run by industrialists, solicitors, businessmen or shopkeepers, sides were soon socially mixed, with miners, old boys and those in professional occupations in the same sides. Rugby bound the new communities together more than the religious dominance of nonconformity, the Welsh language or the Liberal Party, and a newly-invigorated working class soon claimed the game, especially after the South Wales Cup was first contended for in 1877/78.

From the time when a Welsh representative side first played rugby against England at Blackheath in February 1881, the leaders of the Welsh RFU were anxious to avoid overt professionalism and continued to play internationals against the other nations. Winning helped achieve recognition within a British context, while beating the English reinforced their national identity. Internationals in Wales attracted large, socially mixed crowds, while Welsh internationalists, initially middle class, soon included skilled workers, miners, tin-platers, steelworkers and policemen. There was sufficient interest in the composition of the Welsh representative team to attract over 2100 entries to a competition to select it in 1889. By contrast, although soccer took off early in North Wales, where it was the main game, soccer in the more highly populated south was never of a sufficiently high standard seriously to challenge the English.

Rugby largely helped to invent, project and maintain the idea of a single Welsh national identity, in and outside Wales's blurred borders, by mobilising collective identities and passions. It helped to gloss over the different meanings that the people of Wales attached to their nationality. Scottish soccer fulfilled similar functions, but for Welsh males it was increasingly rugby which enabled them to assert their identity in the face of internal divisions and the political, social and cultural shadow of England.[57]

9

The Wider World

British colonialists, traders and tourists tried to make the whole world their sporting playground. In 1860 the *Illustrated Times* claimed that 'the Englishman outvies every nation in the alacrity with which he introduces his sports, wherever he may be located'.[1] Later the *Daily Telegraph* boasted that:

> wherever we go, whatever land we conquer, we found the great national instinct of playing games. Plant a dozen Englishmen anywhere – on an island, in a backwoods clearing or in the Indian hills – and in a wonderfully short time ... the level sward is turned into a cricket field in summer and a football arena in winter.[2]

Britain was the cradle of the sporting world, and its rise as the leading economic world power aided the export of its 'modern' sports. The development of widely-played ball games was a distinctive achievement of Victorian Britain, and the British then taught the world to play them.[3] In so doing they placed themselves at the forefront of developments in contemporary sport. Sport became imperial cultural baggage, and by 1901 organised sport had become central to the daily life of the English-speaking countries. It held the empire together, but also, paradoxically, helped emancipate the subject nations.[4]

For colonists, sports aided the creation of an imagined imperial community and reinforced a British frame of reference. After the English language, soccer, golf, tennis and the many other sports the British first organised and regulated have been amongst Britain's most successful, important and long-lasting cultural exports, playing a key role in the exchange of language and social institutions. The export of British sporting equipment and English thoroughbred stock aided the balance of payments. The cycle industry alone was worth two million pounds to the export trade by 1900. Many countries still show the sporting inheritance of the British colonial diaspora, while soccer has flourished worldwide long after many of the British industries which aided its spread have entered terminal decline.

Military and colonial administrators, and the human flood of missionaries, educators, traders, engineers, merchants and British colonists more generally, were vitally important elements of the varied judicial, educational, economic and religious strands of wider imperial domination, and this aided their role in the spread of sport. They not only played sports amongst themselves but shared an ethnocentric, self-confident certainty that the rest of the world should be converted to their beliefs and sporting institutions. In their baggage they sometimes carried the laws of the games they had played at school. They carried myths, too, that explained how the British had achieved dominance and imperial success because of personal qualities such as superior bravery, rationality, dedication and sporting skill. Cricket, soccer and rugby could be employed as moral tools which aided the propagation of British civilisation, culture and imperial power. Even some of the conquered were won over and came to admire them.

Military and naval officers were mobile sporting shock troops and, along with imperial administrators, key agents of British control. By 1897 there were about 72,000 regular British officers and men in India alone, and some 32,000 in other colonies. Social divisions between officers and other ranks created some reluctance to play against those of a different class or ethnic background, but the early scratch games demonstrated the British enthusiasm for sport to indigenous inhabitants on cantonments, parade grounds and parks. The average Victorian British army officer, often from a gentry and public school background, spent more time on sport than any other activity, including military duties. Officers had a firm belief in its value for developing character, manliness, toughness of heart and muscle and hence its 'invaluable' use in military training.[5] Amongst those adopting an upper-class life style keeping ponies and demonstrating riding skills were generally popular, although such sporting activities could be a financial burden and kept many in debt. Horseracing, cricket and hunting were followed everywhere. In India, first pig-sticking, seen as 'a sport peculiar to India and to the English who live there', and later polo became prestigious sports.[6]

Team games allowed a few officers to mix informally with other ranks during regimental cricket, football and rugby games, and eventually to meet elite members of Indian clubs, but most sports reinforced officers' social position and allowed them to emulate the aristocratic sporting life. Successful participation had positive social and professional importance for officers' careers, especially after the abolition of purchase in 1870. For other ranks, sport provided an aid to physical fitness, an antidote to boredom, a boost to morale, and a confirmation of unit solidarity through informal inter-regimental competitions. By 1888 the Durand Trophy was being competed for by army soccer teams in Simla, and about the same time inter-regimental boxing tournaments were also being used to promote martial spirit. The British Navy on overseas station provided opposition for civilian clubs in the outposts of empire. As the empire spread, newly-recruited administrators were increasingly expected to be sportsmen. Sports learnt on public school playing fields supposedly taught them the moral values and character necessary for effective imperial administration – courage, endurance, initiative, self-reliance, assertion and the inculcation of loyalty and obedience from others.

Christianity, along with education, was another travelling companion of imperialism. Voluntary societies such as the Church Missionary Society (founded in 1799) and the British and Foreign Bible Society (1804) spread throughout the world. As the sea of faith receded in Britain in the later nineteenth century, the twin gospels of Christianity and sport were increasingly spread abroad. The evangelical movement made particular efforts to recruit the 'hearties' and 'bloods' of the public schools and universities, purveying new forms of manly 'missionary' muscularity, combining respectable and reassuring masculinity with a seriousness of purpose and vocation. Anglican clergy were likely to be middle class and public school and Oxbridge educated, Scots missionaries were more likely to be working-class.[7] By the late nineteenth century pious British missionaries and teachers, convinced of their civilising role, had introduced the games ethic and athleticism, which was to play a major role in the mind-set of the empire's ruling elites. These imperial proselytisers preached with fervour, using bat, Bible, behavioural codes and rules of play to inculcate their moral messages. Imperialism had become an article of faith, athleticism the seductive means of its spread.

Athleticism's educational diffusion provided an imperial ideology for sport.[8] Across the empire formidable British sportsman-scholar head teachers transmitted their own educational values and aspirations while also pragmatically promoting loyalty, subservience and obedience, and raising funds for games facilities. They saw sporting codes and morality as bound up with character. Their self-righteous superiority allowed them to ride roughshod over local religious, social and sporting customs in order to introduce games as a significant element of Christian moral training.

Cecil Tyndale-Biscoe (1863–1949) became head of the Church Missionary School in Shrinagar in 1890. His attempts to make his Kashmir pupils play with a leather football in 1891 were initially naturally met with strong religious objections from his pupils. They attempted to avoid contact with, or burst, the ball. Despite his very forceful methods of persuasion, it took some ten years before his game was seen as respectable. The medical missionary Theodore Pennell (1867–1912) boasted in his autobiography, written in 1901, that on the Afghan frontier 'the simpler native games are gradually giving place to the superior attractions of cricket and football, and the tournaments between schools of the provinces are doing much ... to develop among these frontier people a fascination for those sports which have done so much to make Britain what she is'.[9] Many such missionaries provided role models of acceptable sporting behaviour by playing themselves. But different denominations showed differing attitudes. Catholic missions were less interested in sport, Anglican missions espoused cricket and rugby (but had difficulties in terms of physical contact thanks to class and racial attitudes).

British-style elite education spread rapidly. One result was that British interpretations of control, character and conduct were introduced both to the children of colonists and those of wealthier locals. Public school head teachers adopted and adapted a more secularised version of Christian manliness, some for benevolent and idealistic reasons, some with careful calculation, others from a determination to extend their cultural hegemony. As imperial traditions, images and narratives took stronger hold globally in the last decades of the century, more public schools, grammar schools and universities helped to spread them.

Team games were seen as powerful means of inculcating conformity, solidarity and cooperation. They were agents of formal as well as informal socialisation. By the late nineteenth century, many teachers used sport, and especially cricket, as a way of teaching such virtues as perseverance, stoicism and robustness. Cricket supposedly expressed British moral worth and promoted imperial sentiment and unity. It supported a belief that the empire itself was an British exercise in selfless morality. British imperial calculation, self-confidence and benevolence ensured that new Etons were established in India for the sons of chiefs and nobles, albeit on a smaller scale, with four leading 'Chiefs' Colleges' set up by the late 1870s. Facilities, curriculum, rituals and symbols were all based on the British model, with the games field seen as the main instrument of moral and physical fitness and character training. Sporting education was actively encouraged by their financial backers. To take just one example, the financial support given to St Stephen's College in Delhi by English public schools included funds for a cricket pavilion. In New Zealand, cricket's links with the elite school system ensured it was the initial 'national game' in New Zealand until the end of the century, when rugby took off. Even then, the first All Blacks team was largely drawn from elite boys' secondary schools where they had experienced the moral and physical rhetoric of athleticism, and had received encouragement, coaching and playing opportunities.[10]

Throughout the world the heads and assistant masters of schools were propagandists, proselytisers and publicists of sport. Canadian public schools reproduced the house system, prefects and team games, and gave strong support to the games ethic. A *Montreal Gazette* editorial of 1861 claimed that 'sport should constitute an essential part of education in every school and college in Canada, sports that would mould the characters as well as the forms of our youth'. An early advertisement for Canada's Bishop Ridley College fused purpose and provision in claiming that 'special attention is paid to moral training. The facilities for physical development are unrivalled in Canada. Cricket ground of eight acres, well equipped gymnasium, four tennis courts, boat house, bathing crib'.[11] The educationalists of other imperial powers followed suit. Adams College, in South Africa, for example, founded by USA missionaries, was quick to recognise the value of soccer and encouraged it for pupils from the 1870s.[12]

Elite education had its greatest imperialist success in transmitting cricket and the cult of athleticism. More generally, modern British sports found their most fertile homes in conurbations with a modern, urban, trans-national ethos. Soccer spread best not where Britain had had direct political and social control, but where Britain traded or could exploit its commercial, transport and technological expertise. The growth of football may have been linked in part to the spread of engineering techocrats, part of a wider spread of British technical know-how, which presented these new sports as the manifestation of technical progress, much sought after by the middle classes.[13] European examples abound.[14] Scottish workers employed in shipyards along the Swedish coast took football to Gothenburg, Malmo and Stockholm. In Russia, two English brothers, the Charnocks, founded a team at the Morozov cotton mills at Orekhova in 1887, and got a set of Blackburn Rover shirts imported as strip. In Spain football was introduced to Bilbao by English engineers in 1893.

The British were powerful in Argentina, where football took off early. They controlled rail transport, banking and meat production, the key sectors of Argentina's external economy. Scots like Alexander Hutton, known in Argentina as 'el Padre del Futbol Argentinos', or the Brown brothers of the pioneering Alumni team, played a major sporting role.[15] In Uruguay the Central Uruguay Railway Cricket Club, and its foot-balling counterpart Peñarol, were very successful in spreading British sport. When football finally arrived in Western Australia, in the early 1890s, it was first seen in informal matches organised by migrant British coal miners.[16]

Sport was also shaped largely but not exclusively by the popular press. By the beginning of Victoria's reign there was clearly a demand for English sporting newspapers and magazines overseas, and titles, style and much content were copied from British papers. In mid century USA, sports-minded Americans often read a great deal about British sport.[17] Rugby union rules were printed in the *Spirit of the Times* in 1869, and dominated until the 'Boston Rules' of what was to become American football gained a hold in the 1880s. In India, the *India Sporting Review* (circulating round Calcutta from the mid 1840s), and the *Indian Field* (from the 1850s) were good examples of specialist sporting papers with much British material, even though this could take three months or more to arrive. The setting up of the telegraph link to Britain increased the speed of transmission of British sporting results, most importantly the Derby. By the 1870s weekly papers for the expatriate British, such as the *Englishman*, contained sport regularly. By the end of the century, when steamers brought the British press to India in about three weeks, thanks to the Suez canal's construction, there was a well-established weekly sporting press, including the *India Planters' Gazette and Sporting News* and the *Indian Sportsman*.

Australians had specialist sporting papers too. London's *Bell's Life* was emulated by *Bell's Life in Sydney and Sporting Reviewer* in 1845. It was followed in the 1850s and 1860s by equivalents in Victoria, Tasmania and Adelaide, all mixing local with much fondly-reported sporting news from 'Old England'. Other parallels included the monthly New South Wales version of *Sporting Magazine* and the *Illustrated Sporting Gazette*. By the 1880s cheaper sporting papers such as Melbourne's *Sportsman* and Sydney's *Referee* were available, while major daily papers had significant coverage of sport.

Although much of the sport expatriates and people of British descent read about was English, often centred on London, the English role should not be overemphasised. Scots, for example, played a greater role than their numbers allowed, especially in education and medicine. Amongst the empire's migrants, administrators and soldiers, Scots equalled the English in numbers.[18] They were a significant element in colonisation. The sea provided not a barrier but a link with the Americas, and in both Canada and USA exiled Scots were especially keen to celebrate their separate traditions, as they also were in Australia.[19] Like the Welsh, they used their interest in sport to form voluntary associations to sustain their communities and their cultural heritage. The massive Scottish diaspora was a separate and consistently undervalued factor in the spread of sports.[20] In Canada, for example, Scottish innovations, encouragement and entrepreneurship had a substantial effect on the spread of sports such as curling and golf. Golf took off in Canada well before the USA. Lord Dufferin, the Canadian Governor General in the 1870s, made curling increasingly fashionable and respectable, opening it up to women as well as men. The 'traditional' Scottish sports of Caledonian societies across Canada, the United States and the Antipodes were soon opened up to non-Scots and broadened in their scope, giving the Scottish games champion Donald Dinnie opportunities of successful global competition in the 1880s.

If the Scots were important, the British middle classes were even more so in the spread of sports and games. It was they who composed the officer class, the administrators, educationalists and missionaries. Playing sports themselves, they provided global role models. Expatriates' clubs, for bourgeois businessmen, doctors, engineers, consular officials and clerks, often very mobile and well qualified, were amongst the first to play organised matches. The Genoa Cricket and Football Club founded in about 1894 was initially exclusively for British expatriates. Ex-public schoolboys became imperial sportsmen, carrying their enjoyments, physical vigour and competitive energy with them as they assumed new roles – civil service administrators, soldiers and statesmen. School magazines like the *Haileyburian* or *Eton Chronicle* regularly contained reports of the adventures and achievements of nostalgic old boys across the far-flung empire, often boasting of how they were to the fore in games and sports, of the teams they played for, and the sporting offices they held. A typical old boy dinner in Calcutta in 1880 was 'filled with reminiscences of days past interspersed with toasts to "Cricket" and "The Boats", and rounded off … with "the Boating Song"'.[21]

By the end of the century Britain was globalist in its world position, with a passion for imperial rule. Its colonial lands offered the promise of adventure, wealth and status, but the wide range of global British interests transcended any narrow terrritorial view of the world.[22] As Britain reached the apex of power and influence, its political structures, economic organisation, technological know-how, finished goods, ideas and customs were exported worldwide, and it was looked up to by many both inside and outside its empire. Alongside this went a far wider process of imperialistic cultural diffusion in which British sports and their association with manliness, the games ethic and athleticism variously became a cultural bond, a moral metaphor and potent symbol of British power. As British sports were introduced, and steadily extended and expanded their influence, they increasingly provided a key sense of continuity and belonging.

Wherever its colonists settled, sports settled too, although, as we shall see, the patterns soon became complex. Initially, in regions of long-term ever-increasingly white-dominated settlement, such as the United States and Canada, Australia's six colonies, South Africa's Cape and

Natal and New Zealand, British sports were paramount, although cricket had less success in Canada. There was the special case of India where some 100,000 British ruled a vast subcontinent, extorting heavy taxation. Here the princely states occupied a third of the land, and these favoured and flattered monarchs were socially acceptable. There were the various strings of islands and staging posts, taken in earlier centuries, and there were the later nineteenth-century dependent territories in Africa, South-East Asia and the Pacific taken in Britain's period of imperial expansion from the 1870s onwards.

Britain's influence spread still wider through its trading contacts, into South America and Asia, and even into mainland Europe, where the Anglomania of some groups, especially the aristocracy, provided a gentleman-sportsman model of diffusion. In Europe, for example, there were various equivalents to the Jockey Club as administrative and executive authorities of racing.[23] The French upper and middle classes turned increasingly to English sport, following defeat by Germany in 1870, as part of a national revival. Here, however, it caused ideological strife when opposed by more nationalistic gymnasts. For some Frenchmen the infatuation with physical activities seemed ridiculous. For Guy de Maupassant, 'the unfortunate people, the distinguishing mark of whose madness recalls the rattles of the demented buffoons of yore ... infected by a disease of English origin called lawn tennis' revealed 'the hidden bestiality in all human faces' as they raced around the court.[24]

As the British went out to serve the empire they took their sports with them. Sport was a major source of recreation and entertainment. Sport helped to relieve boredom. It integrated British new arrivals, through its recognisable rituals, its common language and convivialities, into the small British colonial social world. It provided a shared pattern of experience, a similarity of outlook, and a boost to morale. Major sporting events like race-meetings brought colonialists and settlers from far-flung areas round about together in mutual solidarity. Many expatriates saw themselves as part of Britain still. They recreated British institutions. Whites only sports clubs emulated familiar British manners and ideals.

Certainly by the 1890s the British press saw sport as a cementing agent, a shared passion, a bond of blood helping to hold the empire together. It reaffirmed ties with the colonies, while enhancing masculinity. The *St James Gazette* argued in 1892 that:

> In the Anglo-Saxon heart is implanted a love of sport and of the fierce delight in competition, and already we are accustomed to visits of Australian cricketers and Canadian football players, while no Colonist who is stopping for a while in England would think of missing the Derby or the Boat Race. Strong is the bond of nationality, strong are the ties of commerce, but stronger than either is the 'union of heart' which comes from devotion to the same forms of recreation.[25]

These colonies were not facsimiles of existing British societies. Colonists were a complex mix which included independent-minded, anti-elitist radicals, aspiring middle-class high achievers, upper-class young men with less money than status, and rural labourers. New social distinctions of one sort and another soon developed. In part sport played a key cohesive and integrating role, providing a common basis of interests and identification. British migrants often retained a strong emotional attachment to their motherland's sports. Australians, like colonists elsewhere, recognised this close relationship: 'in changing our sky we have not lost our old love for the manly sports of the mother country'.[26] Early settlers drew on gambling sports like cockfighting, prize fighting and wrestling, carried out more or less clandestinely away from public view, together with others, like horse racing and cricket, enjoying broad cultural support, even naming their racehorses after famous English ones. Later they adopted new British sports like rugby.

In areas of British settlement throughout the world cricket, aided by its early standardisation of rules, its aesthetics and style, became seen as quintessentially English. The game provided opportunities for emerging elites to establish themselves as arbiters and agents of sporting and imperial philosophy. It was used to emphasise social distinctions, as in the West Indies, where cricket clubs were often restricted in membership, and in return helped restrict social and political change. Gentlemanly conventions of cricket betokened a particular version of Englishness, helping to confirm to both players and spectators the continuance of their cultural identity. British success was seen as linked to sport and to British identity. Love of sport and games and sporting success were seen as running alongside and supporting class consciousness and individualism, while it paradoxically necessitated working in groups. Cricket was a way of transmitting ethical beliefs and standards about 'fair play', honesty and straightforwardness, and respect for authority.

British colonists often had a sense of imperial mission, and wanted to transmit, establish and maintain British culture and 'civilisation' in what they often perceived to be less civilised worlds. Sports became an instrument of imperial purpose, and of social and political stability, with cricket often the main vehicle. When Aborigines began playing cricket on Victorian sheep stations, they were formed into a team by supportive white farmers. Playing first against local clubs, and later touring England in 1868, was presented by whites as a step towards their becoming civilised and respectable.[27] Towards the end of the century elite Hindus and Muslims also began to take cricket up, despite religious concerns about the handling of leather, as did the black middle classes at the Cape.[28] In Calcutta there were six Bengali college sides in the mid 1880s, and other middle-class Bengali sides soon followed, making common cause in promoting cricket in hopes of defeating the English at their national game. Bombay's sectarian teams soon developed communal followings. In the West Indies, while the complex social stratification of Barbadian society was initially reflected in its cricket sides, the English 1895 tour had a broader impact, with men and boys said to be playing in every alley and field.[29]

By 1899 the *Indian Sportsman* could argue that 'sport is one of the greatest civilising forces of the age, for it enables enthusiastic adherents of different nations, climes and races to meet in keen though friendly rivalry [and is] a most powerful aid to amity'.[30] Sporting rules, coupled with a supposedly British way of playing, became an expression of moral worth, Christian belief and British sportmanship. British belief in the value of 'manly games' in providing the physical and moral strength to achieve such supremacy therefore gave strong support to Britain's pivotal role in the development of modern global sport.

British sporting social institutions, architecture and language spread widely. Racing had an early impact. It was recognised that 'a racing governor is bound to become popular' and most major courses had a Governor's Box.[31] Calcutta's course became 'The Epsom of the East'.[32] In Australia from 1861, the Melbourne Cup meeting was modelled on Royal Ascot, and the Victoria Racing Club was formed in 1864, by which time Melbourne was an industrial city.[33] Most major cities acquired

Rugby in Afghanistan, 1879.
The British took their sports with them as part of their imperial mission.

betting clubs. Tattersall's in Sydney was directly modelled on its English equivalent. British sports, from football to cycling or tennis, were taken up avidly.

The international popularity of British sports further aided the global diffusion of spoken and written English. The widespread global adoption of English sporting language provided a lasting linguistic link. Early European clubs, even with no apparent British connection, often adopted British nomenclature such as 'Racing Club' and 'Football Club'. For some, using the English language may have been meant to invoke supposed British qualities and associations. The term 'Sporting Club' was appropriated by leading soccer teams across the world. English became a commanding, unifying language for sport, in which sportsmen everywhere communicated. In Argentina, sporting Spanish was full of Englishisms. Soccer took up English terms enthusiastically, and the Argentine Football Association even began with English as its meeting language.[34] The Australian organising bodies often made their links explicit – the Southern British Football Association in New South Wales, the Anglo-Australian Football Association in Victoria. Within the empire in particular, this common sporting language helped to obscure underlying differences of culture, religion and economic interest. The American fascination for sport first began as a product of its colonial heritage and Anglo-American culture.

Sports also had an impact on the architecture of cities, displaying the sporting culture of empire. It rearranged town planning. Imperial cities offered astonishing material evidence of the importance of sport. Many, like New Delhi, were laid out to reflect the sporting ideologies of imperial planners. Racecourses could be found at the edge of almost all imperial cities, and no significant town was without one. They were prime settings for coming together to socialise, flirt, carry out business or bet, bringing together elite and demotic, separated by enclosure and stand, with the hierarchies made very clear.

Sport's impact on the colonies was complex. The emerging colonies were rarely homogeneous, and sports were often used as an instrument in the preservation and promotion of elite social hierarchies. They, and their codes of behaviour, were increasingly underpinned by beliefs in the moral imperatives of manliness and athleticism. Those British migrants who continued their interest in sport may have been more likely to still define themselves as British, and so, as in Australia, had less incentive to define identities that included the non-British.[35]

Sport offered a model of confrontation and dominance, with sporting British wins supposedly justifying British power and authority in a far broader context, and providing British colonists with a self-confidence engendered by British sporting skills which restricted their willingness and ability to take sports from other nations. When the American Spalding took a baseball exhibition world tour to Australia in 1888/9 he had a clear recognition that Australians were 'taught from infancy' to revere British sports and therefore looked 'somewhat askance at innovations in that line emanating from other shores'.[36] Examples of cross-cultural sporting exchange were rare. Polo was an exception. Developed in Tibet and Manipuri on the North-West frontier, it was initially dismissed in 1842 as 'hockey on horseback', but was copied by soldiers of the East India Company, became popular in the Calcutta region in the 1860s, and was being played in London as an organised sport by the 1870s by teams like the Hussars and Royal Horse Guards.[37] Only at the top levels of society could sporting Britishness literally afford to be inclusive. For many Indian army officers elite sports, however enjoyable, were also a strain on the purse and kept them in debt. Regiments often subscribed annually to racing cups costing at least 100 sovereigns, and the upkeep of polo teams was still more expensive. It cost about £102 in England for an individual to set up and £58 a season afterwards.[38] Yet by 1898, with imperial presumption, the *Indian Sportsman* saw polo overtaking racing and becoming 'as much the national game of India as cricket is in England'.[39] Polo allowed the wealthy of whatever ethnic or social background to enjoy conspicuous competition, and some ethnically mixed teams emerged.[40] It was soon touted as 'a real solvent of race distinctions ... in giving our native fellow-subjects our love for our manly outdoor relations, we insensibly draw closer to them and they to us'.[41] Likewise, tiger hunting, earlier a display of power by Mughal emperors, was taken up as an opportunity for lavish entertainment by viceroys and governors, maharajas and other local rulers.

Sporting tours by the British, or colonial tours of Britain, provided both opportunities for competition and for mutual self-congratulation. Playing British games against the British showed loyalty to traditions. English professional cricketers toured Canada and America in 1859 and the first unofficial team of All-England players to tour Australia (in 1861–62) attracted daily attendances as high as 15,000, creating a large profit for Spiers and Pond, the caterers who sponsored it. The team was feted. As one of the All-England players pointed out in a letter home, 'if the Queen had come out she could not have been treated better than we have been', with a free run of the theatres, free passes on the railways and dinner with the governor.[42] English sides helped raise local standards of play. Any colonial sporting successes conferred status, showed their stock was not degenerating and produced great celebrations.

As colonies forged their own identities there were increasing tensions. The 1861 English cricket tour provided a context in which Australians began to reflect on which parts of their British heritage they really valued, and new notions of identity, federation and nationhood. Initially colonists had feared their culture was inferior, and portrayed English standards of play, ideals and respectability as much higher, putting English sport on an often undeserved pedestal. But as they themselves increasingly achieved sporting success, older feelings of deference and inferiority began to break down. Sport became a surrogate for conflict. Beating the British became a testing mark of manhood. Indeed, the term 'test match' was an Australian invention. Crowds were desperate to see Australian sides triumphant, the English defeated. English touring sides did not always consider it entirely necessary to behave well towards colonials and could feel it was an inversion of the natural order if they did not win. Much of the English press talked disparagingly of the Australian teams as 'the Colonials'. Mutual respect turned to colonial resentment. Once the Australian teams overcame their initial feelings of inferiority, their convincing victories over the English in the 1890s spilled over into a confidence or even arrogance that added salt to the English wounds.[43] The first English rugby tour of Australia and New Zealand, in 1888, was organised by two cricketing entrepreneurs to cash in on the colonists' keenness to defeat the mother country.

Over time emotional ties with Britain loosened. Sporting competitors travelled to Britain more regularly, their progress avidly followed and successes widely feted overseas. There were early contacts with pedestrians from Europe, the USA and beyond, and at least eighteen overseas cricket teams had visited England by 1900. Sporting achievements were a source of power operating on collective consciousness, aiding collective identity, pride and status.[44] In the USA, Harvard and Yale measured themselves both against each other and against Oxford and Cambridge rowers, as did professional rowers like James Hamill in the 1860s, seeing it as 'the trial of the peculiar American physique against the long held supremacy of the English muscular endurance'.[45] The Canadian Ned Hanlan, who dominated professional rowing in the late 1870s, provided for Canadians a symbol that transcended their provincial boundaries. He gave them a sense of being Canadian.[46] Some competitors even stayed. Immigrants found new opportunities, if not for them for their offspring. There were black boxers like Molyneux, the 'Sable Prince', whose 'high character' and scientific boxing ranked him high in the 1830s and early 1840s.[47] There were occasional black footballers, such as Andrew Watson, a top amateur Guyanan player with Queens Park and Scotland in the 1880s, and the talented sprinter, cyclist and goalkeeper Arthur Wharton, from Ghana, who came to study and stayed to play for Darlington, Preston North End and Rotherham Town in the 1880s.[48]

The long distances travelled and the time taken by champion sportsmen built up hope, expectation and interest. They brought Britain and the wider world together in a novel proximity. But, paradoxically, while sports were used by the British to inculcate their own values, sports which boosted colonial self-confidence became a first step on the road to decolonisation. The Australian cricket team long predated the federation of Australian colonies in 1901, helping people move away from defining themselves as from New South Wales or Victoria and towards seeing themselves as Australians. Test matches were a yardstick of Australian strength and fitness for home rule. Even in 1898, the *Bulletin* claimed that the 'ruthless rout' of the English had done 'more to enhance the cause of Australian nationality than could ever have been achieved by miles of erudite essays and impassioned appeal'.[49] Not all agreed. The editor of *Australian Town and Country Journal* felt in 1899 that 'between the excitement of international cricket and international football at the present time, the rising generation of Australians have little energy left to devote even to pressing questions of their national politics' such as federation.[50] Cricket encounters between Australia and New Zealand soon helped to define a separate Australasian world. Impressionistic cultural critics were ambiguous about its effects. In Australia, there were claims that 'Australia was the most sporting nation in the world', with an 'inordinate fondness' for sport at the expense of intellectual pursuits.[51]

As time passed, different attitudes to competition, meritocracy and professionalism within the colonies meant that their sports evolved. They developed characters and identities of their own. When the elite New York Cricket Club played Toronto for $500 in 1840 it still saw itself as amateur. But there was increased antipathy towards British amateurism in the USA. By 1882, when their Hillsdale rowing team was excluded from competitions in London by the Amateur Association, there was much vitriol and abuse from American papers. Their *Turf, Field and Farm* described the Association as one where snobbery ruled, with the English rowing amateur 'a la-de-da or a cad who has never soiled his hands with manual labour'.[52]

Australia was also far less elitist – there was even a Miners' Race Club at Ballarat. Australian cricket, with far less rigid class prejudice or elitist principles, did not follow the rigid formal social segregation of 'gentlemen' and 'players', with their different roles, dressing rooms and titles. Australians found English snobberies irritating. By the 1890s English touring sides, especially amateur 'gentlemen', were being barracked by hostile sections of the crowd on most Australian grounds. And lucre was never filthy in Australia. Colonial 'amateur' Australian touring sides happily received money for touring as the *Sporting Chronicle*, for example, pointed out:

> We wine and dine [the colonists], we dub him 'Esq.' on some of the cricket cards, we treat him to the prefix of 'Mr' in some of our leading newspapers, we elevate him above the pronounced professional, yet the Australian cricketers are on a trip in quest of boodle.[53]

Members of the touring New Zealand Native team in 1888 found London less welcoming than the north of England and south Wales, and found English class notions distasteful. They saw England as 'the rich man's paradise and the poor man's Hades'.[54] By the 1890s there was increased resentment of the way English exclusiveness kept out colonial competition at events like Henley Regatta or the Amateur Athletics Championships.[55]

Equally, geography, climate, and demographic conditions meant sports had to be modified. Governors in Australia, for example, attended hunt clubs, such as the Melbourne Hounds or Adelaide Hunt, but without foxes substitutes such as the kangaroo had to be found. In some colonies various forms of totalisator replaced bookmakers at race meetings. In India racehorses began to be imported from Australia.

In part sport helped to maintain imperial control. The British were convinced that sports like cricket or rugby possessed conservative values and behavioural norms which helped to bind the colonies to Britain, forming an obstacle to nationalism, and helping to impose the economic and political status quo. But sporting relationships between Britain and the empire possessed an essential ambivalence, partly congruent with the imperial programme, but also disruptive and subversive of it. Colonial subjects often wanted to join in and play even in the face of class or ethnic prejudice. Sports were used as agents of social control, but could be turned against the controllers. Sports both divided and united, allied and fractured, and notions of culture, power and oppression were inter-related. The British found American and Australian commercialism, brashness and excessive keenness to win a challenge to gentlemanly standards. Countries elsewhere resented British sports as symbolising British power and pretensions. Contradictions abounded. Racial hierarchies were sometimes breached rather than re-emphasised. Counter-currents involving cultural exchange, resistance and competition were regularly revealed.

Disentangling the various linkages is complex. In Barbados, for example, two years after the Barbadians won a match against the first English touring side, a local male of Afro-Caribbean descent, 'Britannia Bill', turned up to watch the various cricket matches played by a following touring team. He carried a Union Jack, and spent his time praising the side's skills, character, country and monarch. 'Old England forever' was his constant cry. This was interpreted as 'showing an acceptance of cricket and its English cultural provenance'.[56] The touring side attracted good crowds, and cricket was a popular game. Many colonists in Barbados had great loyalty to the empire, while success against the 'mother country' touring side was a measure of the colony's development and themselves. Some of the colonised may have shared such feelings. Yet the Barbadian side was largely composed of members of the colonial elite, and so it is also possible that Britannia Bill's support for the visitors was a symbolic form of resistance to local white dominance.

While British sport mainly played a positive role abroad, its imperial power and dominance created mixed and negative effects. For almost two hundred years Britain dominated the world. During the later nineteenth century it dominated global sport. Its naval supremacy, its industrial might and commercial power enabled Britain to become the centre of a vast empire, the largest yet known.[57] Imperialism was sustained by the ideology of white supremacy, and British success at sport was seen as a vindication of such views. Yet while the white colonies and former colonies were seen as an extension of Britain, the formal empire was often seen back in Britain as conquered territory. Sometimes this was made explicit, as in the *Illustrated Times* of 1860. It stressed that 'the Englishman outvies every nation in the alacrity with which he introduces his sports, wherever he may be located', but explained that 'conquered nations as a matter of course carry with them into subjugated provinces the sports and pastimes which characterise them as a nation', while over time the conquered race's 'tastes and sympathies also become impregnated with the habits and pleasures of the usurpers'.[58]

Indigenous races were largely excluded from sport by racial discrimination and their lack of money. When the future Aboriginal touring team first played the Melbourne Cricket Club in December 1866 they were condescendingly described as 'the savage race' who 'took their beating with the best grace imaginable', although two 'would we think be good enough for a Melbourne first eleven'.[59] Aborigines were also excluded from the rugby codes and Australian rules football. In Barbados, less wealthy blacks were conventionally excluded from playing cricket altogether and blacks had no chance of joining the leading clubs. Yet the majority of spectators at inter-club matches were black, and gave vociferous support to their representatives. By contrast the New Zealand Maoris were involved in rugby sides at local and national level, partly perhaps because of their warrior reputation.

Overt discrimination was less marked for the wealthiest, since the British attempted to create collaborating elites by converting them to the British way of life. In India sport played a leading role, increasingly inducting ethnic groups into its rituals under imperial patronage. There was some fellow-feeling and much collusion between the British elites and Indian rulers. When the new Calcutta race stand was built in 1859, there were sixty-five British and eleven sheiks, rajahs and other Indian subscribers.[60] Rich parents of Indian pupils wanted their sons, in particular, to acquire those materialistic markers of modernity, English language and education, and the occupations, status and salary that they might bring. It is less likely that they valued the sports their children learned. The Indian public schools taught cricket, yet what happened when the boys left? The Parsee touring side which visited Britain in 1886 claimed that they were 'among the most loyal subjects of the Queen', and had come to England to 'pay homage to the centre and home of a noble game' and 'learn some useful lessons in its play'.[61] They were not highly rated in India, where their reception was perceived as being as 'one of the curiosities of cricket'. Indians were keener for 'an invasion' of Britain by a cricket team drawn from a wider Indian constituency, but this proved difficult.[62] In soccer, despite or because of explicit colonial slurs about supposed Bengali 'femininity', Bengalis took up the sport with enthusiasm from the late nineteenth century. But the blatant racism of 'Greater Britain' created social, racial and cultural barriers that ensured indigenous peoples participated at a disadvantage.

There were few overt protests against the destruction of indigenous games, except perhaps in late nineteenth-century Ireland. The work of the Gaelic Athletic Association revived Gaelic sports, such as hurling and Irish football, to preserve and protect what they perceived as an Irish identity dependent on a rural, Catholic and anti-British ideal. Despite their policy of social openness to artisans, police, soldiers and sailors were soon barred from participation. The association pursued an exclusionist, rejectionist and separatist policy after 1888.[63] With rare exceptions, cricket in Ireland symbolised the Anglo-Irish ascendancy and was avoided by rampant nationalists, soccer was dismissed as 'the garrison game', since Ascendancy military officers had an appetite for British sports, and rugby, a more successful import, was taken up largely by the Protestant professional and business middle classes in Dublin, Cork and Belfast. In India, although indigenous sports like kabaddi or wrestling continued, their formalisation and institutionalisation date only from the twentieth century.[64] Tacit resistance to British imperialism in the wider world ensured that cricket clubs were almost all situated either within the empire or were for expatriates.

Even in the colonies there was widespread and increasing resistance to taking up British games on British terms. Soccer has been called England's 'most durable export'.[65] But it did best where Britons simply worked and traded, and worst in the colonies or English-speaking and settled countries, notably the USA, Canada, white South Africa, Australia and New Zealand.[66] In Australia Victorian (later Australian) rules football, codified as early as 1858–59 and symbolising resistance to British pressures, soon dominated both rugby and soccer.[67] The USA was still more resistant to cultural imperialism. While cricket was still an important middle-class summer game in the 1850s, baseball was taking over by the 1880s, largely because cricket was seen as the 'English game', played by immigrant groups still asserting their non-American identity, while in American sporting culture home-grown American sports were higher regarded than overseas impositions.[68] Likewise, American football soon became the winter game.

Just as Victorians dominated the empire, they also wanted to dominate the animal world. Colonial officials, military men and others used hunting as a key means of recreation. This had a major impact on environment.[69] The term 'sport' here meant the shooting of animal prey, often itself seen as noble, located within ever more striking geographical locations from Scotland to Africa and the Arctic. Sporting memoirs provided a stimulus to sporting tourism, and masculine accounts of what was labelled 'real sport', often experienced in the colonies and wild places of the world, continued to have a mythic appeal. Reliable steam transport and increased wealth allowed 'big shots' to travel more widely and escape 'civilisation', pursuing and killing dangerous quarry, and deepening their knowledge of natural history as they wiped it out of existence in acts of gratuitous and massive slaughter.[70] When the Prince of Wales visited India in late 1875, hunting played a key role in his activities. He even participated in the exciting but highly dangerous sport of pig-sticking in Oudh, 'riding over perfectly awful ground' at 'a perfectly awful pace' to claim a first spear.[71] The slaughter of animals and birds across the world was celebrated in those triumphs of the taxidermists' art, the stuffed and mounted trophies and skins, that adorned homes in Britain and overseas. Energetic British big-game hunters in search of sporting adventure increasingly travelled the world for new lands to hunt, pioneering high-risk challenges of physical and mental endurance, and callously clearing out game across wide swathes of territory, causing huge social and economic damage to the lives of indigenous races.

A mass of sporting literature showed their search for new experiences in America, Asia and Africa. Mid-century tourist guides increasingly directed the tourists to game areas, ensuring that soon whole swathes of the imperial dominions were cleared of what had always been relatively rare noble game. Sport was increasingly bound by gentlemanly rules, linking conservation to class and having racial overtones. Imperial guidebooks show how the environment was rearranged to suit hunting tastes. Local administrators imposed game laws in which access was mapped, limited and constrained to ensure hunting could continue for the elite while the indigenous inhabitants were excluded. Subsistence farmers were no longer supposed to kill game. Prosecutions, however, were rare and poaching was rife. By 1901 there was a growing awareness of preservation issues amongst wiser whites.[72]

The whole natural world was unbalanced. Some formerly numerous and widely distributed species, such as the South African quagga or the American bison, were soon in process of being wiped out. Springbok herds in Africa, formerly numbering hundreds of millions, were soon reduced. Lions, tigers and other noble prey were hunted towards extinction, rabbits and camels were introduced to Australia, red deer were exported. Anglers travelled and anglers' societies were formed everywhere. Brown trout were sent to Kashmir and New Zealand to stock fishing waters.

Back in Britain, press reporting of sport helped the dissemination of the imperial ideal, and helped create an imagined imperial community, one where an amateur athletic ethos was valued and Britons enjoyed a class, racial, and national superiority. Sport, like the theatre, juvenile literature, education and the iconography of popular art, became infused with the images of imperialism.[73] Ordinary people came to know and care about the activities of sportsmen throughout the far-flung globe. Sport provided an umbilical bond linking Britain and its empire. The sporting press began using correspondents' reports on colonial sporting events from early in the reign. By 1885 the *Sportsman* could claim in its advertising that 'sport in America, India and Australia [is]descanted upon by specially accredited representatives in those countries'. It reported all major racing in France, and regularly published full returns of the principal continental races in the *Sportsman's Steeplechase and Continental Racing Guide* at sixpence. *Ruff's Guide* provided similar data in its *Lunar Month Annual Summary*. In the same decade the leading cricket magazine, *Cricket*, gave score cards of matches played in Australia, India, the West Indies, South Africa and Ceylon, and mentioned other games elsewhere. British tours were increasingly seen by traditionalists as a cornerstone of empire. Top players in touring Australian cricket sides, like Fred Spofforth, the 'Demon', were reclaimed as really British, and as evidence that British culture could flourish even in remote and less civilised countries.

By 1901 international events could be watched as well as read about. Seized on by advertisers, they provided an animated vehicle for imperial propaganda. Nestle and Lever found an advertising outlet in their short film of the 1897 Sidney test match, with its English victory, after which the progress of cricket tours abroad was regularly recorded on film. The one and a half hour film of the Corbett-Fitzsimmons fight at Carson City, Nevada, deliberately staged with film in mind, generated huge interest. When it opened at the Royal Aquarium Theatre, Westminster, the theatre was besieged by eager crowds. According to one viewer, 'every line of the competitors' faces was clearly traceable, and Corbett's awful look of despairing agony at his defeat was marvellously reproduced'.[74] Sporting films became part of the wider appetite for novelty.

Films largely reinforced images of British success. Audiences basked in imperial glory, and consolidated their already well-established sense of British physical, moral and cultural superiority. The British had pioneered the development of sport, but such attitudes insulated them from changes which might have raised standards. Similar condescension pervaded much British writing, reflecting assumptions of white moral and physical and athletic superiority. Fancy dress charity games often used subordinate 'native' race characters, while after Rorke's Drift in 1879 well-known Sheffield footballers played a series of benefit matches for soldiers' dependants in Zulu costume, dressed in black, with beads, feathers and hair tufts, and carrying assegais, attracting big crowds.

Racist beliefs that foreigners were unethical and lazy, constitutionally lacking patience and resolution, were commonplace, especially from the 1870s, and were applied to sports too. One correspondent wrote to *Cricket*, 'I have instituted your favourite old game, cricket, among the natives, but they are such a lazy race that half-an-hour of it completely does them up'.[75] Many foreign and especially non-white players were belittled by scornful tales about their skills, appearance and knowledge. A Lancashire report of the 1868 Aboriginal tour described it as a 'burlesque upon cricket' while during the Canadian tour of 1880 a journalist pleaded, 'I only hope we shall not be bored with another Canadian team ... for a long time to come'.[76] The leading figures amongst the MCC showed little interest in imperial cricket until the 1890s, when imperialists like Lords Harris and Hawke began arguing for cricket's civilising mission in uniting classes and colonies and uplifting native races.[77] Even though visiting cricket touring sides sometimes claimed victories, only the Australians really commanded attention. Other sides were denigrated as merely on a par with county cricket. Likewise, the British Isles rugby tour of South Africa in 1891 was more of a social event for a predominantly southern English and Edinburgh amateur elite.

To the British, global take up of their sports was naively perceived as evidence that the ruled acquiesced in imperial rule, recognised supposed British superiority and tried to emulate it. The empire was seen in terms of subordination, and its sporting subjugation formed part of that view. Such feelings aided the creation in British self-perception of a new type of patriotism, stressing the cult of sporting celebrity alongside crude notions of sporting social Darwinism, increasingly hostile to foreign sportsmen. The British vision was predominately of an imperial brotherhood of white 'Anglo-Saxon' sportsmen in America or elsewhere, a 'united freemasonry of true friends', part of the wider spread of shared sporting values, a form of globalised campfire camaraderie and fraternal bonding.[78]

As British sports spread, professional British journeymen sportsmen migrated overseas in search of new opportunities and better financial rewards. In horseracing there was significant international traffic in horses and men. British bloodstock, especially the leading stallions, was in demand throughout the world. Jockeys, trainers and grooms found expatriate employment from early in the nineteenth century. In France, the training centre of Chantilly had many resident British trainers and jockeys. In the 1860s, a time when there were over fifty training stables in France, Belgium and Baden, British jockeys still dominated racing all over continental Europe.[79] British jockeys and trainers worked in India from the 1840s, many staying there for long periods. Some at least made sufficient to retire back to England relatively well off. There were some 'native' jockeys, but it was only really towards the end of the century that they began moving successfully into training, often with local maharajas.[80]

Pugilists and pedestrians found rich pickings abroad from the 1840s. North-western pedestrians John Barlow, Thomas Greenhalgh and Ambrose Jackson sailed from Liverpool to compete in the USA in 1844, and their successes brought further invitations for runners such as William Howitt. He toured the USA in 1844–45 and again in 1849–51. Professional British cricket sides first toured North America in 1859, with players each clearing £90 on top of their expenses. They cleared £150 in Australia in 1861–62. Amateur cricket tours, such as the 1882–83 tour of Australia, were rare until the 1890s, a decade which also saw a soccer tour of South Africa by the 'amateur' Corinthians, a sure-fire way of getting a cheap holiday with convivial hospitality.

By then British cricket professionals were finding more regular work abroad. The Parsee touring side of 1886 engaged the services of Robert Henderson of Surrey Cricket Club as coach, while the Maharaja of Patiala employed various English county professionals to coach ethnically mixed sides in the later 1890s.[81] The young Leicestershire bowler Arthur Woodcock, initially engaged as a professional at Mitcham, soon obtained work at Haverford College in Philadelphia (thanks to Alcock, the Surrey secretary), coaching what he described as the 'more gentlemanly element of the community' in cricket between 1887 and 1889.[82]

While the British took their sporting expertise abroad, they had chauvinistic attitudes to most foreign sports, especially those developed in spheres of British influence. Beyond elite sports like polo, cultural exchanges of sport proved difficult. There were a few successes. In Canada tobogganing and ice skating, ice hockey and lacrosse were far better developed; the Canadian touring lacrosse teams who played exhibition matches in Britain in the 1870s and 1880s even put down roots for the sport in London, Manchester and Cheshire. A German gymnastic society was founded in London in 1861. By contrast, baseball's failure to take popular hold in Britain, Canada or Australia shows the then relative weakness of United States global influence. An attempt in 1874 to get baseball adopted in Britain by bringing over the Boston Red Stockings and Philadelphia Athletics to play a series of baseball and cricket matches in London and the provinces was a financial failure, with poor crowds, even though it had been sanctioned by the MCC. The Americans' different approach to principles of sportsmanship and fair play in baseball meant that national newspapers gave very little cover-age and perhaps deterred the public from attending. There may also have been some concern that it would threaten cricket's dominance.

As American economic power grew British sports writers increasingly denigrated baseball as 'rounders made wearisome'. A further American baseball tour of Britain in 1889 received derogatory comments, with one Lancashire paper claiming that baseball was 'as much out of place in England as a nursery frolic in the house of Commons', even though it attracted over seven thousand spectators in London.[83] For a short while baseball had some minor success. A few British professional soccer clubs created a professional National Baseball League to aid summer revenue, while an amateur Baseball Association of Great Britain and Ireland was formed in 1890, and a National Baseball Association in 1892. The base-ball game was strongest in the midlands, as Derby County's Baseball Ground (1894–1997) might remind some readers, and in the north east, where by 1893 a Cleveland and South Durham Baseball Association had eight clubs competing.[84] In 1894 the London Baseball Association was formed with American expatriates playing a key role. The temporary glamour of the American game forced the various British rounders teams of South Wales, Scotland and Lancashire to form associations, and refurbish their game, sometimes, as in the case of Liverpool Rounders Association in 1892, changing the name of their sport to base-ball. But they seem not to have switched codes. When the Minneapolis club visited in 1895, as part of a European tour, there were still only 'upwards of forty clubs' playing baseball.[85] It was, too clearly, the Americans' national game.

Baseball, of course, was not cricket, the sport in which Britain saw itself as pre-eminent. Here, the British believed, colonial sides could be safely welcomed, entertained and usually defeated. Such visits were interpreted as welcome evidence of colonial loyalty to Britain, their assimilation of British values and sportsmanship, and a growing solidity of the British empire. Cricket was probably the first team ball game at which prestigious white teams played against non-white players in Britain. This could be presented as living proof of the success of British civilisation and support for British rule. When Australian Aboriginal cricketers toured England in 1868, there was relatively little sign of culture shock, that profound disorientation of meeting without adequate preparation an alien culture, amongst the British.[86] Supposed evidence of loyalisation amongst the colonised usually resulted in very positive reception in England. Amongst Indians, the Parsees of Bombay were the first to take up the game, and Parsee teams toured England in 1886, taking advantage of the Indian and Colonial Exhibition, and again in 1888. The Parsees' adoption of cricket supposedly indicated that they were 'the most intelligent as well as the most loyal of the races scattered about our Indian possessions', and would doubtless strengthen 'the ties between the governors and the governed'.[87]

Here cricket was being used to assimilate the wealthy in the 'coloured' empire into the wider British social order. In the 1890s the elite Indian, Ranjitsinhji, having learned to play cricket at Rajkumar College in India, played and studied at Cambridge University, before playing for Sussex and England, becoming the leading English amateur batsman. His princely position let him mix socially with the British elite. An elegant player, who scored runs with style and apparent ease, he was hugely popular, attracting the same sort of mass following as had W. G. Grace, with bats, matchboxes, hair restorers and chairs named after him. Such popularity was due to a mixture of his status, his British-style elite education at school and university, his extraordinary skills, and his protestations of imperial loyalty. Paradoxically his non-English batting and appearance helped. It made him appear unique. This was certainly the view of R. H. Lyttelton, who argued that 'the English public ... would have admired Ranjitsinhji as a white batsman, but they worship him because he is black'.[88]

Even in cricket, therefore, the world was proving an apt pupil. Initially British defeats such as *America*'s victory over the best British yachts in 1851 at Cowes for the Royal Yacht Squadron Cup, were relatively rare, although the America's Cup was to take half a century to regain. But as more foreign challengers became successful, elements of self-doubt increasingly competed with sporting self-assurance. French horses first entered British races to derision. One British writer admitted that weight allowances were given to 'enhance our own pride and gratification by showing how superior we were'.[89] These soon had to be withdrawn, and Gladiateur's 1865 Epsom Derby win provided a further shock. When the Australians won a test match in England in August 1882, the *Sporting Life* wrote a mock obituary for English cricket. It had 'died at the Oval ... deeply lamented by a large circle of sorrowing friends and acquaintances'. It suggested the later name for the 'Ashes' trophy created by a group of Melbourne ladies when it announced that 'the Body will be cremated and the ashes taken to Australia'.[90] Cricket was the game of an imperial elite, played by British men, yet the colonials had won. Increased sporting defeats threatened imperial order. They struck at the heart of the imperial spirit, were seen as symptomatic of national ill-health and decline, and reinforced growing beliefs about British physical degeneration. The Australians' aim was 'to play cricket and win matches', and they went into strict training to do so. To compensate, or to save face, British administrators stressed that they 'played the game' for enjoyment, for its own sake. They claimed higher ethical standards and more careful rule-making and observance. Only foreigners played to win, so they could be looked down upon once again. Only foreigners allowed tradesmen, workers and professionals to compete with gentlemen. Britain sportsmen began to retreat from some forms of involvement, and stress more 'amateur' beliefs. In terms of the product cycle, Britain had been an sporting innovator, but it was being overtaken. It turned increasingly to xenophobic isolation, fearing for the future, unwilling to compete outside an imperial context or against more professional opposition. In soccer, a latecomer to widespread popularity, British national teams only played each other. Britain had earlier showed innovative sporting leadership and organisation. Now, unlike the French, the British showed little enthusiasm for playing a leading role in the emerging international federations and organisations, whether in cycling, rowing, football or the Olympic movement.

As the 'Scramble for Africa' reminds us, the Victorian age saw industrialising nations like Britain, Germany, France and the USA becoming cultural imperialists. Their migrants took their sports with them to countries experiencing modernisation and industrial expansion. Sports that then became culturally dominant have largely survived to this day, unless nationalism created a very distinct identity which forced them out. American baseball had some limited success in its sphere of influence. Germans had a flourishing sporting subculture in the USA and South America, often based on Turnverein gymnastic societies and associations. But British sports spread across the world.

Notes

Notes to Preface

1. *Household Words*, 6 (1852), pp. 133–39.
2. Harold Perkin, 'Teaching the Nations How to Play: Sport and Society in the British Empire and Commonwealth', *International Journal of the History of Sport*, 6 (1989), p. 145.
3. Useful introductions to theoretical perspectives on sport are provided in Steven G. Jones, *Sport, Politics and the Working Class* (Manchester: Manchester University Press, 1988), pp. 3–12; Richard Holt, *Sport and the British* (Oxford: Clarendon Press, 1989), pp. 357–67.

Notes to Chapter 1: The Rise of Sport

1. Adrian Harvey, *The Beginnings of a Commercial Sporting Culture in Britain, 1793–1850* (London: Ashgate, 2004) provides a useful overview. For an earlier approach, emphasising attacks on popular sport, and change rather than continuity, see Robert Malcolmson, *Popular Recreations in English Society, 1700–1850* (Cambridge: Cambridge University Press, 1973).
2. See the recent historiographical analysis by Emma Griffin, 'Popular Culture in Industrialising England', *Historical Journal*, 45 (2002), pp. 619–35.
3. See for example, Adrian Harvey, 'Football's Missing Link: The Real Story of the Evolution of Modern Football', in J. A. Mangan, ed., *Sport in Europe: Politics, Class, Gender* (London: Frank Cass, 1999), pp. 92–116; John Goulstone, *Football's Secret History* (Upminster: 3–2 Books, 2001).
4. See Neil Tranter, *Sport, Economy and Society in Britain, 1750–1914* (Cambridge, Cambridge University Press, 1998), pp. 3–12.
5. *Bell's Life*, 26 January 1840.
6. *Bell's Life*, 7 June 1840.
7. *Illustrated Sporting and Dramatic News*, 31 March 1866.
8. See Pamela Horn, *Pleasures and Pastimes in Victorian Britain* (Stroud: Sutton Publishing, 1999), p. 77.

9. Quoted in Derek Birley, *A Social History of English Cricket* (London: Aurum Press, 1999), p. 90.

10. A good discussion of the problematic usage of the phrase 'sporting revolution' is provided in Tranter, *Sport, Economy and Society*, chapter 3. See also Mike Huggins, 'A Tranquil Transformation: Middle-Class Racing "Revolutionaries" in Nineteenth Century England', in J. A. Mangan (ed.), *Reformers, Sport, Modernizers: Middle-Class Revolutionaries* (London: Frank Cass, 2002), pp. 35–57.

11. Daryl Adair and Wray Vamplew, *Sport in Australian Society* (Oxford: Oxford University Press, 1997), p. ix; Tranter, *Sport, Economy and Society*, p. 13.

12. *Land and Water*, 17 March 1866.

13. J. Lowerson and J. Myerscough, *Time to Spare in Victorian England* (Hassocks: Harvester Press, 1977), p. 119.

14. *Bell's Life*, 5 April 1840.

15. H. Shimmin, 'The Aintree Meeting', in J. K. Walton and Alan Wilcox, *Low Life and Moral Improvement in Mid-Victorian England: Liverpool Through the Journalism of H. Shimmin* (Leicester: Leicester University Press, 1991), p. 81.

16. Neil Wigglesworth, *The Evolution of English Sport* (London: Frank Cass, 1996), p. 119, claims that there was a relative change from participation to spectatorship amongst the working classes. The reality is more complex. While sporting events were rare but could be freely watched in the early nineteenth century, a high proportion of local men, women and children would take time off to attend. Once spectators had to pay, the actual proportion of the working-class population watching dropped and took time to recover.

17. *Illustrated Sporting and Dramatic News*, 15 November 1862.

18. David Twydell, *Rejected FC*, iii (Harefield, 1992).

19. *Cricket*, 17 May 1882.

20. *Football*, 4 October 1882.

21. A. E. T. Watson, 'Introduction', in H. Peek, *The Badminton Library of Sports and Pastimes: The Poetry of Sport* (London: Badminton Press, 1896), p. 16.

22. This study owes much of its data on Scotland to Neil Tranter's pioneering researches. The various articles cited in Tranter, *Sport, Economy and Society* provide an avenue into this important material.

23. Parliamentary Papers, Children's Employment Commission, Second Report (1843), xiv, p. 491.

24. F. M. L. Thompson, *Hampstead: Building a Borough, 1650–1964* (London: Routledge, 1974), pp. 384–85.

25. Charles Russell, *Manchester Boys: Sketches of Manchester Lads at Work and Play* (Manchester: Manchester University Press, 1905), p. 70.

26. R. C. Floud and D. McCloskey, *The Economic History of Britain since 1700*, ii (Cambridge: Cambridge University Press, 1981); N. Crofts and T. C. Mills, 'Trends in Real Wages in Britain, 1750–1913', *Explorations in Economic History*, 31 (1994), pp. 176–94.

27. Douglas A. Reid, 'Playing and Praying', in Martin Daunton (ed.), *Cambridge Urban History of Britain*, iii (Cambridge: Cambridge University Press, 2000), provides a useful summary of the process.

28. Steven G. Jones, *Sport, Politics and the Working Class* (Manchester: Manchester University Press, 1988), pp. 22–25.

29. Stephen A. Riess, *City Games: The Evolution of American Urban Society and the Rise of Sports* (Urbana: University of Illinois Press, 1989).

Notes to Chapter 2: Class and Sport

1. See Simon Dentith, *Society and Cultural Forms in Nineteenth Century England* (Basingstoke: Macmillan, 1998).

2. F. G. Afalo (ed.), *The Cost of Sport* (London: John Murray, 1899), p. 289. The Mechanics Golf Club at St Andrews founded in 1865 was an exception.

3. Mike Huggins, *Flat Racing and British Society, 1790–1914* (London: Frank Cass, 2000).

4. Afalo (ed.), *The Cost of Sport*, p. 71. See John Lowerson, 'Brothers of the Angle: Coarse Fishing and English Working Class Culture 1850–1914', in J. A. Mangan (ed.) *Pleasure, Profit and Proselytism: British Culture and Sport at Home and Abroad 1700–1914* (London: Frank Cass, 1988) pp. 105–27.

5. Peter Bailey, 'Will the Real Bill Banks Please Stand Up? Towards a Role Analysis of Mid-Victorian Working-Class Respectability', *Social History*, 12 (1979), pp. 336–53. Mike Huggins and J. A. Mangan (eds) *Disreputable Pleasures: Less Virtuous Victorians at Play* (London: Frank Cass, 2004), provide a more extended critique of 'respectability'.

6. *Illustrated Times*, 31 March 1860.

7. *Illustrated Sporting News*, 29 November 1862.

8. *Illustrated Sporting and Theatrical News*, 23 January, 1869.

9. These draw largely on notions of 'leisure cultures' developed by Hugh Cunningham, 'Leisure and Culture', in F. M. L. Thompson, *The Cambridge Social History of Britain, 1750–1950: People and Their Environment* (Cambridge: Cambridge University Press, 1990).

10. See J. V. Beckett, *The Aristocracy in England, 1660–1914* (Oxford: Basil Blackwell, 1986).

11. Anthony Trollope, *British Sports and Pastimes* (1868), p. 18.

12. David Cannadine, *The Decline and Fall of the British Aristocracy* (London: Papermac, 1996), pp. 8–15.

13. J. Bateman, *The Great Landowners of Great Britain and Ireland* (London: Harrison, 1883).

14. W. D. Rubinstein, *Men of Property: The Very Wealthy in Britain since the Industrial Revolution* (London: Croom Helm, 1981), p. 194.

15. F. M. L. Thompson, *Gentrification and the Enterprise Culture: Britain, 1780–1980* (Oxford: Oxford University Press, 2001), p. 36.

16. E.g. Harry Hieover, *The Sporting World* (London: T. C. Newby, 1858), p. 118.

17. Thompson, *Gentrification*, chapter 3 provides a useful summary of the debate over the extent and nature of such purposes.

18. Keith A. P. Sandiford, 'England', in Brian Stoddard and Keith A. P. Sandiford (eds), *The Imperial Game* (Manchester; Manchester University Press, 1998), p. 12; James Bradley, 'The MCC, Society and Empire: A Portrait of Cricket's Ruling Body, 1860–1914', *International Journal of the History of Sport*, 7 (1990), pp. 3–22.

19. Jill Franklin, 'The Victorian County House', in G. E. Mingay (ed.), *The Victorian Countryside*, ii (London: Routledge, 1981) pp. 402–3. See also Pamela Horn, *Pleasures and Pastimes in Victorian Britain* (Stroud: Sutton Publishing, 1999), chapter 5.

20. See J. Stovin (ed.), *Journals of a Methodist Farmer, 1871–75* (London: Croom Helm, 1977).

21. E.g. *The Times*, 7 March 1883; ibid., 18 August 1883. See also M. A. Kellett, 'The Power of Princely Patronage: Pigeon Shooting in Victorian Britain', *International Journal of the History of Sport*, 11 (1994), pp. 63–85. For rabbit shooting see *The Days' Doings*, 8 January 1870.

22. Raymond Carr, 'Country Sports', in Mingay (ed.), *The Victorian Countryside*, p. 484.

23. For his life see D. Sutherland, *The Yellow Earl* (London: Molendinar Press, 1965).

24. Hieover, *The Sporting World*, p. 4. Raymond Carr, *English Foxhunting: A History* (London: Weidenfeld and Nicolson, 1976) pp. 116, 124; F. G. Afalo (ed.), *The Cost of Sport* (London: John Murray, 1899), pp. 137–57.

25. *Sporting Chronicle*, 10 and 11 February 1899.

26. Mike Benborough Jackson, 'Landlord Careless? Landowners, Tenants and Agriculture on Four Estates in West Wales, 1850–1875', *Rural History* 14 (2003), pp. 81–98.

27. George Plumtre, *The Fast Set* (London: André Deutsch, 1985), pp. 43–45. Cannadine *Decline and Fall*, pp. 360–61.

28. Mike Huggins, 'Cumberland and Westmorland Wrestling *c.* 1800–2000', *Sports Historian*, 21 (2001) pp. 35–55; Mike Huggins, *Flat Racing and British Society*, p. 155. For a Scottish example see Lorna Jackson, 'Sport and Patronage: Evidence from Nineteenth Century Argyllshire', *Sports Historian*, 18 (1998), pp. 95–106.

29. Mark Girouard, *The Return to Camelot: Chivalry and the English Gentleman* (Newhaven, Connecticut: Yale University Press, 1981), p. 236.

30. Mike Huggins, *Flat Racing and British Society, 1790–1914* (London: Frank Cass, 2000).

31. M. A. Simpson, 'The West End of Glasgow, 1830–1914', in M. A. Simpson and T. H. Lloyd (eds), *Middle-Class Housing in Britain* (Newton Abbot: David and Charles, 1977), p. 54.

32. In Leeds in 1832 over a fifth of the population could claim middle-class status. R. J. Morris, 'Middle-Class Culture, 1700–1914', in Derek Frazer (ed.), *A History of Modern Leeds* (Manchester: Manchester University Press, 1980) p. 201.

33. Harold Perkin, *The Rise of Professional Society* (London: Routledge, 1989), pp. 28–29. See also John Lowerson, *Sport and the English Middle Classes, 1850–1914* (Manchester: Manchester University Press, 1993), ch. 1. Simon Gunn, *The Public Culture of the Victorian Middle Class* (Manchester: Manchester University Press, 2000), ch. 2.

34. Norman McCord, *British History, 1815–1906* (1991), p. 99.

35. Eric J. Hobsbawm, 'The Example of the English Middle Class', in J. Kocka and A. Mitchell (eds) *Bourgeois Society in Nineteenth-Century Europe* (Oxford: Berg, 1993), p. 133; R. J. Morris, *Class, Sect and Party. The Making of the British Middle Class: Leeds, 1820–1850* (Manchester: Manchester University Press, 1990); Gunn, *Public Culture*, ch. 2.

36. 1881 Census of England and Wales, General Report, 1883 (C.3797), lxxx, p. 30; 1891 Census of England and Wales, General Report, 1893–94 (C.7222), cv, p. 38.

37. Perkin, *Rise of Professional Society*, chapters 2 and 3.

38. 'Foreword' to the new edition of J. A. Mangan, *Athleticism in the Victorian and Edwardian Public School* (London: Frank Cass 2000).

39. J. Horne, A. Tomlinson and G. Whannel, *Understanding Sport: An Introduction to the Sociological and Cultural Analysis of Sport* (London: Spon, 1999), p. 8.

40. The full complexity of the process of athleticism's diffusion, which can only be hinted at here, has been explored in seminal books and articles by

J. A. Mangan including *Athleticism*, and his *The Games Ethic and Imperialism* (Harmondsworth: Viking, 1986).

41. Colm Hickey, 'Athleticism and the London Training Colleges', Ph.D. thesis, University of Strathclyde; J. A. Mangan, 'Grammar Schools and the Games Ethic in the Victorian and Edwardian Eras', *Albion*, 15 (1983), pp. 313–24.

42. Timothy Chandler, 'Games at Oxbridge and the Public Schools, 1830–80: The Diffusion of an Innovation', *International Journal of the History of Sport*, 8 (1991), pp. 171–204.

43. *Illustrated Sporting News*, 17 May 1862.

44. Cannadine, *Decline and Fall*, p. 361.

45. *Bell's Life*, 5 April 1840.

46. Mike Huggins, 'A Tranquil Transformation: Middle-Class Racing 'Revolutionaries' in England', in J. A. Mangan (ed.), *Reformers, Sport, Modernisers: Middle Class Revolutionaries* (London: Frank Cass, 2002), pp. 35–57.

47. Neil Tranter, 'The Chronology of Organised Sport in Nineteenth-Century Scotland: A Regional Study. Patterns', *International Journal of the History of Sport*, 7 (1990), p. 189.

48. See A. Durie and M. Huggins, 'Sport, Social Tone and the Seaside Resorts of Great Britain', *International Journal of the History of Sport*, 15 (1998), pp. 173–87.

49. Richard Holt, *Sport and the British* (Oxford: Oxford University Press, 1989), p. 143.

50. Wray Vamplew, *Pay Up and Play the Game: Professional Sport in Britain, 1875–1914* (Cambridge: Cambridge University Press, 1988).

51. J. Lowerson, 'Opiate of the People and Stimulant for the Historian? Some Issues in Sports History', in W. Lamont (ed.), *Historical Controversies and Historians* (London: UCL, 1998), p. 209.

52. *Northern Review*, 12 January 1889. Richard Holt has taken a different view, suggesting that 'association football did not attract a significant non-working-class audience until well after the Second World War'. See Holt, 'Cricket and Englishness: The Batsman as Hero', *International Journal of the History of Sport*, 13 (1996), p. 48.

53. *Grasshopper*, 21 January 1895 and 5 May 1895.

54. I have explored the leisure life of the less respectable middle classes in a number of publications. See Mike Huggins, 'More Sinful Pleasures? Leisure, Respectability and the Male Middle Classes in Victorian England', *Journal of Social History*, 33 (2000), pp. 585–600; Mike Huggins, 'Second-Class Citizens? English Middle-Class Culture and Sport, 1850–1910: A

Reconsideration', *International Journal of the History of Sport*, 17 (2000) pp. 1–35; Huggins and Mangan (eds), *Disreputable Pleasures*.

55. David Cannadine, *Class in Britain*, p. 121. See also Geoffrey Crossick (ed.), *The Lower Middle Class in Britain, 1870–1914* (London: Macmillan, 1977).

56. Peter Bailey, 'White Collars, Grey Lives? The Lower Middle Class Revisited', *Journal of British Studies*, 38 (1999), pp. 273–90.

57. Bailey, 'White Collars, Grey Lives?'

58. Frederick Gale, *Modern English Sports: Their Use and Abuse* (London, 1885) p. 60.

59. Reid, 'Playing and Praying', p. 766.

60. David Nash, *Secularism, Art and Freedom* (Leicester: Leicester University Press, 1992), p. 97.

61. *Liverpool Mercury*, 27 February 1839.

62. *Derby Mercury*, 28 February 1844. See Antony Delves 'Popular Recreation and Social Conflict in Derby, 1800–1850', in Stephen Yeo and Eileen Yeo (eds), *Popular Culture and Class Conflict, 1590–1914: Explorations in the History of Labour and Leisure* (Brighton: Harvester, 1981).

63. See R. W. Malcolmson, 'Leisure', in Mingay (ed.), *The Victorian Countryside*, p. 612.

64. Andy Croll, *Civilising the Urban: Popular Culture and Public Space in Merthyr, c. 1870–1914* (Cardiff: University of Wales Press, 2000), p. 141.

65. *Manchester Guardian*, 9 August 1858.

66. Mike Huggins, 'An Early North-East Football Club, 1878–1887', *Bulletin of the Cleveland and District Local History Society* 51 (1986), pp. 28–40.

67. See, for example, the comments of Ernest Ensor, 'The Football Madness', *Contemporary Review*, 74 (November 1898), pp. 753–60.

68. Geoffrey Crossick, *An Artisan Elite in Victorian Society* (London: Croom Helm, 1978), p. 135.

69. *Bell's Life*, 2 August 1840.

70. D. A. Reid, 'The Decline of St Monday', *Past and Present*, 71 (1976), pp. 76–98; D. A. Reid, 'Weddings, Workdays, Work and Leisure in Urban England, 1791–1911: The Decline of St Monday Revisited', *Past and Present*, 153 (1996), pp. 135–63.

71. *The Day's Doings*, 3 December 1870.

72. Thomas Wright, *Some Habits and Customs of the Working Classes* (first published 1867; New York: Augustus Kelly, 1967), p. 256.

73. Wright, *Habits and Customs*, p. 7.

74. Sport and games aided working-class recruitment. See Hugh Cunningham, *Leisure in the Industrial Revolution* (London: Croom Helm, 1980), p. 182.

75. Malcolmson, 'Leisure', in Mingay (ed.), *The Victorian Countryside*, p. 604.

76. Alfred Williams, *A Wiltshire Village* (London: Duckworth, 1912), p. 234.

77. Lyn Murfin, *Popular Leisure in the Lake Counties* (Manchester: Manchester University Press, 1990), pp. 105–10.

78. See Dennis R. Mills, *Lord and Peasant in Nineteenth Century Britain* (London: Croom Helm, 1980).

79. See Raphael Samuel, *Village Life and Labour* (London: Routledge and Kegan Paul, 1975), pp. 162–63.

80. *Cricket Weekly Record*, 28 April 1892.

81. William Plomer (ed.), *Kilvert's Diary, 1870–1879* (London: Cape, 1973), p. 159.

82. Richard Jeffries, *The Toilers in the Field* (London: MacDonald Futura, 1981 edn), p. 68. See also Mary Mitford, *Our Village* (London: Walter Scott, 1891 edn).

83. Raphael Samuel, 'Quarry Roughs; Life and Labour in Headington Quarry 1860–1920', in Samuel, *Village Life and Labour*, p. 148.

84. Mark Girouard, *Life in the English Country House* (Newhaven, Connecticut: Yale University Press, 1978).

85. F. M. L. Thompson, 'Landowners and the Rural Community', in Mingay (ed.), *The Victorian Countryside*, p. 464.

86. F. M. L. Thompson, *The Cambridge Social History of Britain, 1750–1940*, i, *Regions and Communities* (Cambridge: Cambridge University Press, 1990), p. 71. Neville Kirk, *Change, Continuity and Class: Labour in British Society, 1850–1920* (Manchester: Manchester University Press, 1998). Many historians still fall into the trap of presenting the working classes as relatively homogenous in their interests and identity.

87. Nigel Tranter, 'The Social and Occupational Structure of Organised Sport in Central Scotland during the Nineteenth Century', *International Journal of the History of Sport*, 4 (1987), p. 303.

88. Nigel Tranter, *Sport, Economy and Society in Britain, 1750–1914* (Cambridge: Cambridge University Press, 1998), pp. 26–31, summarises and provides references for this debate. He sees the diffusionist model as 'too restricted to be acceptable'.

89. Charles Booth, *Life and Labour of the People of London*, i (London: Macmillan, 1892), pp. 35, 62.

90. B. Seebohm Rowntree, *Poverty: A Study of Town Life* (London: Longman, 1901), pp. 115–18.

91. Henry Mayhew said rat catching was a favourite sport of London costermongers in the 1850s. So did Charles Manby Smith, *Curiosities of London Life* (London: A. W. Bennett, 1853). Descriptions of a Liverpool sparring

match and dog fight in the later 1850s can be found in John Walton and Alastair Wilcox (eds), *Low Life and Moral Improvement in Mid-Victorian England* (Leicester: Leicester University Press, 1991), pp. 59–70. See also James Burnley, *Two Sides of the Atlantic* (London: 1880), part 2, for Bradford examples in the late 1870s.

92. *Merthyr Evening News*, 15 November 1890, quoted in Andy Croll, *Civilising the Urban: Popular Culture and Public Space in Merthyr, c. 1870–1914* (Cardiff: University of Wales Press, 2000), p. 138.

93. Charles Russell, *Manchester Boys: Sketches of Manchester Lads at Work and Play* (Manchester: Manchester University Press, 1905), p. 66.

94. Bailey, *Leisure and Class*, chapter 4.

Notes to Chapter 3: Amateurs and Professionals

1. *Spectator*, 20 April 1901, p. 566.
2. *Cricket*, 10 May 1882.
3. *Athletic News*, 28 October 1876.
4. *Illustrated Sporting and Dramatic News*, 20 April 1889.
5. See Harvey Taylor, 'Play Up, but Don't Play the Game: English Amateur Elitism, 1863–1910', *Sports Historian*, 22 (2002), pp. 75–97; Richard Holt, *Sport and the British* (Oxford: Clarendon, 1989), chapter 2; Neil Wigglesworth, *The Evolution of English Sport* (London: Frank Cass, 1996), chapter 6.
6. Eric Halliday, *Rowing in England: A Social History* (Manchester: Manchester University Press, 1990), p. 30.
7. *The Times*, 16 April 1840.
8. *Bell's Life*, 11 October 1846.
9. London Rowing Club minutes, 20 March 1872, quoted in Wigglesworth, *The Evolution of English Sport*, p. 89.
10. *Illustrated Sporting News*, 8 February 1866.
11. *Athletic News Cricket Annual* (London: Athletic News, 1896), p. 97.
12. Holt, *Sport and the British*, p. 104.
13. Earl of Suffolk, 'Gentlemen Riders', *Badminton Magazine*, 11 April 1896, p. 478.
14. *Grasshopper*, 21 January 1895.
15. J. M. Richardson and Finch Mason, *Gentleman Riders Past and Present* (London: Vinton, 1909), p. 313.
16. *Illustrated Sporting and Dramatic News*, 20 April 1889.
17. Quoted in T. Delaney, *Rugby Disunion* (Keighley: privately printed, 1993), p. 54.

18. Rev J. E. C. Welldon, *Church Monthly*, 1899, quoted in Keith Booth, *The Father of Modern Sport: The Life and Times of Charles W. Alcock* (Manchester: Parrs Wood Press, 2002), p. 185.

19. RFU President Arthur Budd, quoted in Gareth Evans, 'How Amateur Was My Valley: Professional Sport and National Identity in Wales, 1890–1914', *British Journal of Sports History*, 2 (1985), pp. 249–69.

20. *Sporting Chronicle*, 11 February 1899.

21. *Football*, 4 October 1882

22. *Northern Review*, 9 February 1889.

23. See Mike Huggins, 'Cartoons and the Comic Periodical, 1841–1901: A Satirical Sociology of Victorian Sporting Life', in Mike Huggins and J. A. Mangan (eds), *Disreputable Pleasures: Less Virtuous Victorians at Play* (London: Frank Cass, 2004).

24. *Lancaster Gazette*, 19 February 1870.

25. Quoted in Eric Halladay, *Rowing in England: A Social History* (Manchester: Manchester University Press, 1990), p. 81.

26. Argonaut (E. D. Brickwood), *The Art of Rowing and Training* (1866), quoted in Halladay, *Rowing in England*, pp. 75–76.

27. See Win Hayes, 'The Professional Swimmer, 1860–1880s', *Sports Historian*, 22 (2002), pp. 119–48 especially p. 133.

28. *Cricketers' Companion* (London: Lillywhite, 1880), p. 8.

29. Booth, *The Father of Modern Sport*, pp. 180–82, 197–200; *Yorkshireman*, 9 May 1888.

30. *Athletic News*, 19 March 1879.

31. Dominic Malcolm, 'Cricket Spectator Disorder: Myths and Historical Evidence', *Sports Historian*, 19 (1999) pp. 22–23.

32. Tony Mason, *Association Football and English Society, 1863–1915* (Brighton: Harvester Press, 1980), p. 77.

33. *Athletic News*, 5 February 1879.

34. Keith Warsop, 'Researching the Game's Past: The Quest for Early FA Cup Finalists', *Soccer History* 2 (2002), pp. 34–40.

35. Quoted in Warsop, 'Researching the Game's Past', p. 37.

36. *Athletic News*, 12 February 1879.

37. *Northern Review*, 9 February 1889.

38. *Bell's Life*, 1 April 1882

39. *Bell's Life*, 2 December, 1882.

40. Charles W. Alcock, *The Football Annual* (London: Wright and Co, 1884).

41. *Sporting Life*, 15 September 1884.

42. See Dave Russell, *Football and the English* (Preston: Carnegie Publishing, 1997), p. 27, for a different view.

43. 'Pa' Jackson, quoted in Booth, *The Father of Modern Sport*, p. 230.

44. Dave Russell, *Football and the English* (Carnegie: Preston, 1997), p. 28.

45. The standard work is Tony Collins, *Rugby's Great Split: Class, Culture and the Origins of Rugby Football League* (London: Frank Cass, 1998).

46. Charles W. Alcock (ed.), *Football Annual* (London: Wright and Co, 1886), p. 161.

47. A. J. Arnold, 'The Belated Entry of Professional Soccer into the Textile District of Northern England', *International Journal of the History of Sport*, 6 (1989), pp. 319–34.

48. P. Greenhalgh, 'The Work and Play Principle: The Professional Regulations of the Northern Rugby Football Union, 1898–1905', *International Journal of the History of Sport*, 9 (1992), p. 359; Geoffrey Moorhouse, *A People's Game: The Official History of Rugby League* (London: Hodder and Stoughton, 1995), pp. 46–47.

49. Paul Blackledge, 'Rational Capitalist Concerns: William Cail and the Great Rugby Split of 1895', *International Journal of the History of Sport*, 18 (2001), pp. 35–53.

50. *Sporting Chronicle*, 11 February 1899.

51. *Swimming, Rowing and Athletic Record*, 23 August 1873.

52. *Illustrated Sporting and Theatrical News*, 29 May 1869.

53. *Bell's Life*, 5 January 1862.

54. For example *Bell's Life*, 3 August 1862 at Nottinghamshire claimed 'we heard no betting ... at the commencement but we understand 6 to 4 had been laid on Notts'.

55. *Cricket*, 10 May 1882.

56. *Northern Review*, 21 August 1888.

57. See John Lowerson, *Sport and the English Middle Classes, 1870–1914* (Manchester: Manchester University Press, 1993), pp. 268ff.

58. David Nash, *Secularism, Art and Freedom* (Leicester: Leicester University Press, 1992), p. 98.

59. *The Hour*, 11 May, 1874; *Cricket*, 22 June 1882.

60. Norbert Elias, *The Civilising Process* (Oxford: Blackwell, 1982); R. W. Malcolmson, *Popular Recreation and English Society, 1700–1850* (Cambridge: Cambridge University Press, 1973). The work of Eric Dunning has been particularly influential. See, for example, Eric Dunning and K. Sheard, *Barbarians, Gentlemen and Players* (London: Martin Robinson, 1979).

61. See Malcolmson, *Popular Recreation*, pp. 118–38.

62. *Liverpool Mercury*, 27 February 1839, quoted in Derek Birley, *Sport and the Making of Britain* (Manchester: Manchester University Press, 1993), p. 206.

63. See, for example, *Daily Telegraph*, 18 December 1869; *Pall Mall Gazette*, 7 January 1870.

64. *The Day's Doings*, 21 January 1871.

65. Dunning and Sheard, *Barbarians, Gentlemen and Players*, pp. 113ff. See also T. J. Chandler, 'The Structuring of Manliness and the Development of Rugby Football at the Public Schools and Oxbridge, 1830–1880', in John Nauright and T. J. Chandler (eds), *Making Men: Rugby and Masculine Identity* (London: Frank Cass, 1996).

66. See *Athletic News*, 4 November 1876.

67. See Collins, *Rugby's Great Split*, for details.

68. *Northern Review*, 17 November 1888.

69. Quoted in Roberta J. Park, 'Mended or Ended? Football Injuries and the British and American Medical Press, 1870–1910', *International Journal of the History of Sport* 18 (2001), pp. 110–33.

70. Historians disagree about violence's extent. See Neil Tranter, *Sport, Economy and Society in Britain, 1750–1914* (Cambridge: Cambridge University Press, 1998), pp. 46–48. Joe Maguire, 'Images of Manliness and Competing Ways of Living in Late Victorian and Edwardian Britain', *British Journal of Sports History*, 3 (1986), pp. 265–87, provides a class-based analysis of manliness.

71. *Northern Review*, 24 December 1887.

72. Quoted in R. W. Lewis, 'Football Hooliganism in England before 1914: A Critique of the Dunning Thesis', *International Journal of the History of Sport*, 13 (1996), pp. 310–39. See also Patrick Murphy, Eric Dunning and Joseph Maguire, 'Football Spectator Violence and Disorder before the First World War: A Reply to R. W. Lewis', ibid., 15 (1998), pp. 141–62.

73. For details of current research on the place of women in Victorian sport see the succinct summary in Tranter, *Sport, Economy and Society*, chapter 6.

74. *Punch*, July 26 1890.

75. *Grasshopper*, 19 April 1895.

76. *Punch*, 6 December 1899, p. 268.

Notes to Chapter 4: Sporting Pleasures

1. See for example, Gustave Doré and Blanchard Jerrold, *London: A Pilgrimage* (London: Grant, 1872), chapters 5 and 6.

2. *The Day's Doings*, 1 April 1871.

3. *Sporting Life*, 28 May 1859.

4. Hippolyte Taine, *Notes on England* (London: Caliban Books, 1995), pp. 32–36.

5. Jeremy Crump, 'The Great Carnival of the Year: The Leicester Races in the Nineteenth Century', *Transactions of the Leicestershire Historical and Archaeological Society*, 58 (1982–83), pp. 58–74.

6. *Doncaster Reporter*, 11 September 1867.

7. Tony Collins and Wray Vamplew, *Mud, Sweat and Beers: A Cultural History of Sport and Alcohol* (Oxford: Berg, 2002), p. 71.

8. Charles Dickens and W. H. Wills, 'Epsom', *Household Words* 3, 63, June 7 1851.

9. *The Free Lance*, 15 June 1867, p. 202.

10. *The Day's Doings*, 27 May 1871.

11. Dennis Brailsford, *Sport, Time and Society: The British at Play* (London: Routledge 1991), pp. 2–11.

12. *Wolverhampton Chronicle*, 29 December, 1875.

13. *Northern Review*, 8 January 1887.

14. *Baily's Magazine*, November 1895, p. 396.

15. *Northern Review*, 24 April 1889.

16. See Lyn Murfin, *Popular Leisure in the Lake Counties* (Manchester: Manchester University Press, 1990), p. 49.

17. *Sporting Chronicle*, 8 August 1899.

18. *Illustrated Times*, 12 May 1860.

19. Roy Lomas, *Grasmere Sports: The First 150 Years* (Kendal: MTP publications, 2002); J. D. Marshall and John K. Walton, *The Lake Counties from 1830 to the Mid-Twentieth Century* (Manchester: Manchester University Press, 1981), p. 162.

20. *Sporting Chronicle*, 6 February 1899.

21. *Illustrated Sporting and Dramatic News*, 26 June 1874.

22. Patrick Joyce, *Work, Society and Politics: The Culture of the Factory in Late Victorian England* (Brighton: Harvester, 1980), p. 338.

23. *Football*, 29 March 1893.

24. *Illustrated Sporting and Dramatic News*, 7 July 1866.

25. Quoted in F. S. Ashley-Cooper, *Cricket Highways and Byways* (London: Allen and Unwin, 1927), p. 107.

26. David Kennedy, 'The Split of Everton Football Club 1892', *Sport in History*, 23 (2003), pp. 1–26.

27. Helen E. Meller, *Nottingham in the 1880s: A Study in Social Change* (Nottingham: University of Nottingham, 1971). The National Archives' BT31 file of failed companies has a significant number of such clubs.

28. John Lowerson, *Sport and the English Middle Classes* (Manchester: Manchester University Press, 1993) is the most complete and authoritative analysis available of this middle-class adult sporting life.

29. Doug A. Reid, 'Playing and Praying', in M. Staunton (ed.), *Cambridge Urban History of Britain*, iii (Cambridge: Cambridge University Press, 2000), p. 784.

30. *Sporting Chronicle*, 9 February 1899.

31. See advertisement in *Doncaster Gazette*, 17 September 1841.

32. Kelly and Co., *Post Office Directory of Lancashire with Liverpool and Manchester* (London: Kelly and Co., 1881).

33. *Northern Review*, 15 September 1888.

34. *Bicycling News and Tricycling Gazette*, 14 January 1895.

35. Herbert and Mary Jackson (eds), *Lakeland's Pioneer Rock-Climbers* (Clapham: Dalesman Books, 1980), p. 12.

36. J. Fairfax Blakeborough, *Northern Sport and Sportsmen*, 5 (London: Hunter and Longhurst, n.d.), p. 109.

37. Hugh Keevins and Kevin McCarra, *100 Cups: The Story of the Scottish Cup* (Edinburgh: Mainstream Publishing, 1985), p. 42.

38. *Cricket and Football Times*, 15 July 1880.

39. Peter Bailey (ed.), *Music Hall: The Business of Pleasure* (Milton Keynes: Open University Press, 1986).

40. See Collins and Vamplew, *Mud, Sweat and Beers*; John Burnett, *Riot, Revelry and Rout: Sport in Scotland before 1860* (East Lothian; Tuckwell Press, 2000).

41. *Northern Review*, 27 October 1887.

42. See Andy Croll, *Civilising the Urban: Popular Culture and Public Space in Merthyr, c. 1870–1914* (Cardiff: University of Wales Press, 2000), p. 144.

43. *Grasshopper*, 17 May 1895.

44. *Scottish Athletic Journal*, 1 February 1887.

45. *North Wales Observer and Express*, 17 February 1888.

46. *Northern Echo*, 23 March 1889.

47. John Arlott (ed.), *The Oxford Companion to Sports and Games* (Oxford: Oxford University Press, 1975), p. 28.

48. F. G. Afalo (ed.), *The Cost of Sport* (London: John Murray, 1999), gives further details.

49. Mike Huggins, *Flat Racing and British Society, 1790–1914* (London: Frank Cass, 2000).

50. Richard Holt, *Sport and the British* (Oxford: Oxford University Press, 1989), pp. 153–59.

51. H. Seton-Carr, *My Sporting Holidays* (London: Edward Arnold, 1904), p. 97.

52. John Crosfield, *A History of the Cadbury Family*, ii (Cambridge: Cambridge University Press, 1985), p. 437.

53. The academic study of women's sport has yet to really explore the enjoyments women gained. See Neil Tranter, *Sport, Economy and Society in Britain, 1750–1914* (Cambridge: Cambridge University Press, 1998), chapter 6.

54. *Athletic News*, 21 February 1888.

Notes to Chapter 5: Money

1. *Sporting Magazine*, October 1853, pp. 252–60.

2. Wray Vamplew, *Pay Up and Play the Game: Professional Sport in Britain, 1875–1914* (Cambridge: Cambridge University Press, 1988), p. 77; R. D. Walker, 'Lord's Up to Date', *Badminton Magazine*, 10 (1900), p. 325, quoted in Keith Sandiford and Wray Vamplew, 'The Peculiar Economics of English Cricket before 1914', *British Journal of Sports History*, 3 (1986), pp. 311–26.

3. *Athletic News*, 29 April 1901.

4. Wray Vamplew, 'The Economics of a Sports Industry: Scottish Gate Money Football, 1890–1914', *Economic History Review*, 35 (1982), pp. 549–67, especially pp. 549–50; John Lowerson, *Sport and the English Middle Classes, 1870–1914* (Manchester: Manchester University Press, 1993), p. 225.

5. Neil Wigglesworth, *The Evolution of English Sport* (London: Frank Cass, 1996), p. 60.

6. 1891 Census, General Report, 1893–94 (C.7222), cvi, p. 40; and 1893–94 (C.7058), cvi, p. xxvii.

7. Vamplew, *Pay Up and Play the Game*, provides a thorough economic treatment. See also Neil Tranter, *Sport, Economy and Society in Britain, 1850–1914* (Cambridge: Cambridge University Press, 1998); Lowerson, *Sport and the English Middle Classes, 1870–1914*, chapter 8; Wigglesworth, *The Evolution of English Sport*, chapters 3 and 4.

8. See Derek Birley, *Sport and the Making of Britain* (Manchester: Manchester University Press, 1993), pp. 117–18. Dennis Brailsford, *A Taste for Diversions: Sport in Georgian England* (Cambridge: Lutterworth Press, 1999).

9. John Lowerson and John Myercough, *Time to Spare in Victorian England* (Hassocks, Harvester Press, 1977).

10. *Doncaster Reporter*, 11 September 1867.

11. Warren Roe, 'The Athletic Capital of England: The White Lion, Hackney Wick, 1857–1875', *British Society for Sports History Bulletin*, Winter 2002–3, pp. 39–53.

12. *Bell's Life*, 14 April 1844.

13. *Sporting Life*, 25 June 1859.

14. *Bell's Life*, 6 April 1862.

15. *Sporting Chronicle*, 8 February 1899.

16. *The Times*, 11 September 1876.

17. Mike Huggins, 'The First Generation of Street Bookmakers in Victorian England: Demonic Fiends or Decent Fellers?', *Northern History*, 36 (2000), pp. 129–45.

18. Wray Vamplew, *The Turf* (London: Allen Lane, 1976), p. 27.

19. Tony Collins and Wray Vamplew, 'The Pub, the Drinks Trade and the Early Years of Modern Football', *Sports Historian*, 20 (2000), pp. 1–17, esp. p. 8.

20. *Bell's Life*, 6 April 1863

21. These are held in the BT31 files at Kew.

22. Harding Cox et al., *Coursing and Falconry* (London: The Field, 1892), p. 99.

23. See Tony Collins, *The Great Split* (London: Frank Cass, 1998), p. 99.

24. Andrew Ritchie, 'The Origins of Bicycle Racing in England: Technology, Entertainment, Sporsorship and Advertising in the Early History of the Sport', *Journal of Sports History*, 26 (1999), pp. 487–518.

25. Andrew Done and Richard Muir, 'The Landscape History of Grouse Shooting in the Yorkshire Dales', *Rural History*, 12 (2001), pp. 195–210.

26. See Peter Bailey, *Popular Culture and Performance in the Victorian City* (Cambridge: Cambridge University Press, 1999), p. 143; Peter Bailey, *Music Hall: The Business of Pleasure* (Milton Keynes: Open University, 1986), p. 38.

27. *Northern Review*, 20 October 1888.

28. *Northern Review*, 29 December 1888.

29. Matthew Taylor and John Coyle, 'The Election of Clubs to the Football League, 1888–1939', *Sports Historian*, 19 (1999), pp. 1–24. See also Dave Russell, *Football and the English* (Preston: Carnegie Publishing, 1997), pp. 31–33.

30. Mike Huggins, 'The Spread of Soccer in North-East England, 1876–90', *International Journal of the History of Sport*, 6 (1989), pp. 299–318.

31. *Northern Review*, 19 May 1888.

32. John Coyle, 'From Minor to Major', *Association of Sports Historians Newsletter*, July 2000, pp. 10–19.

33. Mike Huggins, 'Sport and the Social Construction of Identity in North-East England, 1800–1914', in Neville Kirk (ed.), *Northern Identities* (Aldershot: Ashgate, 2000), pp. 132–62, p. 157.

34. Wigglesworth, *The Evolution of English Sport*, p. 109.

35. K. C. Edwards, 'The Park Estate, Nottingham', in M. A. Simpson and

T. H. Lloyd (eds), *Middle-Class Housing in Britain* (Newton Abbot: David and Charles, 1977), pp. 161–62.

36. David Hunt, *A History of Preston North End: The People, the Power and the Politics* (Preston: Preston North End Publications, 2000).

37. Figures based on data in *Ruff's Guide to the Turf* and the *Racing Calendar.*

38. Anthony Trollope, *British Sports and Pastimes* (1868), quoted in Birley, *Sport and the Making of Britain*, p. 226.

39. There has been substantial research on professional incomes. See Tranter, *Sport, Economy and Society*, pp. 67–71, for a guide into the literature.

40. *Barnet Gazette*, 8 September 1860; *Bell's Life*, 13 October 1861.

41. *Cricket*, 22 November 1887.

42. Keith A. P. Sandiford, 'The Birth of the Professional Cricketer's Benefit Match', *International Journal of the History of Sport*, 8 (1991), pp. 111–23.

43. Tony Mason, *Association Football and English Society, 1863–1915* (Brighton: Harvester Press, 1980), p. 95.

44. Matthew Taylor, 'Beyond the Maximum Wage: The Earnings of Football Professionals in England, 1900–1939', *Soccer and Society*, 2 (2001), pp. 102–3, provides a useful summary of existing research.

45. *Sunderland News*, 4 June 1889.

46. *Sporting Chronicle*, 11 February 1899.

47. *Sporting Chronicle*, 26 February 1899.

48. John Pinfold, *Hoylake Race Course and the Beginnings of the Royal Liverpool Golf Club* (Prenton: I. & M. Boumphrey, 2002), p. 31.

49. Mike Huggins, *Kings of the Moor* (Middlesbrough: Teesside Polytechnic Papers, 1991), p. 28; *Middlesbrough Daily Exchange*, 29 January 1886; *Baily's Magazine*, July 1895, p. 70; ibid. September 1895, p. 230.

50. See Lowerson, *Sport and the English Middle Classes*, chapter 8.

51. *Bell's Life*, 29 October 1848.

52. *Midland Sporting News*, 26 August 1873.

53. Donald Dallas, *Holland & Holland, the Royal Gunmaker: The Complete History* (London: Quiller Press, 2003).

54. Charles Smith, *Curiosities of London Life* (London: A. W. Bennett, 1853).

55. Anon., *London Characters and the Humorous Side of London Life* (London: Slaley Rivers, 1871).

56. Lowerson, *Sport and the English Middle Classes*, p. 229.

57. *Cricket and Football Times*, 4 November 1880.

58. *Bell's Life*, 10 September 1848.

59. Birley, *Sport and the Making of Britain*, p. 276.

60. Rachael Low and Roger Manvell, *The History of the British Film, 1896–1906* (London: George Allen, 1948).

61. *Sporting Chronicle*, 11 February 1899.

62. *North-Eastern Daily Gazette*, 16 November 1889.

63. *Northern Review*, 9 February 1889.

64. Andrew Horrall, *Popular Culture in London, c.1890–1918* (Manchester: Manchester University Press, 2001), p. 107.

Notes to Chapter 6: The Media

1. 'The W. G. Grace Testimonial', *The Times*, 17 June 1895.

2. Richard Holt, *Sport and the British* (Oxford, Oxford University Press, 1989), p. 12.

3. Those few historians who have explored this field have concentrated largely but not exclusively on the sporting press, and this chapter owes much to their pioneering work. See Tony Mason, *Association Football and English Society, 1863–1915* (Brighton: Harvester Press, 1980), pp. 187–95; Tony Mason, 'Sporting News, 1860–1914', in Michael Harris and Alan Lee, *The Press in English Society from the Seventeenth to the Nineteenth Centuries* (London: Associated Universities Press, 1986), pp. 168–86; Tony Mason, *Sport in Britain* (London: Faber and Faber, 1988), pp. 46–50; John Lowerson, *Sport and the English Middle Classes, 1870–1914* (Manchester: Manchester University Press, 1993), esp. pp. 251–57; See also I. Nannestad, 'Researching the Game's Past: The National Sporting Press in England to 1900', *Soccer History*, 4 (2003), pp. 39–43.

4. John Mackenzie, *Propaganda and Empire: The Manipulation of British Public Opinion, 1880–1960* (Manchester: Manchester University Press, 1984), p. 17.

5. *Cricket*, May 17 1882.

6. C. Mitchell and Co., *The Newspaper Press Directory* (London: Mitchell, 1882), p. 200.

7. Report of the House of Commons Select Committee on the Post Office (Telegraph Department) 176 (357), xiii, q. 1765.

8. Deacon's *Newspaper Handbook* (London: Deacon, 1881); Joseph Hatton, *Journalistic London* (London: Sampson Lowe, 1882), p. 207.

9. *Bell's Life*, 1 August 1852.

10. *Midland Sporting News*, 4 January 1873.

11. Joe Wilson, *Tyneside Songs and Drolleries* (Newcastle: Allen, 1970), p. 267.

12. *Newcastle Daily Chronicle*, 26 June 1861.

13. *Bell's Life*, 1 April 1882.

14. See Keith Booth, *The Father of Modern Sport: The Life and Times of Charles W. Alcock* (Manchester: Parrs Wood Press, 2002).

15. Bill Murray, *The Old Firm* (Edinburgh: John Donald, 2000), p. 17.

16. Hatton, *Journalistic London*, p. 207.

17. *Illustrated Sporting and Dramatic News*, 25 March 1899.

18. Virginia Berridge, 'Content Analysis and Historical Research on Newspapers', in Harris and Lee (eds), *The Press in English Society*, p. 212; David S. Camper, 'Popular Sunday Newspapers, Respectability and Working-Class Culture in Late-Victorian Britain', in Mike Huggins and J. A. Mangan (eds), *Disreputable Pleasures: Less Virtuous Victorians at Play* (London: Frank Cass, 2004).

19. Mason, 'Sporting News', p. 177.

20. *Newsagent and Booksellers' Review*, 28 January 1893, p. 101.

21. *Northern Review*, 1 September 1888.

22. *Illustrated Sporting and Dramatic News*, 19 May 1866.

23. C. Mitchell and Co., *The Newspaper Press Directory* (London: Mitchell, 1851) pp. 185, 268.

24. Andrew Walker, 'Reporting Play: The Local Newspaper and Sports Journalism, c. 1870–1914', paper delivered at the Social History Conference, Leicester, 2003.

25. See Mason, *Association Football*, pp. 192–93.

26. *Sunderland Echo*, 24 September 1888.

27. The following comments are based on the numbers of books acquired by the British Library at this time.

28. E. W. Bovill, *The England of Nimrod and Surtees, 1815–1854* (London: Oxford University Press, 1959).

29. But note the cricket match at Dingley Dell in Charles Dickens, *Pickwick Papers* (London: Dent, 1998).

30. Antony Trollope, *An Autobiography* (Oxford: Oxford University Press, 1961), p. 54. See also his *Hunting Sketches* (London: Chapman and Hall, 1865).

31. George Eliot, *Daniel Deronda* (London: J. M. Dent, 1964), pp. 72–73.

32. John MacAloon, *This Great Symbol: Pierre de Coubertin and the Origins of the Modern Olympic Games* (Chicago: University of Chicago Press, 1981).

33. See Jeffery Richards, *Imperialism and Juvenile Literature* (Manchester: Manchester University Press, 1989).

34. Diana Dixon, 'Children and the Press, 1866–1914', in Harris and Lee, *The Press in English Society*, p. 135.

35. Good overviews of this material are provided in E. S. Turner, *Boys Will be Boys* (London: Michael Joseph, 1957); P. W. Musgrave, *From Brown to Bunter* (London: Routledge and Kegan Paul, 1985).

36. Peter Bailey, *Popular Culture and Performance in the Victorian City*

(Cambridge: Cambridge University Press, 1998); See also Lynda Nead, *Victorian Babylon* (Newhaven; Yale University Press, 2000).

37. See for example, Arthur M. Binstead and Ernest Wells, *A Pink 'Un and a Pelican* (London: Sands and Co., 1898), or J. B. Booth, *Old Pink 'Un Days* (London: Grant Richards, 1924), which both describe the social life of the *Sportsman*'s staff from its inception.

38. See Keith Gregson and Mike Huggins, 'Sport, Music Hall Culture and Popular Song in Nineteenth Century England', *Culture, Sport, Society*, 2 (1999), pp. 82–102.

39. *The Days' Doings*, 15 October 1870.

40. Andrew Horrall, *Popular Culture in London, c. 1890–1914* (Manchester: Manchester University Press, 2001), pp. 156–57.

41. John Barnes, *The Beginning of the Cinema in England*, v, *1900* (Exeter: University of Exeter Press, 1997) p. xvi.

42. *Star* (Newport), 10 November 1896.

43. *Era*, 2 October 1897, quoted in John Barnes, *The Beginnings of the Cinema in England*, ii, *1897* (Exeter: Exeter University Press, 1996), p. 150.

Notes to Chapter 7: Stars

1. Chris Rojek, *Celebrity* (London: Reaktion, 2001), provides useful theoretical analysis, and Ellis Cashmore, *Beckham* (Cambridge: Polity, 2002), a sporting example. A post-modernist approach is exploited by Margery Houriham, *Deconstructing the Hero* (London: Routledge, 1997).

2. Thomas Carlyle, *On Heroes, Hero Worship and the Heroic in History* (London: Chapman and Hall, 1904), p. 11.

3. See Richard Holt and J. A. Mangan, 'Prologue: Heroes of a European Past', in Richard Holt, J. A. Mangan and Pierre Lanfranchi, *European Heroes: Myth, Identity, Sport*, a special issue of the *International Journal of the History of Sport*, 13 (1996), pp. 1–13.

4. Keith Gregson and Mike Huggins, 'Sport, Music Hall Culture and Popular Song in Nineteenth-Century England', *Culture, Sport Society*, 2 (1999), pp. 96–97.

5. The Druid, *Saddle and Sirloin* (London: Vinton, 1895), pp. 65–78.

6. Thormanby, *Kings of the Turf* (London: Hutchinson, 1898), p. v.

7. J. Robinson and S. Gilpin, *Wrestling and Wrestlers* (London: Bemrose, 1893).

8. *Bell's Life*, 6 April 1862.

9. H. Shimmin, *Liverpool Life* (Liverpool: 1856), p. 99.

10. H. Allingham and D. Radford, *William Allingham: A Diary, 1824–1889* (London: Macmillan, 1907).

11. *Illustrated Sporting News*, 15 November 1862.

12. *Bell's Life*, 5 January 1862; ibid., 6 April 1862; ibid., 3 August 1862.

13. *Cricket and Football Times*, 21 October 1880.

14. Holt and Mangan, 'Prologue: Heroes of a European Past', p. 3.

15. Holt and Mangan, 'Prologue: Heroes of a European Past', p. 9.

16. *Newcastle Daily Chronicle*, 5 June 1868.

17. Richard Holt, 'Cricket and Englishness: The Batsman as Hero', *International Journal of the History of Sport*, 13 (1996), p. 50.

18. *Illustrated Sporting News*, 29 November 1862.

19. *Illustrated Sporting News*, 7 July 1866.

20. *Bell's Life*, 3 August 1862.

21. *Newcastle Weekly Chronicle*, 26 August 1871.

22. *Newcastle Courant*, 25 August 1871.

23. *Newcastle Daily Chronicle*, 11 September 1871; *Newcastle Weekly Chronicle*, 16 September 1871.

24. J. Fairfax-Blakeborough, *Northern Turf History: Hambledon and Richmond* (London: J. A. Allen, 1948), p. 317.

25. J. Radcliffe, *Ashgill: The Life and Times of John Osborne* (London: Sands and Co., 1905), pp. 391–93.

26. Roger Mortimer et al. (eds), *Biographical Encyclopaedia of British Flat Racing* (London: MacDonald, 1978), p. 578.

27. Peter Wynne-Thomas, *'Give Me Arthur': A Biography of Arthur Shrewsbury* (London: Arthur Barker, 1985).

28. *Grasshopper*, 15 February 1895.

29. *Essex Review* (1904), quoted in Callum McKenzie, 'The British Big-Game Hunting Tradition: Masculinity and Fraternalism with Particular Reference to the Shikar Club', *Sports Historian*, 20 (2000), pp. 70–96, p. 71.

30. Jeffrey Richards, *Imperialism and Juvenile Literature* (Manchester: Manchester University Press, 1989), pp. 75–76.

31. The following section largely draws on Eric Midwinter, *W. G. Grace: His Life and Times* (London: George Allen and Unwin, 1981), and Simon Rae, *W. G. Grace* (London: Faber and Faber, 1998).

32. Quoted in *Athletic News*, 5 June 1888.

33. Such figures are not without dispute, given the problems of definition of 'first class' and the disagreements about scores in primary sources. See Rae, *W. G. Grace*, p. 496.

34. Holt, 'Cricket and Englishness', p. 49.

35. *British Medical Journal*, 22 June 1895, p. 1406.

36. *Athletic News*, 20 January 1879.

37. Gareth Williams, 'How Amateur Was My Valley: Professional Sport and National Identity in Wales 1890–1914', *International Journal of the History of Sport*, 2 (1985), p. 252.

38. *Bell's Life*, 7 December 1862.

39. J. Fairfax Blakeborough, *The Analysis of the Turf* (London: Philip Allan, 1927), p. 306.

40. Wray Vamplew, *The Turf* (London: Allen Lane, 1976), p. 148.

41. *Bell's Life*, 6 April 1862.

42. Letter of Fordham to Charley Wood, 1 October 1887, in York Racing Museum, quoted in Vamplew, *The Turf*, p. 172.

43. See Vamplew, *The Turf*, pp. 171–72.

44. *Cricket and Football Times*, 3 June 1880.

45. James S. Curl, *The Victorian Celebration of Death* (Newton Abbot: David and Charles, 1972); John Wolffe, *Great Deaths: Grieving, Religion and Nationhood in Victorian and Edwardian Britain* (Oxford: Oxford University Press, 2000).

46. *Bell's Life*, 18 November 1865; *Croydon Weekly Standard*, 25 November 1865.

47. *Illustrated Sporting and Theatrical News*, 20 November 1865.

48. *The Times*, 13 November 1886.

49. *Newmarket Journal*, 20 November 1886.

50. *Newcastle Journal*, 18 July 1870; *Newcastle Daily Chronicle*, 19 July 1870.

51. *The Day's Doings*, 16 September 1871.

52. Scott's memorial received subscriptions inter alia from at least thirty-three titled individuals, and sixty calling themselves esquire, including three clergymen. *Bell's Life*, 7 December 1872.

53. Peter Seddon, *Steve Bloomer: The Story of Football's First Superstar* (Derby, 1999).

Notes to Chapter 8: Loyalties

1. The Liverpool journalist Hugh Shimmin, 'The Aintree Carnival', quoted in J. K. Walton and A. Wilcox (eds), *Low Life and Moral Improvement in Mid-Victorian England Through the Journalism of Hugh Shimmin* (Leicester: Leicester University Press, 1991), pp. 74–75.

2. The classic work is Eric Hobsbawm and Terence Ranger (eds), *The Invention of Tradition* (Cambridge: Cambridge University Press, 1993). In general I have avoided overuse of the term 'identity', to avoid confusion for those readers without a background in cultural studies.

3. *Tonbridgian*, July 1858, p. 13, quoted in Timothy Chandler, 'Games at

Oxbridge and the Public Schools, 1830–80: The Diffusion of an Innovation', *International Journal of the History of Sport*, 8 (1991), p. 196.

4. Graham Curry, 'The Trinity Connection: An Analysis of the Role of Members of Cambridge University in the Development of Football in the Mid Nineteenth Century', *Sports Historian* 22 (2002); Eric Dunning, *Barbarians, Gentlemen and Players: A Sociological Study of the Development of Rugby Football* (Oxford: Martin Robertson, 1979).

5. Tony Mason, *Association Football and English Society, 1863–1915* (Brighton: Harvester Press, 1980), p. 25.

6. *Illustrated Sporting and Theatrical News*, 26 May 1866.

7. *Cleveland News*, 25 March 1881.

8. Jeff Hill, 'Rite of Spring: Cup Finals and Community in the North of England', in Jeff Hill and Jack Williams (eds), *Sport and Identity in the North of England* (Keele: Keele University Press, 1996), p. 106.

9. See Jack Williams, 'One Could Literally Have Walked on the Heads of the People Congregated There: Sport, the Town and Identity', in Keith Laybourne (ed.), *Social Conditions, Status and Community, 1860–c.1920* (Stroud: Sutton Publishing, 1997), pp. 127–28.

10. David Smith and Gareth Williams, *Fields of Praise: the Official History of the Welsh Rugby Union, 1881–1981* (Cardiff: University of Wales Press, 1980), p. 5.

11. *Preston Herald*, 2 April 1884.

12. *Lincolnshire Echo*, 6 February 1892.

13. *Sunderland Echo*, 23 December 1887, 14 and 21 January 1888.

14. *Newcastle Daily Chronicle*, 10 April 1888, *Sunderland Echo*, 15 and 17 September 1888.

15. *Grasshopper*, 30 August 1895.

16. *Grasshopper*, 5 July 1895.

17. *Grasshopper*, 21 January 1895.

18. *Sheffield Daily Telegraph*, 5 March 1887, quoted in Mason, *Association Football*, p. 159.

19. *Pastime*, 13 May 1891.

20. See Asa Briggs, *Victorian Cities* (Harmondsworth: Pelican, 1977), p. 326.

21. *Bell's Life*, 7 June 1840 and 6 April 1862.

22. See Gerry Redmond, *The Caledonian Games in Nineteenth Century America* (Rutherford, New Jersey: Fairleigh Dickinson University Press, 1971).

23. Paul Beken and Stephen Jones, *Dragon in Exile: The Centenary History of London Welsh RFC* (London: Springwood Books, 1985).

24. J. D. Marshall and John K. Walton, *The Lake Counties from 1830 to the Mid-Twentieth Century* (Manchester: Manchester University Press, 1981), p. 168.

25. Thomas Thacker, *The Courser's Annual Remembrancer and Stud Book* (London: Longman, 1842), p. 146.

26. *Athletic News*, 15 January, 19 February and 7 May 1879.

27. See Alan Metcalfe, 'Football in the Mining Communities of East Northumberland, 1882–1914', *International Journal of the History of Sport*, 5 (1988), pp. 65–79.

28. *Sporting Chronicle*, 6 February 1899.

29. *The Day's Doings*, 5 November 1870; *Midland Sporting News*, 4 January and 21 October 1873; *Illustrated Sporting and Dramatic News*, 14 March 1874.

30. *The Times*, 2 May 1882.

31. *Grasshopper*, 28 June 1895.

32. *Bell's Life*, 2 December 1882.

33. *Sunderland Echo*, 24 November 1888.

34. *Illustrated Sporting and Theatrical News*, 24 November 1866.

35. *Illustrated Sporting and Dramatic News*, 17 October 1874.

36. *Athletic News*, 1895, quoted by Neil Wigglesworth, *The Evolution of English Sport* (London: Frank Cass, 1996), p. 98.

37. Geoffrey Green, *History of the Football Association* (London: Naldrett Press, 1953), p. 117.

38. Mike Huggins, 'Sport and the Social Construction of Identity in North-East England, 1800–1914', in Neville Kirk (ed.), *Northern Identities: Historical Interpretations of 'The North' and 'Northernness'* (Aldershot: Ashgate, 2000), pp. 132–62.

39. *The Times*, 17 July 1850; ibid., 2 May 1882.

40. Hill and Williams, *Sport and Identity*, p. 6.

41. Dave Russell, 'Amateurs, Professionals and Aspects of Northern Identity', *Sports Historian*, 16 (1996), pp. 64–80.

42. Reprinted report of 20 January 1872 in *Athletic News*, 15 January 1879.

43. Richard Holt, 'Heroes of the North: Sport and the Shaping of Regional Identity', in Hill and Williams, *Sport and Identity*, pp. 137–64.

44. Quoted in Mason, *Association Football and English Society*, p. 75.

45. *Tinsley's Magazine*, 1889/90, quoted in Mason, 'Football, Sport of the North?', in Hill and Williams, *Sport and Identity*, p. 50.

46. Mason, *Association Football and English Society*, p. 80.

47. *Athletic News*, 11 July 1888.

48. *Illustrated Times*, 12 May 1860.

49. Jeffrey Hill, 'Cocks, Cats, Caps and Cups: A Semiotic Approach to Sport and National Identity', *Culture, Sport, Society*, 2 (1999), pp. 1–21.

50. Linda Colley, *Britons: Forging the Nation, 1807–1837* (Newhaven, Connecticut: Yale University Press, 1992), p. 5.

51. Derek Birley, *Sport and the Making of Britain* (Manchester: Manchester University Press, 1993), p. 339.

52. See Grant Jarvie and John Burnett (eds), *Sport, Scotland and the Scots* (East Lothian: Tuckwell Press, 2000).

53. *Highlander*, 1 January 1876, quoted in Irene A. Reid, 'Shinty, Nationalism and Celtic Politics, 1870–1922', *Sports Historian*, 18 (1998), p. 115.

54. See Bill Murray, *The Old Firm: Sectarianism, Sport and Society in Scotland* (Edinburgh: John Donald, 1984); G. Finn, 'Racism, Religion and Social Prejudice: Irish Catholic Clubs, Soccer and Scottish Society', *International Journal of the History of Sport*, 8 (1991) pp. 72–95. G. Finn, 'Faith, Hope and Bigotry: Case Studies of Anti-Catholic Prejudice in Scottish Soccer and Society', in Grant Jarvie and Graham Walker (eds), *Ninety Minute Patriots? Scottish Sport and the Making of a Nation* (Leicester: Leicester University Press, 1994); Joseph Bradley, 'Football in Scotland: A History of Political and Ethnic Identity', *International Journal of the History of Sport*, 12 (1995), pp. 81–98; Joseph Bradley, 'Integration or Assimilation? Scottish Society, Football and Irish Immigrants', ibid., 13 (1996), pp. 61–79; Daniel Burdsley and Robert Chappell, 'An Examination of the Formation of Football Clubs in Scotland', *Sports Historian*, 21 (2001), pp. 94–106.

55. See Emma Lile, 'Professional Pedestrianism in South Wales during the Nineteenth Century', *Sports Historian*, 20 (2000), p. 97.

56. Gareth Williams, 'How Green Was My Valley: Professional Sport and National Identity in Wales, 1890–1914', *British Journal of Sports History*, 2 (1985), pp. 248–69.

57. Martin Johnes, *Soccer and Society: South Wales, 1900–1939* (Cardiff, University of Wales Press, 2002), pp. 1–4; David Andrews, 'Sport and the Masculine Hegemony of the Modern Nation: Welsh Rugby, Culture and Society, 1890–1914', in John Nauright and Timothy J. L. Chandler (eds), *Making Men: Rugby and Masculine Identity* (London: Frank Cass, 1996), pp. 50–69.

Notes to Chapter 9: The Wider World

1. *Illustrated Times*, 26 May 1860.

2. *Daily Telegraph*, 28 September 1888.

3. Sir Charles Tennyson, 'They Taught the World to Play', *Victorian Studies*, 2 (1959), pp. 211–22.

4. Harold Perkin, 'Teaching the Nations How to Play: Sport and Society in the British Empire and Commonwealth', *International Journal of the*

History of Sport, 6 (1989), p. 146; J. A. Mangan (ed.), *The Cultural Bond: Sport, Empire, Society* (London: Frank Cass, 1992), pp. 6–9.

5. J. D. Campbell, 'Training for Sport is Training for War: Sport and the Transformation of the British Army, 1860–1914', *International Journal of the History of Sport*, 17 (2000), pp. 21–58.

6. *Illustrated Times*, 31 March 1860.

7. I owe this point to Professor John Mackenzie (personal communication).

8. The cultural historian J. A. Mangan is the leading figure in the field. See J. A. Mangan, *The Games Ethic and Imperialism* (London: Viking, 1985), and Mangan (ed.), *The Cultural Bond*.

9. Theodore L. Pennell, *Amongst the Wild Tribes of the Afghan Frontier* (London, 1901), p. 157, quoted in J. A. Mangan, 'Christ and the Imperial Games Fields: Evangelical Athletes of the Empire', *British Journal of Sports History*, 1 (1984), p. 188.

10. Greg Ryan, *The Making of New Zealand Cricket, 1832–1914* (London: Frank Cass, 2003). Greg Ryan, 'Rural Myth and Urban Actuality: The Anatomy of All Black and New Zealand Rugby, 1884–1934', *New Zealand Journal of History*, 3 (2001), pp. 45–69, esp. p. 62.

11. Mangan, *The Games Ethic*, pp. 126, 146, 155 and passim.

12. Ossie Stuart, 'The Lion Roars, Football in African Society', in S. Wragg (ed.), *Giving the Game Away: Football, Politics and Culture in Five Continents* (London: Leicester University Press, 1995).

13. Pierre Lanfranchi, 'Exporting Football: Notes on the Development of Football in Europe', in Richard Guilianotti and John Williams (eds), *Game Without Frontiers: Football, Identity and Modernity* (Aldershot: Arena, 1994), pp. 23–46.

14. Stephen Wragg, 'On the Continent: Football in the Societies of N. W. Europe', in Wragg, *Giving the Game Away*, pp. 103–24.

15. Richard McBrearty, 'Scotland's Football Pioneers in Argentina', *Soccer History*, 3 (2003), pp. 23–25.

16. Phillip Moore, 'Soccer and the Politics of Culture in Western Australia', in Noel Dyke (ed.), *Games, Sports and Cultures* (Oxford: Berg, 2000), p. 123.

17. John R. Betts, *America's Sporting Heritage, 1850–1950* (Reading, Massachusetts, 1974), chapter 1.

18. Andrew Porter (ed.), *The Oxford History of the British Empire: The Nineteenth Century* (Oxford: Oxford University Press, 1999), p. 19.

19. Carl Martin and Benjamin Kline, 'British Emigration and New Identities', in P. J. Marshall (ed.), *Cambridge Illustrated History of the British Empire* (Cambridge: Cambridge University Press, 1996), p. 267.

20. Gerald Redmond, *The Sporting Scots of Nineteenth-Century Canada* (Toronto: Associated University Presses, 1982). See also Gerald Redmond, *The Caledonian Games in Nineteenth-Century America* (Rutherford, New Jersey: Fairleigh Dickinson University Press, 1971).

21. *Eton Chronicle*, July 1890, p. 1270; quoted in Mangan, *The Games Ethic*, p. 65.

22. Porter, *The Oxford History of the British Empire*, p. 4.

23. J. A. Roy, *Histoire du Jockey-Club de Paris* (Paris: Rivière, 1959).

24. Guy de Maupassant, *Gil Blas*, 6 June 1887, quoted in Jean-Michel Faure, 'National Identity and Sporting Champion: Jean Borotra and French History', *International Journal of the History of Sport*, 13 (1996), p. 87.

25. Quoted in Mangan, *The Games Ethic*, p. 53.

26. *Bell's Life in Victoria*, 28 December 1861.

27. Ashley Mallett, *Lord's Dreaming* (London: Souvenir Press, 2002), provides a full study of the tour.

28. Mihir Bose, *A History of Indian Cricket* (London: Deutsch, 1990).

29. Hilary McD. Beckles and Brian Stoddard, *Liberation Cricket: West Indies Cricket Culture* (Manchester: Manchester University Press, 1995), p. 23.

30. *Indian Sportsman*, 28 January 1899.

31. Nat Gould, *On and Off the Turf in Australia* (London: Routledge, 1895), p. 12.

32. 'The Turf in India', *Illustrated Times*, 26 May 1860, p. 325.

33. M. Cavanough and M. Davies, *Cup Day: The Story of the Melbourne Cup, 1861–1900* (Melbourne: F. W. Cheshire, 1960).

34. Eduardo Archetti,' Masculinity and Football: The Formation of National Identity in Argentina', in Guilianotti and Williams (eds), *Game Without Frontiers*, pp. 225ff. See also Tony Mason, *Passion of the People: Football in South America* (London: Verso, 1995), chapters 1 and 2.

35. Ged Martin and Benjamine Kline, 'British Emigration and New Identities', in Marshall (ed.), *Cambridge Illustrated History of the British Empire*, p. 274.

36. Albert Spalding, quoted in Glenn Moore, 'The Great Baseball Tour of 1888–9: A Tale of Image Making, Intrigue and Labour Relations in the Gilded Age', *International Journal of the History of Sport*, 11 (1994), p. 450.

37. G. Vigne, *Travels in Kashmir* (London: 1842), quoted by Derek Birley, *Sport and the Making of Britain* (Manchester: Manchester University Press, 1993), p. 309. For polo see Allen Guttman and H. E. Chehabi, 'Polo, the Asian Innovation: Emergence and Diffusion', in J. A. Mangan and Fan Hong (eds), *Sport in Asian Society: Past and Present* (London: Cass, 2002).

38. F. G. Afalo (ed.), *The Cost of Sport* (London: John Murray, 1899).

39. *Indian Sportsman*, 3 December 1898.
40. Patrick McDevitt, 'The King of Sport: Polo in Late Victorian and Edwardian India', *International Journal of the History of Sport*, 20 (2003), pp. 1–27.
41. T. F. Dale, 'Polo and Politics', *Blackwoods Magazine*, 165, June 1899, pp. 1033–36.
42. *Bell's Life*, 6 April 1862.
43. Derek Birley, *The Willow Wand* (London: Queen Anne Press, 1979), p. 74.
44. John M. Mackenzie, 'Heroic Myths of Empire', in John M. Mackenzie, *Imperialism and the Military, 1850–1950* (Manchester: Manchester University Press, 1993), p. 110.
45. Steven Riess, *Sport in Industrial America, 1850–1920* (Wheeling, Illinois: Harlan Davison, 1995), p. 85.
46. Alan Metcalfe, *Canada Learns to Play* (Toronto: McClelland and Stewart, 1987), p. 177.
47. See *Bell's Life*, 14 June 1840.
48. Richard McBrearty, 'Andrew Watson: The World's First Black Football Internationalist', *Soccer History*, 2 (2002), pp. 3–6; Phil Vasili, *The First Black Footballer* (London: Frank Cass, 1998).
49. Quoted in Birley, *The Willow Wand*, p. 76.
50. Quoted in the *Sporting Chronicle*, 12 August 1899.
51. See Daryl Adair and Wray Vamplew, *Sport in Australian History* (Oxford: Oxford University Press, 1997), pp. 6–7.
52. Quoted in *Bell's Life*, 5 August 1882.
53. *Sporting Chronicle*, 12 August. 1899.
54. Greg Ryan, 'Handsome Physiognomy and Blameless Physique: Indigenous Colonial Sporting Tours and British Racial Consciousness, 1868 and 1888', *International Journal of the History of Sport*, 14 (1997), p. 78.
55. The columns of the *Indian Sportsman*, 31 December, 1898, reported such press complaints.
56. Brian Stoddard, 'Cricket and Colonialism in the Caribbean', in Beckles and Stoddard, *Liberation Cricket*, pp. 11–24.
57. See Trevor Lloyd, *Empire: A History of the British Empire* (London: Hambledon, 2001).
58. *Illustrated Times*, 26 May 1860.
59. *Bell's Life in Victoria*, 29 December 1866.
60. *Indian Field*, 16 April 1859.
61. *Cricket*, 9 August 1886.
62. *Indian Sportsman*, 25 March 1899. The extent of the existence of counter-communities of students and other radical groups amongst the colonised

has still to be fully probed in the vernacular newspapers of the time. See Boria Majumdar, 'The Vernacular in Sports History', *International Journal of the History of Sport*, 20 (2003), pp. 107–25.

63. Michael Mullen, 'The Devolution of the Irish Economy in the Nineteenth Century and the Bifurcation of Irish Sport', *International Journal of the History of Sport*, 13 (1996), pp. 42–60; Joseph Bradley, 'Unrecognised Middle-Class Revolutionary? Michael Cusack, Sport and Cultural Change in Nineteenth Century Ireland', in J. A. Mangan (ed.), *Reformers, Sport, Modernizers: Middle-Class Revolutionaries* (London: Frank Cass, 2002), pp. 58–72. For a broader perspective see J. Sugden and A. Bairner, *Sport, Sectarianism and Society in a Divided Ireland* (Leicester: Leicester University Press, 1993), and Mike Cronin, *Sport and Nationalism in Ireland* (Dublin: Four Courts Press, 1999).

64. J. A. Alter, 'Kabbadi, A National Sport of India', in Noel Dyck (ed.), *Games, Sports and Cultures* (Oxford: Berg, 2000), pp. 81–116.

65. Jim Walvin, *The People's Game* (London: Allen Lane, 1975), p. 92.

66. See Tony Mason, 'Some Englishmen and Scotsmen Abroad; The Spread of World Football', in Alan Thomlinson and Garry Whannel (eds), *Off the Ball* (London: Pluto Press, 1986).

67. Rob Hess and Bob Stewart (eds), *More than a Game: An Unauthorised History of Australian Rules Football* (Melbourne; Melbourne University Press, 1998).

68. Tom Melville, *The Tented Field: A History of Cricket in America* (Bowling Green; Bowling Green State University Press, 1998).

69. John M. McKenzie, *The Empire of Nature: Hunting, Conservation and British Imperialism* (Manchester: Manchester University Press, 1988).

70. Sporting memoirs of this period survive in large numbers in the British Library.

71. *Englishman* (Calcutta), 3 March 1876.

72. Peter Star, 'Native Bird Protection, National Identity and the Rise of Preservation in New Zealand to 1914', *New Zealand Journal of History*, 36 (2002) pp. 123–36, provides a useful case study.

73. See John MacKenzie (ed.), *Imperialism and Popular Culture* (Manchester: Manchester University Press, 1998).

74. *Era*, 2 October 1897.

75. *Cricket*, 28 October 1886.

76. *Bury Times*, 25 July 1868, *Cricket and Football Times*, 8 July 1880.

77. James Bradley, 'The MCC, Society and Empire: A Portrait of Cricket's Ruling Body, 1860–1914', *International Journal of the History of Sport*, 7 (1990), pp. 3–22.

78. J. A. Mangan and Callum McKenzie, 'Radical Conservatives: Middle-Class Masculinity, the Shikar Club and Big-Game Hunting', in Mangan (ed.), *Reformers, Sport, Modernizers*, pp. 188–89.

79. *Sporting Life*, 27 December 1862.

80. *Indian Sportsman*, 31 December 1898, gave publicity to one of the first, Jaffer Khan, who became trainer to His Highness the Koer Sahib of Patiala, and wrote *A New Book on Racing from 1855 to Date* (Calcutta, 1898).

81. *Indian Planters' Gazette*, 9 March 1886.

82. Leicestershire Record Office, DE 5051/3, scrapbook of Arthur Woodcock.

83. *Lancashire Evening Post*, 14 March 1889. See Daniel Bloyce, 'Just Not Cricket: Baseball in England, 1874–1900', *International Journal of the History of Sport*, 14 (1997), pp. 207–18.

84. *Newcastle Daily Chronicle*, 8 May 1893.

85. *Midland Sporting News*, 24 August 1895.

86. See Rupert Christianson, *The Visitors: Culture Shock in Nineteenth-Century Britain* (London: Pimlico Press, 2001).

87. *Cricket Chat*, 1886, and *Cricket*, 23 August 1888, quoted in Jack Williams, *Cricket and Race* (Oxford: Berg, 2001) p. 29.

88. *Field*, 27 June 1896, quoted in Williams, *Cricket and Race*, p. 27.

89. *Illustrated Sporting and Dramatic News*, 7 November 1874.

90. Derek Birley, *A Social History of English Cricket* (London: Aurum Press, 1999), p. 137.

Bibliography

MANUSCRIPT SOURCES

The amount of Victorian sports material in archive holdings has increased substantially in recent years as sport's importance has become more widely recognised. Readers who would find guidance to such sources helpful are referred to Richard William Cox's excellent book *History of Sport: A Guide to Historiography, Research Methodology and Sources of Information* (London: Frank Cass, 2003).

NEWSPAPERS

Athletic News
Badminton Magazine
Baily's Magazine
Barnet Gazette
Bell's Life
Bell's Life in Victoria
Bicycling News and Tricycling Gazette
Blackwood's Magazine
British Medical Journal
Bury Times
Cleveland News
Contemporary Review
Cricket
Cricket and Football Times
Cricket Weekly Record
Croydon Weekly Standard
Daily Telegraph

Day's Doings

Derby Mercury

Doncaster Gazette

Doncaster Reporter

Englishman

Field

Football

Free Lance

Grasshopper

Hour

Household Words

Illustrated Sporting and Dramatic News

Illustrated Sporting and Theatrical News

Illustrated Times

Indian Field

Indian Planters' Gazette

Indian Sportsman

Lancashire Evening Post

Lancaster Gazette

Land and Water

Lincolnshire Echo

Liverpool Mercury

Manchester Guardian

Midland Sporting News

Middlesbrough Daily Exchange

Newcastle Courant

Newcastle Daily Chronicle

Newcastle Journal

Newcastle Weekly Chronicle

Newmarket Journal

Newsagent and Booksellers' Review

North-Eastern Daily Gazette

Northern Echo

Northern Review

North Wales Observer and Express

Pall Mall Gazette

Pastime

Preston Herald

Punch

Racing Calendar

Scottish Athletic Journal

Spectator

Sporting Chronicle

Sporting Life

Sporting Magazine

Star

Sunderland Echo

Sunderland News

Swimming, Rowing and Athletic Record

The Times

Wolverhampton Chronicle

Yorkshireman

PRINTED PRIMARY SOURCES

Afalo, G. (ed.), *The Cost of Sport* (London: John Murray, 1899).

Alcock, Charles W. (ed.), *Football Annual* (London: Wright and Co., 1884).

Alcock, Charles W. (ed.), *Football Annual* (London: Wright and Co., 1886).

Allingham, H. and Radford, D., *William Allingham: A Diary, 1824–1889* (London: Macmillan, 1907).

Anon., *London Characters and the Humorous Side of London Life* (London: Slaley Rivers, 1871).

Ashley-Cooper, S., *Cricket Highways and Byways* (London: Allen and Unwin 1927).

Athletic News, *Athletic News Cricket Annual* (London: Athletic News, 1896).

Bateman, J., *The Great Landowners of Great Britain and Ireland* (London: Harrison, 1883).

Booth, Charles, *Life and Labour of the People of London*, i (London: Macmillan, 1892).

Booth, J. B., *Old Pink 'Un Days* (London: Grant Richards, 1924).

Binstead, Arthur M. and Wells, Ernest, *A Pink 'Un and a Pelican* (London: Sands and Co., 1898).

Burnley, James, *Two Sides of the Atlantic* (London: Simpkin, Marshall, 1880).

Carlyle, Thomas, *On Heroes, Hero Worship and the Heroic in History* (London: Chapman and Hall, 1904).

Cox, Harding et al., *Coursing and Falconry* (London: The Field, 1892).

Deacon's *Newspaper Handbook* (London: Deacon, 1881).

Dickens, Charles, *Pickwick Papers* (London: Dent, 1998).

Doré, Gustave and Jerrold, Blanchard, *London: A Pilgrimage* (London: Grant, 1872).

Druid, *Saddle and Sirloin* (London: Vinton, 1895).

Eliot, George, *Daniel Deronda* (London: J. M. Dent, 1964).

Gale, Frederick, *Modern English Sports: Their Use and Abuse* (London: 1885).

Gould, Nat, *On and Off the Turf in Australia* (London: Routledge, 1895).

Hatton, Joseph, *Journalistic London* (London: Sampson Lowe, 1882).

Hieover, Harry, *The Sporting World* (London: T. C. Newby, 1858).

Jeffries, Richard, *The Toilers in the Field* (London: MacDonald Futura, 1981).

Lillywhite, John, *John Lillywhite's Football Annual* (London: Lillywhite, 1868–1901).

Lillywhite, *Cricketers' Companion* (London: Lillywhite, 1880).

Mitchell and Co., *The Newspaper Press Directory* (London: Mitchell, 1851–1901).

Mitford, Mary, *Our Village* (London: Walter Scott, 1891 edn).

Kelly and Co., *Post Office Directory of Lancashire with Liverpool and Manchester* (London: Kelly and Co., 1881).

Peek, H., *The Badminton Library of Sports and Pastimes: The Poetry of Sport* (London: Badminton Press, 1896).

Plomer, William (ed.), *Kilvert's Diary, 1870–1879* (London: Cape, 1973).

Radcliffe, J., *Ashgill: The Life and Times of John Osborne* (London: Sands and Co., 1905).

J. M. Richardson and Finch Mason, *Gentleman Riders Past and Present* (London: Vinton, 1909).

Robinson J. and Gilpin, S., *Wrestling and Wrestlers* (London: Bemrose, 1893).

Ruff, William, *Ruff's Guide to the Turf* (London: Ruff, 1846–1901).

Russell, Charles, *Manchester Boys: Sketches of Manchester Lads at Work and Play* (Manchester: Manchester University Press, 1905).

Rowntree, Seebohm, *Poverty: A Study of Town Life* (London: Longman, 1901).

Seton-Carr, H., *My Sporting Holidays* (London: Edward Arnold, 1904).

Shimmin, H., *Liverpool Life* (Liverpool: 1856).

Smith, Charles Manby, *Curiosities of London Life* (London: A. W. Bennett, 1853).

Stovin, J. (ed.), *Journals of a Methodist Farmer, 1871–75* (London: Croom Helm, 1977).

Taine, Hippolyte, *Notes on England* (London: Caliban Books, 1995).

Thacker, Thomas, *The Courser's Annual Remembrancer and Stud Book* (London: Longman, 1842).

Thormanby, *Kings of the Turf* (London: Hutchinson, 1898).

Trollope, Anthony, *An Autobiography* (Oxford: Oxford University Press, 1961).

Trollope, Anthony, *British Sports and Pastimes* (London: Virtue, 1868).

Trollope, Anthony, *Hunting Sketches* (London: Chapman and Hall, 1865).

Williams, Alfred, *A Wiltshire Village* (London: Duckworth, 1912).

Wilson, Joe, *Tyneside Songs and Drolleries* (Newcastle: Allen, 1870).

Wright, Thomas, *Some Habits and Customs of the Working Classes* (first published 1867; New York: Augustus Kelly, 1967).

SECONDARY SOURCES: BOOKS

Adair, Daryl and Vamplew, Wray, *Sport in Australian History* (Oxford: Oxford University Press, 1997).

Arlott, John (ed.), *The Oxford Companion to Sports and Games* (Oxford: Oxford University Press, 1975).

Bailey, Peter (ed.), *Music Hall: The Business of Pleasure* (Milton Keynes: Open University Press, 1986).

Bailey, Peter, *Popular Culture and Performance in the Victorian City* (Cambridge: Cambridge University Press, 1999).

Barnes, John, *The Beginnings of the Cinema in England*, ii, *1897* (Exeter: Exeter University Press, 1996).

Barnes, John, *The Beginning of the Cinema in* England, v, *1900* (Exeter: University of Exeter Press, 1997).

Beckles, Hilary McD. and Stoddard, Brian, *Liberation Cricket: West Indies Cricket Culture* (Manchester: Manchester University Press, 1995).

Beckett, J. V., *The Aristocracy in England, 1660–1914* (Oxford: Basil Blackwell, 1986).

Beken, Paul and Jones, Stephen, *Dragon in Exile: The Centenary History of London Welsh RFC* (London: Springwood Books, 1985).

Betts, John R., *America's Sporting Heritage, 1850–1950* (Reading, Massachusetts, 1974).

Birley, Derek, *A Social History of English Cricket* (London: Aurum Press, 1999).

Birley, Derek, *Sport and the Making of Britain* (Manchester: Manchester University Press, 1993).

Birley, Derek, *The Willow Wand* (London: Queen Anne Press, 1979).

Booth, Keith, *The Father of Modern Sport: The Life and Times of Charles W. Alcock* (Manchester: Parrs Wood Press, 2002).

Bose, Mihir, *A History of Indian Cricket* (London: Deutsch, 1990).

Bovill, W., *The England of Nimrod and Surtees, 1815–1854* (London: Oxford University Press, 1959).

Brailsford, Dennis, *A Taste for Diversions: Sport in Georgian England* (Cambridge: Lutterworth Press, 1999).

Brailsford, Dennis, *Sport, Time and Society: The British at Play* (London: Routledge, 1991).

Briggs, Asa, *Victorian Cities* (Harmondsworth: Pelican, 1977).

Burnett, John, *Riot, Revelry and Rout: Sport in Scotland before 1860* (East Lothian; Tuckwell Press, 2000).

Cannadine, David, *The Decline and Fall of the British Aristocracy* (London: Papermac, 1996).

Carr, Raymond, *English Foxhunting: A History* (London: Weidenfeld and Nicolson, 1976).

Cashmore, Ellis, *Beckham* (Cambridge: Polity, 2002).

Cavanough M. and Davies, M., *Cup Day: The Story of the Melbourne Cup, 1861–1900* (Melbourne: F. W. Cheshire, 1960).

Christianson, Rupert, *The Visitors: Culture Shock in Nineteenth-Century Britain* (London: Pimlico Press, 2001).

Colley, Linda, *Britons: Forging the Nation, 1807–1837* (New Haven, Connecticut: Yale University Press, 1992).

Collins, Tony, *Rugby's Great Split: Class, Culture and the Origins of Rugby Football League* (London: Frank Cass, 1998).

Collins, Tony and Vamplew, Wray, *Mud, Sweat and Beers: A Cultural History of Sport and Alcohol* (Oxford: Berg, 2002).

Croll, Andy, *Civilising the Urban: Popular Culture and Public Space in Merthyr, c. 1870–1914* (Cardiff: University of Wales Press, 2000).

Cronin, Mike, *Sport and Nationalism in Ireland* (Dublin: Four Courts Press, 1999).

Crosfield, John, *A History of the Cadbury Family*, ii (Cambridge: Cambridge University Press, 1985).

Crossick, Geoffrey, *An Artisan Elite in Victorian Society* (London: Croom Helm, 1978).

Crossick, Geoffrey (ed.), *The Lower Middle Class in Britain, 1870–1914* (London: Macmillan, 1977).

Cunningham, Hugh, *Leisure in the Industrial Revolution* (London: Croom Helm, 1980).

Curl, James S., *The Victorian Celebration of Death* (Newton Abbot: David and Charles, 1972).

Delaney, T., *Rugby Disunion* (Keighley: privately printed, 1993).

Dallas, Donald, *Holland & Holland, the Royal Gunmaker: The Complete History* (London: Quiller Press, 2003).

Dentith, Simon, *Society and Cultural Forms in Nineteenth-Century England* (Basingstoke: Macmillan, 1998).

Dunning, Eric, and Sheard, K., *Barbarians, Gentlemen and Players* (London: Martin Robinson, 1979).

Dyke, Noel (ed.), *Games, Sports and Cultures* (Oxford: Berg, 2000).

Elias, Norbert, *The Civilising Process* (Oxford: Blackwell, 1982).

Fairfax-Blakeborough, Jack, *Northern Sport and Sportsmen Part 5* (London: Hunter and Longhurst, n.d.).

Fairfax-Blakeborough, Jack, *Northern Turf History: Hambledon and Richmond* (London: J. A. Allen, 1948).

Fairfax Blakeborough, Jack, *The Analysis of the Turf* (London: Philip Allan, 1927).

Floud, R. and McCloskey, D., *The Economic History of Britain since 1700*, ii (Cambridge: Cambridge University Press, 1981).

Jarvie, Grant and Burnett, John (eds), *Sport, Scotland and the Scots* (East Lothian: Tuckwell Press, 2000).

Girouard, Mark, *Life in the English Country House* (Newhaven: Yale University Press, 1978).

Girouard, Mark, *The Return to Camelot: Chivalry and the English Gentleman* (New Haven, Connecticut: Yale University Press, 1981).

Goulstone, John, *Football's Secret History* (Upminster: 3–2 Books, 2001).

Green, Geoffrey, *History of the Football Association* (London: Naldrett Press, 1953).

Guilianotti, Richard and Williams, John (eds), *Game Without Frontiers: Football, Identity and Modernity* (Aldershot: Arena, 1994).

Gunn, Simon, *The Public Culture of the Victorian Middle Class* (Manchester: Manchester University Press, 2000).

Halliday, Eric, *Rowing in England: A Social History* (Manchester: Manchester University Press, 1990).

Harvey, Adrian, *The Beginnings of a Commercial Sporting Culture in Britain, 1793–1850* (London: Ashgate, 2004).

Hess, Rob and Stewart, Bob (eds), *More than a Game: An Unauthorised History of Australian Rules Football* (Melbourne; Melbourne University Press, 1998).

Hill, Jeff and Williams, Jack (eds), *Sport and Identity in the North of England* (Keele: Keele University Press, 1996).

Hobsbawm, Eric and Ranger, Terence (eds), *The Invention of Tradition* (Cambridge: Cambridge University Press, 1993).

Holt, Richard, *Sport and the British* (Oxford: Clarendon Press, 1989).

Horn, Pamela, *Pleasures and Pastimes in Victorian Britain* (Stroud: Sutton Publishing, 1999).

Horne, J., Tomlinson, A. and Whannel, G., *Understanding Sport: An Introduction to the Sociological and Cultural Analysis of Sport* (London: Spon, 1999).

Houriham, Margery, *Deconstructing the Hero* (London: Routledge, 1997).

Horrall, Andrew, *Popular Culture in London, c. 1890–1918* (Manchester: Manchester University Press, 2001).

Huggins, Mike, *Flat Racing and British Society, 1790–1914* (London: Frank Cass, 2000).

Huggins, Mike, *Kings of the Moor* (Middlesbrough: Teesside Polytechnic Papers, 1991).

Huggins, Mike and Mangan, J. A. (eds), *Disreputable Pleasures: Less Virtuous Victorians at Play* (London: Frank Cass, 2004).

Hunt, David, *A History of Preston North End: The People, the Power and the Politics* (Preston: Preston North End Publications, 2000).

Jackson, Herbert and Mary (eds), *Lakeland's Pioneer Rock-Climbers* (Clapham: Dalesman Books, 1980).

Johnes, Martin, *Soccer and Society: South Wales, 1900–1939* (Cardiff, University of Wales Press, 2002).

Jones, Steven G., *Sport, Politics and the Working Class* (Manchester: Manchester University Press, 1988).

Joyce, Patrick, *Work, Society and Politics; The Culture of the Factory in Late Victorian England* (Brighton: Harvester, 1980).

Keevins, Hugh and McCarra, Kevin, *100 Cups: The Story of the Scottish Cup* (Edinburgh: Mainstream Publishing, 1985).

Kirk, Neville, *Change, Continuity and Class: Labour in British Society, 1850–1920* (Manchester: Manchester University Press, 1998).

Lloyd, Trevor, *Empire: A History of the British Empire* (London: Hambledon, 2001).

Lomas, Roy, *Grasmere Sports: The First 150 Years* (Kendal: MTP publications, 2002).

Low, Rachael and Manvell, Roger, *The History of the British Film, 1896–1906* (London: George Allen, 1948).

Lowerson, John, *Sport and the English Middle Classes, 1850–1914* (Manchester: Manchester University Press, 1993).

Lowerson, John and Myerscough, J., *Time to Spare in Victorian England* (Hassocks: Harvester Press, 1977).

MacAloon, John, *This Great Symbol: Pierre de Coubertin and the Origins of the Modern Olympic Games* (Chicago: University of Chicago Press, 1981).

McCord, Norman, *British History, 1815–1906* (Oxford: Oxford University Press, 1991).

Mackenzie, John (ed.), *Imperialism and Popular Culture* (Manchester: Manchester University Press, 1998).

Mackenzie, John, *Imperialism and the Military, 1850–1950* (Manchester: Manchester University Press, 1993).

Mackenzie, John, *Propaganda and Empire: The Manipulation of British Public Opinion, 1880–1960* (Manchester: Manchester University Press, 1984).

Mackenzie, John, *The Empire of Nature: Hunting, Conservation and British Imperialism* (Manchester: Manchester University Press, 1988).

Malcolmson, Robert, *Popular Recreations in English Society, 1700–1850* (Cambridge: Cambridge University Press, 1973).

Mallett, Ashley, *Lord's Dreaming* (London: Souvenir Press, 2002).

Mangan, J. A., *Athleticism in the Victorian and Edwardian Public School* (London: Frank Cass 2000).

Mangan, J. A. (ed.), *The Cultural Bond: Sport, Empire, Society* (London: Frank Cass, 1992).

Mangan, J. A., *The Games Ethic and Imperialism* (Harmondsworth: Viking, 1986).

Mangan, J. A. and Hong, Fan (eds), *Sport in Asian Society: Past and Present* (London: Cass, 2002).

Marshall, J. D. and Walton, John K., *The Lake Counties from 1830 to the Mid-Twentieth Century* (Manchester: Manchester University Press, 1981).

Marshall, P. J. (ed.), *Cambridge Illustrated History of the British Empire* (Cambridge: Cambridge University Press, 1996).

Mason, Tony, *Association Football and English Society, 1863–1915* (Brighton: Harvester Press, 1980).

Mason, Tony, *Passion of the People: Football in South America* (London: Verso, 1995).

Mason, Tony, *Sport in Britain* (London: Faber and Faber, 1988).

Meller, Helen E., *Nottingham in the 1880s: A Study in Social Change* (Nottingham: University of Nottingham, 1971).

Melville, Tom, *The Tented Field: A History of Cricket in America* (Bowling Green: Bowling Green State University Press, 1998).

Metcalfe, Alan, *Canada Learns to Play* (Toronto: McClelland and Stewart, 1987).

Midwinter, Eric, *W. G. Grace: His Life and Times* (London: George Allen and Unwin, 1981).

Mills, Dennis R., *Lord and Peasant in Nineteenth-Century Britain* (London: Croom Helm, 1980).

Mingay, G. E. (ed.), *The Victorian Countryside*, ii (London: Routledge, 1981).

Moorhouse, Geoffrey, *A People's Game: The Official History of Rugby League* (London: Hodder and Stoughton, 1995).

Morris, R. J., *Class, Sect and Party: The Making of the British Middle Class. Leeds, 1820–1850* (Manchester: Manchester University Press, 1990).

Mortimer, Roger et al. (eds), *Biographical Encyclopaedia of British Flat Racing* (London: MacDonald, 1978).

Murfin, Lyn, *Popular Leisure in the Lake Counties* (Manchester: Manchester University Press, 1990).

Murray, Bill, *The Old Firm: Sectarianism, Sport and Society in Scotland* (Edinburgh: John Donald, 1984).

Musgrave, P. W., *From Brown to Bunter* (London: Routledge and Kegan Paul, 1985).

Nash, David, *Secularism, Art and Freedom* (Leicester: Leicester University Press, 1992).

Nead, Lynda, *Victorian Babylon* (New Haven, Connecticut: Yale University Press, 2000).

Perkin, Harold, *The Rise of Professional Society* (London: Routledge, 1989).

Pinfold, John, *Hoylake Race Course and the Beginnings of the Royal Liverpool Golf Club* (Prenton: I. & M. Boumphrey, 2002).

Plumtre, George, *The Fast Set* (London: Andrew Deutsch, 1985).

Porter, Andrew (ed.), *The Oxford History of the British Empire: The Nineteenth Century* (Oxford: Oxford University Press, 1999).

Rae, Simon, *W. G. Grace* (London: Faber and Faber, 1998).

Redmond, Gerald, *The Caledonian Games in Nineteenth-Century America* (Rutherford, New Jersey: Fairleigh Dickinson University Press, 1971).

Redmond, Gerald, *The Sporting Scots of Nineteenth-Century Canada* (Toronto: Associated University Presses, 1982).

Richards, Jeffery, *Imperialism and Juvenile Literature* (Manchester: Manchester University Press, 1989).

Riess, S., *City Games: The Evolution of American Urban Society and the Rise of Sports* (Urbana: University of Illinois Press, 1989).

Riess, S., *Sport in Industrial America, 1850–1920* (Wheeling, Illinois: Harlan Davison, 1995).

Rojek, Chris, *Celebrity* (London: Reaktion, 2001).

Roy, J. A., *Histoire du Jockey-Club de Paris* (Paris: Rivière, 1959).

Rubinstein, William D., *Men of Property: The Very Wealthy in Britain since the Industrial Revolution* (London: Croom Helm, 1981).

Russell, Dave, *Football and the English* (Preston: Carnegie Publishing, 1997).

Ryan, Greg, *The Making of New Zealand Cricket, 1832–1914* (London: Frank Cass, 2003).

Samuel, Raphael, *Village Life and Labour* (London: Routledge and Kegan Paul, 1975).

Seddon, Peter, *Steve Bloomer: The Story of Football's First Superstar* (Derby: Breedon, 1999).

Smith, David and Williams, Gareth, *Fields of Praise: The Official History of the Welsh Rugby Union, 1881–1981* (Cardiff: University of Wales Press, 1980).

Stoddard, Brian and Sandiford, Keith A. P. (eds), *The Imperial Game* (Manchester; Manchester University Press, 1998).

Sugden, J. and Bairner, A., *Sport, Sectarianism and Society in a Divided Ireland* (Leicester: Leicester University Press, 1993).

Sutherland, D., *The Yellow Earl* (London: Molendinar Press, 1965).

Thompson, F. M. L., *Gentrification and the Enterprise Culture: Britain, 1780–1980* (Oxford: Oxford University Press, 2001).

Thompson, F. M. L., *Hampstead: Building a Borough, 1650–1964* (London: Routledge, 1974).

Thompson, F. M. L. (ed.), *The Cambridge Social History of Britain, 1750–1940*, i, *Regions and Communities* (Cambridge: Cambridge University Press, 1990).

Tranter, Neil, *Sport, Economy and Society in Britain, 1750–1914* (Cambridge, Cambridge University Press, 1998).

Turner, E. S., *Boys Will Be Boys* (London: Michael Joseph, 1957).

Twydell, David, *Rejected FC*, iii (Harefield, 1992).

Vamplew, Wray, *Pay Up and Play the Game: Professional Sport in Britain, 1875–1914* (Cambridge: Cambridge University Press, 1988).

Vamplew, Wray, *The Turf* (London: Allen Lane, 1976).

Vasili, Phil, *The First Black Footballer* (London: Frank Cass, 1998).

Walton, J. K. and Wilcox, Alan (eds), *Low Life and Moral Improvement in Mid-Victorian England: Liverpool Through the Journalism of H. Shimmin* (Leicester: Leicester University Press, 1991).

Walvin, James, *The People's Game* (London: Allen Lane, 1975).

Wigglesworth, Neil, *The Evolution of English Sport* (London: Frank Cass, 1996).

Williams, Jack, *Cricket and Race* (Oxford: Berg, 2001).

Wolffe, John, *Great Deaths: Grieving, Religion and Nationhood in Victorian and Edwardian Britain* (Oxford: Oxford University Press, 2000).

Wragg, S. (ed.), *Giving the Game Away: Football, Politics and Culture in Five Continents* (London: Leicester University Press, 1995).

Wynne-Thomas, Peter, *'Give Me Arthur': A Biography of Arthur Shrewsbury* (London: Arthur Barker, 1985).

SECONDARY SOURCES:
ARTICLES AND CHAPTERS IN EDITED EDITIONS

Alter, J. A., 'Kabbadi, A National Sport of India', in Noel Dyck (ed.), *Games, Sports and Cultures* (Oxford: Berg, 2000), pp. 81–116.

Andrews, David, 'Sport and the Masculine Hegemony of the Modern Nation: Welsh Rugby, Culture and Society, 1890–1914', in John Nauright and Timothy J. L. Chandler (eds), *Making Men: Rugby and Masculine Identity* (London: Frank Cass, 1996), pp. 50–69.

Arnold, A. J., 'The Belated Entry of Professional Soccer into the Textile District of Northern England', *International Journal of the History of Sport*, 6 (1989), pp. 319–34.

Bailey, Peter, 'Will the Real Bill Banks Please Stand Up? Towards a Role Analysis of Mid-Victorian Working-Class Respectability', *Social History*, 12 (1979), pp. 336–53.

Bailey, Peter, 'White Collars, Grey Lives? The Lower Middle Class Revisited', *Journal of British Studies*, 38 (1999), pp. 273–90.

Blackledge, Paul, 'Rational Capitalist Concerns: William Cail and the Great Rugby Split of 1895', *International Journal of the History of Sport*, 18 (2001), pp. 35–53.

Bloyce, Daniel, 'Just Not Cricket: Baseball in England, 1874–1900', *International Journal of the History of Sport*, 14 (1997), pp. 207–18.

Bradley, Joseph, 'Football in Scotland: A History of Political and Ethnic Identity', *International Journal of the History of Sport*, 12 (1995), pp. 81–98.

Bradley, Joseph, 'Integration or Assimilation? Scottish Society, Football and Irish Immigrants', *International Journal of the History of Sport*, 13 (1996), pp. 61–79.

Bradley, James, 'The MCC, Society and Empire: A Portrait of Cricket's Ruling Body, 1860–1914', *International Journal of the History of Sport*, 7 (1990), pp. 3–22.

Bradley, Joseph, 'Unrecognised Middle-Class Revolutionary? Michael Cusack, Sport and Cultural Change in Nineteenth-Century Ireland', in J. A. Mangan (ed.), *Reformers, Sport, Modernizers: Middle-Class Revolutionaries* (London: Frank Cass, 2002), pp. 58–72.

Burdsley, Daniel and Chappell, Robert, 'An Examination of the Formation of Football Clubs in Scotland', *Sports Historian*, 21 (2001), pp. 94–106.

Campbell, J. D., 'Training for Sport is Training for War: Sport and the Transformation of the British Army, 1860–1914', *International Journal of the History of Sport*, 17 (2000), pp. 21–58.

Chandler, Timothy, 'Games at Oxbridge and the Public Schools, 1830–80: The Diffusion of an Innovation', *International Journal of the History of Sport*, 8 (1991), pp. 171–204.

Chandler, Timothy, 'The Structuring of Manliness and the Development of Rugby Football at the Public Schools and Oxbridge, 1830–1880', in John Nauright and T. J. Chandler (eds), *Making Men: Rugby and Masculine Identity* (London: Frank Cass, 1996), pp. 13–31.

Collins, Tony and Vamplew, Wray, 'The Pub, the Drinks Trade and the Early Years of Modern Football', *Sports Historian*, 20 (2000), pp. 1–17.

Curry, Graham, 'The Trinity Connection: An Analysis of the Role of Members of Cambridge University in the Development of Football in the Mid Nineteenth Century', *Sports Historian* 22 (2002), pp. 46–74.

Coyle, John, 'From Minor to Major', *Association of Sports Historians Newsletter*, July 2000, pp. 10–19.

Crump, Jeremy, 'The Great Carnival of the Year: The Leicester Races in the Nineteenth Century', *Transactions of the Leicestershire Historical and Archaeological Society*, 58 (1982–83), pp. 58–74.

Cunningham, Hugh, 'Leisure and Culture', in F. M. L. Thompson (ed.), *The Cambridge Social History of Britain, 1750–1950: People and Their Environment* (Cambridge: Cambridge University Press, 1990), pp. 279–340.

Crofts, N. and Mills, T. C., 'Trends in Real Wages in Britain, 1750–1913', *Explorations in Economic History*, 31 (1994), pp. 176–94.

Delves, Antony, 'Popular Recreation and Social Conflict in Derby, 1800–1850', in Stephen Yeo and Eileen Yeo (eds), *Popular Culture and Class Conflict, 1590–1914: Explorations in the History of Labour and Leisure* (Brighton: Harvester, 1981).

Done, Andrew and Muir, Richard, 'The Landscape History of Grouse Shooting in the Yorkshire Dales', *Rural History*, 12 (2001), pp. 195–210.

Durie, Alastair and Huggins, M., 'Sport, Social Tone and the Seaside Resorts of Great Britain', *International Journal of the History of Sport*, 15 (1998), pp. 173–87.

Edwards, K. C., 'The Park Estate, Nottingham', in M. A. Simpson and T. H. Lloyd (eds), *Middle-Class Housing in Britain* (Newton Abbot: David and Charles, 1977), pp. 153–69.

Evans, Gareth, 'How Amateur Was My Valley: Professional Sport and National Identity in Wales, 1890–1914', *British Journal of Sports History*, 2 (1985), pp. 249–69.

Finn, G., 'Faith, Hope and Bigotry: Case Studies of Anti-Catholic Prejudice in Scottish Soccer and Society', in Grant Jarvie and Graham Walker (eds), *Ninety Minute Patriots? Scottish Sport and the Making of a Nation* (Leicester: Leicester University Press, 1994), pp. 91–112.

Finn, G., 'Racism, Religion and Social Prejudice: Irish Catholic Clubs, Soccer and Scottish Society', *International Journal of the History of Sport*, 8 (1991), pp. 72–95.

Greenhalgh, Paul, 'The Work and Play Principle: The Professional Regulations of the Northern Rugby Football Union, 1898–1905', *International Journal of the History of Sport*, 9 (1992), pp. 356–77.

Gregson, Keith and Huggins, Mike, 'Sport, Music Hall Culture and Popular Song in Nineteenth-Century England', *Culture, Sport, Society*, 2 (1999), pp. 82–102.

Griffin, Emma, 'Popular Culture in Industrialising England', *Historical Journal*, 45 (2002), pp. 619–35.

Harvey, Adrian, 'Football's Missing Link: The Real Story of the Evolution of Modern Football', in J. A. Mangan (ed.), *Sport in Europe: Politics, Class, Gender* (London: Frank Cass, 1999), pp. 92–116.

Hayes, Win, 'The Professional Swimmer, 1860–1880s', *Sports Historian*, 22 (2002), pp. 119–48.

Hill, Jeffrey, 'Rite of Spring: Cup Finals and Community in the North of England', in Jeff Hill and Jack Williams (eds), *Sport and Identity in the North of England* (Keele: Keele University Press, 1996), pp. 85–112.

Hill, Jeffrey, 'Cocks, Cats, Caps and Cups: A Semiotic Approach to Sport and National Identity', *Culture, Sport, Society*, 2, 2 (1999), pp. 1–21.

Holt, Richard, 'Cricket and Englishness: The Batsman as Hero' *International Journal of the History of Sport*, 13 (1996), pp. 48–70.

Holt, Richard and Mangan, J. A., 'Prologue: Heroes of a European Past', *International Journal of the History of Sport*, 13 (1996), pp. 1–13.

Huggins, Mike, 'An Early North-East Football Club, 1878–1887', *Bulletin of the Cleveland and District Local History Society*, 51 (1986), pp. 28–40.

Huggins, Mike, 'A Tranquil Transformation: Middle-Class Racing "Revolutionaries" in Nineteenth-Century England', in J. A. Mangan (ed.), *Reformers, Sport, Modernizers: Middle-Class Revolutionaries* (London: Frank Cass, 2002), pp. 35–57.

Huggins, Mike, 'Cartoons and the Comic Periodical, 1841–1901: A Satirical Sociology of Victorian Sporting Life', in Mike Huggins and J. A. Mangan (eds), *Disreputable Pleasures: Less Virtuous Victorians at Play* (London: Frank Cass, 2004), pp. 124–50.

Huggins, Mike, 'More Sinful Pleasures? Leisure, Respectability and the Male Middle Classes in Victorian England', *Journal of Social History*, 33 (2000), pp. 585–600.

Huggins, Mike, 'Cumberland and Westmorland Wrestling, c. 1800–2000', *Sports Historian* 21, 1 (2001) pp. 35–55.

Huggins, Mike, 'Second-Class Citizens? English Middle-Class Culture and Sport, 1850–1910: A Reconsideration', *International Journal of the History of Sport*, 17 (2000), pp. 1–35.

Huggins, Mike, 'Sport and the Social Construction of Identity in North-East England, 1800–1914', in Neville Kirk (ed.), *Northern Identities* (Aldershot: Ashgate, 2000), pp. 132–62.

Huggins, Mike, 'The First Generation of Street Bookmakers in Victorian England: Demonic Fiends or Decent Fellers?', *Northern History*, 36 (2000), pp. 129–45.

Huggins, Mike, 'The Spread of Soccer in North-East England, 1876–90', *International Journal of the History of Sport*, 6 (1989), pp. 299–318.

Jackson, Lorna, 'Sport and Patronage: Evidence from Nineteenth-Century Argyllshire', *Sports Historian* 18, 2 (1998), pp. 95–106.

Jackson, Mike Benborough, 'Landlord Careless? Landowners, Tenants and Agriculture on Four Estates in West Wales, 1850–1875', *Rural History*, 14 (2003), pp. 81–98.

Kellett, M. A., 'The Power of Princely Patronage: Pigeon Shooting in Victorian Britain', *International Journal of the History of Sport*, 11 (1994), pp. 63–85.

Kennedy, David, 'The Split of Everton Football Club, 1892', *Sport in History*, 23 (2003), pp. 1–26.

Lewis, R. W., 'Football Hooliganism in England before 1914: A Critique of the Dunning Thesis', *International Journal of the History of Sport*, 13 (1996), pp. 310–39.

Lile, Emma, 'Professional Pedestrianism in South Wales during the Nineteenth Century', *Sports Historian*, 20 (2000), pp. 94–105.

Lowerson, John, 'Brothers of the Angle: Coarse Fishing and English Working Class Culture, 1850–1914' in J. A. Mangan (ed.), *Pleasure, Profit and Proselytism: British Culture and Sport at Home and Abroad, 1700–1914* (London: Frank Cass, 1988), pp. 105–27.

Lowerson, John, 'Opiate of the People and Stimulant for the Historian? – Some Issues in Sports History', in W. Lamont (ed.), *Historical Controversies and Historians* (London: UCL, 1998), pp. 201–14.

McBrearty, Richard, 'Andrew Watson: The World's First Black Football Internationalist', *Soccer History*, 2 (2002), pp. 3–6.

McBrearty, Richard, 'Scotland's Football Pioneers in Argentina', *Soccer History*, 3 (2003), pp. 23–25.

McDevitt, Patrick, 'The King of Sport: Polo in Late Victorian and Edwardian India', *International Journal of the History of Sport*, 20 (2003), pp. 1–27.

McKenzie, Callum, 'The British Big-Game Hunting Tradition: Masculinity and Fraternalism with Particular Reference to the Shikar Club', *Sports Historian*, 20 (2000), pp. 70–96.

Malcolm, Dominic, 'Cricket Spectator Disorder: Myths and Historical Evidence', *Sports Historian*, 19 (1999), pp. 16–37.

Maguire, Joe, 'Images of Manliness and Competing Ways of Living in Late Victorian and Edwardian Britain', *British Journal of Sports History*, 3 (1986), pp. 265–87.

Majumdar, Boria, 'The Vernacular in Sports History', *International Journal of the History of Sport*, 20 (2003), pp. 107–25.

Mangan, J. A., 'Christ and the Imperial Games Fields: Evangelical Athletes of the Empire', *British Journal of Sports History*, 1 (1984), pp. 184–201.

Mangan, J. A., 'Grammar Schools and the Games Ethic in the Victorian and Edwardian Eras', *Albion*, 15 (1983), pp. 313–24.

Mangan, J. A. and McKenzie, Callum, 'Radical Conservatives: Middle-Class Masculinity, the Shikar Club and Big-Game Hunting', in J. A. Mangan (ed.), *Reformers, Sport, Modernizers: Middle-Class Revolutionaries* (London: Frank Cass, 2002), pp. 185–209.

Mason, Tony, 'Some Englishmen and Scotsmen Abroad: The Spread of World Football', in Alan Thomlinson and Garry Whannel (eds), *Off the Ball* (London: Pluto Press, 1986).

Mason, Tony, 'Sporting News, 1860–1914', in Michael Harris and Alan Lee (eds), *The Press in English Society from the Seventeenth to the Nineteenth Centuries* (London: Associated Universities Press, 1986), pp. 168–86.

Metcalfe, Alan, 'Football in the Mining Communities of East Northumberland, 1882–1914', *International Journal of the History of Sport*, 5 (1988), pp. 65–79.

Moore, Moore, 'The Great Baseball Tour of 1888–9: A Tale of Image Making, Intrigue and Labour Relations in the Gilded Age', *International Journal of the History of Sport*, 11 (1994), pp. 431–56.

Morris, R. J., 'Middle-Class Culture, 1700–1914', in Derek Fraser (ed.), *A History of Modern Leeds* (Manchester: Manchester University Press, 1980), pp. 200–22.

Mullen, Michael, 'The Devolution of the Irish Economy in the Nineteenth Century and the Bifurcation of Irish Sport', *International Journal of the History of Sport*, 13 (1996), pp. 42–60.

Murphy, Patrick, Dunning, Eric and Maguire, Joseph, 'Football Spectator Violence and Disorder before the First World War: A Reply to R. W. Lewis', *International Journal of the History of Sport*, 15 (1998), pp. 141–62.

Nannestad, Ian, 'Researching the Game's Past: The National Sporting Press in England to 1900', *Soccer History*, 4 (2003), pp. 39–43.

Park, Roberta J., 'Mended or Ended? Football Injuries and the British and American Medical Press, 1870–1910', *International Journal of the History of Sport*, 18 (2001), pp. 110–33.

Perkin, Harold, 'Teaching the Nations How to Play: Sport and Society in the British Empire and Commonwealth', *International Journal of the History of Sport*, 6 (1989), pp. 145–55.

Reid, Douglas A., 'Playing and Praying', in Martin Daunton (ed.), *Cambridge Urban History of Britain*, iii (Cambridge: Cambridge University Press, 2000), pp. 745–807.

Reid, D. A., 'The Decline of St Monday', *Past and Present*, 71 (1976), pp. 76–98.

Reid, D. A., 'Weddings, Workdays, Work and Leisure in Urban England, 1791–1911: The Decline of St Monday Revisited', *Past and Present*, 153 (1996), pp. 135–63.

Reid, Irene A., 'Shinty, Nationalism and Celtic Politics, 1870–1922', *Sports Historian*, 18 (1998), pp. 107–30.

Ritchie, Andrew, 'The Origins of Bicycle Racing in England: Technology, Entertainment, Sporsorship and Advertising in the Early History of the Sport', *Journal of Sports History*, 26 (1999), pp. 487–518.

Russell, Dave, 'Amateurs, Professionals and Aspects of Northern Identity', *Sports Historian*, 16 (1996), pp. 64–80.

Roe, Warren, 'The Athletic Capital of England: The White Lion, Hackney Wick, 1857–1875', *British Society for Sports History Bulletin* (Winter 2002–3), pp. 39–53.

Ryan, Greg, 'Handsome Physiognomy and Blameless Physique: Indigenous Colonial Sporting Tours and British Racial Consciousness, 1868 and 1888', *International Journal of the History of Sport*, 14 (1997), pp. 67–81.

Ryan, Greg, 'Rural Myth and Urban Actuality: The Anatomy of All Black and New Zealand Rugby, 1884–1934', *New Zealand Journal of History*, 3 (2001), pp. 45–69.

Sandiford, Keith and Vamplew, Wray, 'The Peculiar Economics of English Cricket before 1914', *British Journal of Sports History*, 3 (1986), pp. 311–26.

Sandiford, Keith A. P., 'The Birth of the Professional Cricketer's Benefit Match', *International Journal of the History of Sport*, 8 (1991), pp. 111–23.

Simpson, M. A., 'The West End of Glasgow, 1830–1914', in M. A. Simpson and T. H. Lloyd (eds), *Middle-Class Housing in Britain* (Newton Abbot: David and Charles, 1977), pp. 44–85.

Star, Peter, 'Native Bird Protection, National Identity and the Rise of Preservation in New Zealand to 1914', *New Zealand Journal of History*, 36 (2002) pp. 123–36.

Taylor, Harvey, 'Play Up, but Don't Play the Game: English Amateur Elitism, 1863–1910', *Sports Historian*, 22 (2002), pp. 75–97.

Taylor, Matthew, 'Beyond the Maximum Wage: The Earnings of Football Professionals in England, 1900–1939', *Soccer and Society*, 2 (2001), pp. 101–18.

Taylor, Matthew and Coyle, John, 'The Election of Clubs to the Football League, 1888–1939', *Sports Historian*, 19 (1999), pp. 1–24.

Tennyson, Sir Charles, 'They Taught the World to Play', *Victorian Studies*, 2 (1959), pp. 211–22.

Tranter, Neil, 'The Chronology of Organised Sport in Nineteenth-Century Scotland: A Regional Study. Patterns', *International Journal of the History of Sport*, 7 (1990), pp. 188–203.

Tranter, Neil, 'The Social and Occupational Structure of Organised Sport in Central Scotland during the Nineteenth Century', *International Journal of the History of Sport*, 4 (1987), pp. 301–14.

Vamplew, Wray, 'The Economics of a Sports Industry: Scottish Gate Money Football, 1890–1914', *Economic History Review*, 35 (1982), pp. 549–67.

Warsop, Keith, 'Researching the Game's Past: The Quest for Early FA Cup Finalists', *Soccer History*, 2 (2002), pp. 34–40.

Williams, Gareth, 'How Amateur Was My Valley: Professional Sport and National Identity in Wales, 1890–1914', *British Journal of Sports History*, 2 (1985), pp. 248–69.

Williams, Jack, 'One Could Literally Have Walked on the Heads of the People Congregated There: Sport, the Town and Identity', in Keith Laybourne (ed.), *Social Conditions, Status and Community, 1860–c. 1920* (Stroud: Sutton Publishing, 1997), pp. 128–38.

UNPUBLISHED PAPERS

Hickey, Colm, 'Athleticism and the London Training Colleges', Ph.D thesis, University of Strathclyde.

Walker, Andrew, 'Reporting Play: The Local Newspaper and Sports Journalism, c. 1870–1914', paper delivered at the Social History Conference, Leicester 2003.

Index

and prize value 59
professionals and amateurs 57, 60,
    61, 62, 100
seasonal patterns 90–91
weekly patterns 12
Atkinson, George 131
August Bank Holiday 91
Australia 150, 224, 231, 237, 239
    and colonisation 225, 226, 228, 229,
        233
    cricket in 234, 235, 246
Australian Town and Country Journal
    234
Aylesford, Earl of, seventh 26

badger-baiting 4, 48
badminton 82
Badminton Library of Sports and
    Pastimes 11
*Badminton Magazine of Sports and
    Pastimes* 66, 77, 156
*Bailey's Magazine of Sports and
    Pastimes* 156
ball games, development of 219
Ballantyne, R. M. 161
Ballywater Park, Ulster 28
Barbados 229, 236, 237
Barlow, John 243
Barron, H. J. 171
Barry, Felix 63
baseball 122, 232, 239, 243–44, 247
Baseball Association of Great Britain
    and Ireland 244
Baum, James 115
Baum, John 115
Bedford High School 82
Bedford Park housing estate, Ealing
    126
Beers, Frank 133
Bell's Life 1–4, 13, 19, 42, 145–51
    passim, 170
    and challenges 91
    on FA Cup final 64

on regatta membership 55
on spectator accommodation 117
*Bell's Life in London and Sporting
    Chronicle see Bell's Life*
*Bell's Life in Sydney and Sporting
    Reviewer* 225
benefit matches, cricket 130–31
Bengal 229, 238
Bentley, J. J. 152
Bergman-Osterberg, Madam 82
Bessingborough, Earl of 189
betting 4, 37, 43, 70–72, 108, 136–38
    and angling 48, 57, 70, 71, 108
    and athletics 57
    betting clubs 101–2, 116
    by working-class 6
    and horse-racing 2, 57, 70, 71, 108
    illegal 116
    and rowing 57, 70, 71, 108, 116
    and women 48
Betting House Act (1851) 137
Betting House Act (1853) 71, 72
Bicycling News 153
big-game hunting 239–40
billiards 103, 104
bird-shooting 3, 4, 12, 25, 120
    see also pigeon-shooting; shooting
Birmingham 10, 15, 16, 42, 118, 195
    and civic pride 201–2
    and cycle racing 119
    and football 65, 77, 119
Birmingham Cricket League 122
Birmingham Daily Post 155
Birmingham and District Football
    Association 77
Birmingham race course 126
Biscoe, Cecil Tynedale 222
Bishop Auckland 66
Black Bull Recreational Ground,
    Sheffield 117
Blackburn 98
Blackburn Olympic football club 63,
    98

Taylor, Tom 164
technology 1, 17, 137, 144, 224
Temperance groups 41–43, 72, 73, 106, 216
tennis 6, 30, 35, 100, 103, 126
  and concept of manliness 74
  in education 82
  membership 35, 108
  seasonal patterns 12
  as a social event 107
  and Sunday sport 73
  trophies 150
  weekly patterns 41
  women participants 8, 82, 110
Tennyson, Alfred 158
Thames Regatta 21
theatre 116, 163, 164–65
Third Lanark football club 90
three-day cricket 123–24
Thring, Edward 31
Tibet 232
Times 2, 6, 20, 187, 206
  on dog-racing 116
  on pigeon shoots 26
  on steeplechasing 55
tipsters 112, 137
tobogganing 243
Tom Brown's Schooldays (Hughes) 160
Tottenham 13, 132, 211
tourism 113, 239, 240
Townsend, W. Thompson 161
traditional sporting events 44, 45, 88, 89, 91, 93
transport 17, 46, 144, 239
  coach 113, 114
  rail 35, 46, 114
Trent Bridge cricket ground 123
Trollope, Anthony 21, 158
trophies 98, 150, 197
trotting 12
Turf Club 28, 102
Turf, Field and Farm 235

Turf Herald and Yorkshire Field 146
Tysoe village 40

Umpire 154
Underwood, Bill 45
unemployment 48
United London Scottish soccer club 203
University Foot Ball Club, Cambridge 193
Uppingham school 31
urban culture 46–49, 196
urbanisation 1, 13, 16, 112, 116
Uruguay 224
USA 16, 231, 234, 239, 240
  and colonisation 225, 226, 227

Vane Tempest, Lord Harry 106
Vaughan, Charles 31, 113
Victoria, Queen 28, 97
Victorian parks 13
voluntary societies 34, 43, 46, 99, 101, 122
  and imperialism 221

wages, real 14, 47
Wakefield Trinity Rugby Club 41
Wales 70, 216, 225
  and loyalties 199, 213, 216, 217
Wales, prince of 22, 23, 25, 28, 97, 239
Wallsend 48
Wanderers amateur football club, London 64
Warwickshire 34
Warwickshire Cricket Ground 118
Watson, A. E. T. 11
Watson, Andrew 234
Watson, Thomas 132
Webb, Matthew 172
Weekly Dispatch 145, 155
Wells, H. G. 158
Welsh football clubs 65